ENCHANTING A
DISENCHANTED WORL

3rd
EDITION

With much love to Dylan Tyler Ritzer
My grandson and my friend

3rd
EDITION

ENCHANTING A DISENCHANTED WORLD

Continuity and Change in the Cathedrals of Consumption

GEORGE RITZER

University of Maryland

Los Angeles | London | New Delhi
Singapore | Washington DC

For information:

Pine Forge Press
An Imprint of SAGE
   Publications, Inc.
2455 Teller Road
Thousand Oaks,
   California 91320
E-mail: order@sagepub.com

SAGE Publications India Pvt. Ltd.
B 1/I 1 Mohan Cooperative
   Industrial Area
Mathura Road,
   New Delhi 110 044
India

SAGE Publications Ltd.
1 Oliver's Yard
55 City Road
London EC1Y 1SP
United Kingdom

SAGE Publications
   Asia-Pacific Pte. Ltd.
33 Pekin Street #02-01
Far East Square
Singapore 048763

Printed in the United States of America

Library of Congress Cataloging-in-Publication Data

Ritzer, George.
Enchanting a disenchanted world : continuity and change in the cathedrals of consumption / George Ritzer.—3rd ed.
    p. cm.
Includes bibliographical references and index.
ISBN 978-1-4129-7581-0 (pbk.)
   1. Consumption (Economics)—United States. 2. Consumption (Economics) 3. Marketing—United States. 4. Marketing. I. Title.

HC110.C6R58 2010
339.4'70973—dc22   2009031759

This book is printed on acid-free paper.

09   10   11   12   13   10   9   8   7   6   5   4   3   2   1

Acquisitions Editor:	David Repetto
Editorial Assistant:	Nancy Scrofano
Production Editor:	Astrid Virding
Copy Editor:	Gillian Dickens
Typesetter:	C&M Digitals (P) Ltd.
Proofreader:	Dennis W. Webb
Indexer:	William Ragsdale
Cover Designer:	Candice Harman
Marketing Manager:	Jennifer Reed Banando

Brief Contents

Detailed Contents

Preface

When I began working on this third edition of *Enchanting a Disenchanted World* in late 2008 and 2009, we were well into the "Great Recession."[1] The economic world had been turned topsy-turvy with entire countries (e.g., Iceland) going bankrupt, legendary Wall Street firms (e.g., Bear Stearns, Lehman Brothers) disappearing overnight, banks failing (IndyMac) or being nationalized (Royal Bank of Scotland in Great Britain), major corporations in bankruptcy (General Motors, Chrysler) or being saved by government bailouts (AIG), individuals in the United States losing much of their retirement savings in 401k plans, and the U.S. unemployment rate jumping every month and on target to reach 10%, or more, in late 2009.

Similarly, in part as a result of the above, and in part as a contributor to it, consumption in the United States—and much of the rest of world—had, at least for the time being, tanked (and, amazingly, the savings rate, which had approached zero, increased dramatically). This stood in stark contrast to the 1990s through late 2007, a period that was characterized by a boom (now better seen as a bubble) in the economy, including such a dramatic acceleration in consumption that I labeled it *hyperconsumption*. Furthermore, it was an epoch that saw the massive expansion of the settings—what I called the *cathedrals of consumption*—needed to accommodate *and* fuel hyperconsumption.

In fact, it could be argued that both hyperconsumption (and the cathedrals of consumption) were important causes of the Great Recession. Because of excessively high levels of consumption of housing, automobiles, and other consumables, people took on unsustainable levels of mortgage, automobile,

---

[1]Note I am not using the term *recession* here in its technical sense, nor am I arguing that we are not or will not move into a depression as that is defined technically. I like the phrase *Great Recession* because it indicates that the current economic decline is greater, and of more widespread significance, than other recessions. It is especially consequential for the concerns in this book—consumption and the settings in which it occurs.

and credit card debt. Housing prices skyrocketed, and when they collapsed, many people were ruined financially.

However, as the economic crisis gained steam, consumption dropped precipitously, making it impossible to think of the contemporary reality as approaching anything close to hyperconsumption. Furthermore, the cathedrals of consumption felt the pain, and some disappeared and others experienced great difficulties as a result of the decline in consumption.

Despite this decline, it is clear that while they are changing in various ways, consumption and the cathedrals of consumption are not disappearing and will continue to play a central role in society. However, the changes wrought by the Great Recession have taught laypeople and scholars alike some important lessons that need to be thought through and incorporated into this new edition. In the end, the Great Recession helped me to refine and advance the conceptual analysis of consumption and the cathedrals of consumption presented in these pages.

That reconceptualization is captured in the change in the subtitle of this book. While the main title—*Enchanting a Disenchanted World*—remains the same, the subtitle has been changed to *Continuity and Change in the Cathedrals of Consumption*. By continuity, I mean that most of the revolutionary changes in consumption and consumption settings that occurred between the end of World War II and the onset of the current recession—and described in these pages—remain in place. Furthermore, it is entirely possible that once the current economic crisis passes, we will see both resume their expansion. However, both consumption and consumption settings have changed, and it is also possible that we will see a long-term decline in both. Thus, for example, I discuss in the concluding chapter whether many of the largest and most significant cathedrals of consumption are in danger of becoming "dinosaurs of consumption" that are too large and cumbersome to adapt to the new economic realities.

The above suggests major changes in this book, and while there are such changes, a surprisingly large portion, including the most central analytic chapters, remains largely intact. The main focus of the book was, and is, a theoretical analysis of the ways in which the cathedrals of consumption deal with the perils of rationalization and disenchantment through enchantment derived from spectacles produced by simulations, implosions, and manipulations of time and space. While at least some of these spectacles may now be in the process of being downsized (even the usually garish Academy Awards opened its 2009 program with a production number that was made to appear low in cost, even homemade), and there may be efforts to produce them in new ways, the cathedrals of consumption cannot avoid relying on spectacles. In the short run, the cathedrals of consumption will focus on reducing costs and prices, but they will be resistant to doing this for long, as they have in the past, since it leads to price competition and therefore to lower, if not low or nonexistent, profits.

The Great Recession will force various changes on the nature of spectacle in the cathedrals of consumption (also to be discussed in the concluding chapter). For example, in some cases, "underwhelming" spectacles (e.g., Main Street in Disney World) will replace the current emphasis on those that overwhelm the consumer. In other cases, new technologies will be used to heighten the spectacle and lower costs (e.g., by relying less on costly employees). In other words, we will see more *economical spectacles*. Some methods discussed in this book for creating spectacles (e.g., implosion, simulation) are likely to be used more because they can be cost-effective, while others (reliance on great expanses of space) will be used less because of the high cost associated with them. Finally, hard economic times will lead to the discovery of new methods of creating spectacle, especially those that rely on advanced technologies. Many of these technologies will be associated with the Internet and the likelihood that an increasing number of cathedrals of consumption will be found there.

However, changes in the cathedrals of consumption will be far from uniform. For one thing, they will vary by type with some (e.g., shopping malls) changing more dramatically than others (e.g., Disney World). For another, the degree and nature of the change will vary by area of the world. The United States is likely to see more than its share of change. For one thing, it was the site of the invention of many of the cathedrals of consumption, and a number of them may have outlived their useful lives (e.g., strip malls). For another, many of the cathedrals of consumption witnessed massive overbuilding, with the result that there is excess capacity in many domains (e.g., an excessive number of electronics superstores led to the demise of one large chain—Circuit City—while another, Best Buy, survives). Finally, it is possible, perhaps even likely, that the wealth of the United States is in decline relative to the likely growth of other economies (China, India, the Arab world, Brazil), and it will not be in a position to afford as many cathedrals of consumption as well as the hyperconsumption that is closely associated with them.

This points to another important source of variation in the fate of the cathedrals of consumption. That is, while some parts of the world will witness a relative decline in consumption and the settings in which it occurs, others will see an expansion of both. For example, as I was writing this new edition, I spent some time in Dubai looking at the creation there of countless extraordinary cathedrals of consumption (see Chapter 7). The effects of the current economic crisis were certainly being felt there, including a decline in consumption and in the building of new cathedrals of consumption. However, I came away from my visit with the conclusion that both would resume their expansion as the current crisis ebbs and especially as the price of oil[2] climbs back to its former heights and likely beyond. Thus, while the United States and other areas may see a relative decline in consumption and cathedrals of consumption, other parts of the world such as Dubai (another is Macau with its access to the growing Chinese market) are likely to see an expansion of both.

Chapter 1 continues to describe the major cathedrals of consumption of focal concern in this book. While many of these have experienced problems lately (e.g., superstores, shopping malls, Las Vegas casino-hotels, cruise ships), and some (e.g., superstores such as Circuit City and Linens 'n Things) have even disappeared, most remain significant forces in the economy and in consumer culture. There have been some changes in the discussion to reflect recent changes—especially declines—but the vast majority of it remains intact and of continuing relevance. Chapter 2 describes, as before, the revolutionary changes that took place until recently in consumption, as well as the reasons for those changes. The most theory-driven chapters (3–6) remain largely intact because they continue to be of great utility in understanding this book's major focus—the disenchantment (rationalization) of the cathedrals of consumption and the mechanisms (spectacle and extravaganza through the use of simulations, implosion, and manipulations of time and space) needed to reenchant them.

There are three major changes in this book. The first is found Chapter 7 on the "landscapes of consumption" (geographic locales that encompass two or more cathedrals of consumption). New to the chapter is a discussion of the impact of the recession on these areas, as well as of two new landscapes of consumption in Dubai and Macau. The discussion is now oriented around three types of such landscapes. The first type, exemplified by the area around the Duomo in Milan, Italy, illustrates a fairly stable landscape of consumption. The second involves new landscapes of consumption that are being threatened by the current recession and includes Easton Town Center in Columbus, Ohio; Dubai in the United Arab Emirates; and the Cotai Strip in Macau, China. The third type deals with a landscape of consumption in decline, as exemplified by Pigeon Forge, Tennessee.

The second major change is the elimination of what was Chapter 8 in the last edition ("Societal Implications and the Future of the New Means of Consumption"). While many important issues were discussed there, the chapter had to be eliminated in order to make space for the third major change, the new Chapter 8—"The Cathedrals (and Landscapes) of Consumption:

---

[2]Dubai is not rich in oil, but other emirates, as well as surrounding Arab states (e.g., Saudi Arabia), are, and much of the money for Dubai's development, as well as many of its visitors, comes from those areas.

Continuity and Change"—dealing with the current economic downturn and its likely effect on the cathedrals of consumption. While there are certainly now significant signs of trouble in the cathedrals of consumption (some have become dinosaurs and others are threatened by "dinosaurization") and even some signs of devolution (e.g., the return of some "mom-and-pop" shops to the malls replacing chain stores; some chains moving away from large outlets and opening much smaller ones), it seems likely that stability and even expansion will eventually return to the cathedrals of consumption. However, that growth will be nothing like that which occurred in the past two decades. Those who own and run the cathedrals of consumption have learned some important lessons and, in any case, have fewer resources and less access to credit. Much the same can be said of the consumer. Yet people will continue to need and to want to consume, and the cathedrals of consumption will be there to meet their needs and wants and even to inflame them once again.

I would like to thank my two terrific assistants, Nathan Jurgenson and Jillet Sam, for their many contributions to this revision. I would also like to thank the other students in my spring 2009 graduate seminar—Heather Marsh, Beverly Pratt, P. J. Rey, and Cagri Tanyol—for their thoughts on the book and their contributions to it. I would also like to thank the following reviewers who made truly important contributions to the final phase of this revision:

D. Reber Dunkel, *Randolph-Macon College*

Leslie R. S. Elrod, *University of Cincinnati*

Brenda Forster, *Elmhurst College*

Douglas J. Goodman, *Stonehill College*

Bruce Hoffman, *Ohio University*

Douglas Kellner, *University of California, Los Angeles*

Ryan Moore, *Florida Atlantic University*

Beau Niles, *University of Florida*

Johanna K. Pabst, *Boston College*

Sara Raley, *McDaniel College*

Jean Van Delinder, *Oklahoma State University*

Robert E. Wood, *Rutgers University*

As usual, my editor at Pine Forge Press, Jerry Westby, has been both supportive and encouraging. It is always a pleasure to work with him and the rest of the staff at Pine Forge.

1

A Tour of the New
Means of Consumption

We consume many obvious things—fast food, T-shirts, a day at Walt Disney World—and many others that are not so obvious—a lecture, medical service, a day at the ballpark. We consume many goods and services that we must have in order to live and more that we simply want or think we need. Often we must go to particular settings to obtain these goods and services (although, as we will see, more and more of them are coming to us). This book is concerned with those settings: home-shopping television, shopping malls, online shopping sites, fast-food restaurants, theme parks, and cruise ships, to name a few.

Unlike many treatments of the subject of consumption, this is *not* a book about the consumer[1] or the increasing profusion of goods and services.[2] Rather, it is about the settings[3] that allow, encourage, and even compel us to consume so many of those goods and services. The settings of interest will be termed the *new means of consumption*. These are, in the main, locales that came into existence or took new forms after the end of World War II and that, building on but going beyond earlier settings, dramatically transformed the nature of consumption. Because of important continuities, it is not always easy to distinguish clearly between new and older means of consumption,[4] but it is the more contemporary versions, singly and collectively, that will concern us.[5]

To get a better sense of the new means of consumption, let us first look at Walt Disney World and the larger Disney operation of which it is part. Disney's worlds and lands are important not only in themselves but also because they have served—through a process that has been labeled "Disneyization"[6]—as a model for other amusement parks, as well as many other new means of consumption.

DISNEY'S WORLD

Building on late-19th- and early 20th-century efforts, including world exhibitions (and fairs) and Coney Island in New York, Walt Disney and his company created a revolutionary new type of amusement park, the theme park, defined by areas, or even an entire park, devoted to a given motif (e.g., the various lands at Disney World to be discussed below). The first of its theme parks, Disneyland (renamed Disneyland Park in 2007), opened in Southern California in 1955 (a second, adjacent theme park, Disney's California Adventure, as well as a shopping area [basically a mall]—Downtown Disney—were added in 2001).[7] It was followed by Disney World in Florida in 1971, Tokyo Disneyland in 1983 (the adjoining DisneySea opened in 2001),[8] and Disneyland Resort Paris in 1992 (Walt Disney Studios Paris joined it in 2002). In addition, the Hong Kong Disneyland was opened in 2005, and another is planned for Shanghai in 2014. The Disney theme parks (even the initially financially troubled Paris Disney) have, of course, been enormous successes, in great part because they built, and greatly expanded, on the bases of the success of the early amusement parks. This includes entertainment for the masses, great spectacles, use of advanced technology for consumption rather than production, the commercialization of "fun," and the offer of a safety valve where people can expend their energies without threatening society. In addition, Disney systematically eliminated the "seedy" and risqué elements that characterized and played a major role in the decline of many amusement parks in the first half of the 20th century.

Disney transformed amusement parks by, among other things, cleaning them up, creating a far more "moral" order than most of the early parks ever had, and making them acceptable as family entertainment.[9] Disney offered a self-contained, controlled environment free from the kinds of problems that had undermined earlier parks. It pioneered the order and constraint that are characteristic of virtually all contemporary theme parks.[10] Although visitors arriving at earlier amusement parks felt a sense of looseness, even danger, tourists arriving at Disney World know and take comfort in the fact that inside the gates lies a tightly regulated world. The primary appeal of early amusement parks such as Coney Island was that they offered visitors "a respite from . . . formal, highly regulated social situations,"[11] but the main attraction at Disney World is just such tight regulation.[12] To put it another way, although parks such as Coney Island provided "a moral holiday,"[13] Disney World created a new morality emphasizing conformity to external demands.

Disney World is highly predictable. For example, there are no midway scam artists to bilk the visitor. There are teams of workers who, among their other cleaning chores, follow the nightly parades cleaning up debris—including animal droppings—so that an errant step should not bring with it an unpleasant surprise. There is no sexual titillation of the kind that characterized many early amusement parks. The park is continually cleaned, repaired, and repainted; there is nothing tacky about Disney World. The steep admission charge, the high cost of eating, shopping, hotels (especially many of those on park premises) and so forth, as well as the costs involved in getting there, have succeeded in keeping "undesirables" out. A Disney executive said, "Think of Disney World as a medium-sized city with a crime rate of zero."[14] As a result of this sanitizing of the park experience, Disney parks have become a favorite destination for middle-class families and many other people as well.

The heart of Disney World is the Magic Kingdom (a telling name given, as you will see, our interest in this book in enchantment) and its seven themed "lands." The trek through Disney World begins (and ends) in Main

Street, U.S.A. (basically an outdoor shopping mall), which leads to the six other themed lands—Tomorrowland[15] (with, among other things, a roller-coaster-like space adventure on "Space Mountain"), Fantasyland ("It's a Small World," among other attractions), Adventureland ("Pirates of the Caribbean," etc.), Frontierland (anchored by such traditional favorites as "Country Bear Jamboree"), Liberty Square (with, among others, "The Hall of Presidents"), and Mickey's Toontown Fair (with "Minnie's and Mickey's Country Houses").

Epcot Theme Park has Future World, which includes "Mission: Space Pavilion." Reminiscent of world fairs, Epcot's World Showcase has pavilions featuring exhibits from a number of nations, including China ("Reflections of China"), France ("Impressions de France"), and Mexico ("Grand Fiesta Tour").

Another set of major attractions at Disney World is Disney Hollywood Studios, which includes the "Great Movie Ride," "Indiana Jones: Epic Stunt Spectacular," and "The American Idol Experience."

Animal Kingdom encompasses 500 acres, nearly five times the area of the Magic Kingdom. Visitors enter through the Oasis, a lush jungle-like setting that leads to the themed lands of Animal Kingdom and includes a branch of the chain of Rainforest Cafe theme restaurants. Discovery Island offers the centerpiece of Animal Kingdom, the massive "Tree of Life." Several hundred hand-carved animals seem to grow out of the tree, inside of which is a multimedia theater. Dinoland USA attempts to depict life as it existed millions of years ago and includes the "Boneyard," a children's playground with equipment made out of what appear to be giant dinosaur bones. Africa includes the "Kilimanjaro Safari" involving a trip through the countryside and a high-speed automobile chase across, among other things, a collapsing bridge over a "crocodile-infested" river. Asia has the "Maharajah Jungle Trek," and there is also Rafiki's Planet Watch as well as Camp Minnie Mouse, which includes "Festival of the Lion King."

Beyond the four theme parks, there are two water parks (Typhoon Lagoon and Blizzard Beach); DisneyQuest (loaded with games of all sorts); Downtown Disney, which features a shopping area (Downtown Disney Marketplace); an area that is more oriented to entertainment (Downtown Disney West Side with Cirque de Soleil La Nouba and a 24-screen AMC movie theater); Pleasure Island (in transition but with more shopping and dining); Disney's Boardwalk modeled after turn-of-the century boardwalks like the one at Coney and with still more shops, restaurants, and entertainment; about two dozen "resort" hotels divided into four categories (deluxe villas, deluxe resort hotels, moderate resort hotels, and value resort hotels), as well as campgrounds; the town of Celebration (although in recent years, Disney has been divesting itself of its interest in the town);[16] and even a huge sports complex (Disney's Wide World of Sports, to be renamed ESPN Wide World of Sports Complex)—all means of consumption in their own right.[17]

Disney has become a global presence not only through its many products (the CEO claimed that worldwide, more than one billion people use a Disney product in a given month[18]) and theme parks but also through its many other enterprises, such as its movies (Walt Disney Studios, among others), television shows (Disney Channel), and cable television network. Of greater relevance to the concerns of this book are the 229 Disney stores that are found in innumerable shopping malls and online, Radio Disney (a children's radio network), Disney Mobile (wireless phones, which are extremely popular in Japan despite failing in the United States market), the Disney Cruise Line, Disney's ownership of ABC and ESPN (expanded to include ESPN2, ESPN Classic, ESPNEWS), Disney publishing (the world's largest publisher of children's books), Disney theatrical producing live stage musicals in several locales throughout the world, the Disney Catalog, and even the Disney Credit Card. All of these are employed synergistically to sell one another in a tightly integrated system that ultimately sells the Disney brand name and yields huge profits. Disney in general and its theme parks in particular are revolutionary in many senses, but perhaps above all they are part of a "selling machine" capable of marketing Disney to an unprecedented degree.[19] Said the CEO, "It is virtually impossible to travel anywhere in the world and not see someone wearing a piece of clothing adorned with Mickey's smiling face."[20]

Disney is a potent force, and its power is reflected in the opening of the acclaimed Disney Concert Hall in Los Angeles (with a startling design by legendary architect Frank Gehry) and the central role it played in the resuscitation of the area around Times Square and 42nd Street in New York City.[21] Prior to Disney's arrival, this area was all but dead as a commercial center, dominated by peep shows and street hustlers. In fact, Rolling Stone dubbed 42nd Street "the sleaziest block in America."[22] Many previous high-profile efforts to rebuild the area never got off the ground. But in 1993, Disney agreed to invest what is for it the paltry sum of $8 million in the renovation of the New Amsterdam Theater to serve as a site for Broadway productions of Disney shows. In addition, a Disney Store was opened. Because of the luster of the Disney name, theme restaurants, a 25-screen movie theater, Madame Tussaud's wax museum, B. B. King Blues Club, a Virgin Mega-Store, Starbucks, and major hotels (Westin New York, Times Square Hilton), among others, have since opened in this area. The result is that Times Square has been revived as a consumption and business center, and this helped to revivify other areas of New York City. For its part, Disney gained more stature and a theater, yet another means of consumption and way of selling itself and its products.

THE NEW MEANS OF CONSUMPTION

Disney World (and many other aspects of Disney's world) is of interest to us because it represents a model of a new *means of consumption* or, in other words, the settings or structures[23] that enable us to consume all sorts of things. As a new means of consumption, Disney World has many continuities with older settings, as do many of the other new means of consumption. The predecessors to today's cruise lines were the legendary ocean liners of the past. Las Vegas casinos had precursors such as the great casino at Monte Carlo. Shopping malls can be traced back to the markets of ancient Greece and Rome, the souks of the ancient Arab and Muslim worlds, and the arcades of 19th-century France. At the same time, these new means also exhibit a number of important and demonstrable differences from their predecessors.

The means of consumption are part of a broader set of phenomena related to goods and services: production, distribution, advertising,[24] branding,[25] marketing,[26] sales, individual taste,[27] style,[28] and fashion.[29] Our concern is with the process leading up to, and perhaps including, an exchange of money (or equivalents such as checks, electronic debits to bank or credit card accounts, etc.) for goods or services between buyers and sellers.[30] This is often dealt with under the rubric of shopping,[31] but our interests are broader than that and include the consumer's relationship with not only shops and malls but also theme parks, casinos, cruise lines, and other settings, including athletic stadiums,[32] universities, hospitals, and museums,[33] which surprisingly are coming to resemble the more obvious new means of consumption. In most cases, an exchange occurs;[34] people do purchase and receive goods and services. This process may take place instantaneously or over a long period of time and may involve many steps—perception of a want, arousal of a desire by an advertisement, study of available literature (e.g., *Consumer Reports* and ConsumerReports.org), comparison of available options, and ultimately perhaps an actual purchase. Of course, the process need not stop there; it is not unusual for people to take things home, find them wanting, return them, and perhaps begin the process anew.

Many of the new settings have attracted a great deal of attention individually, but little has been said about them collectively. I undertake to analyze them not only because of their growing importance and inherent interest but also because they have played a central role in dramatically altering the nature of consumption. Americans, especially, and increasingly many others throughout the world, consume very differently, and they consume on a larger scale (at least until the recession that rages as I write in 2009; much more will be said in Chapter 8 about this and its implications for the analysis presented in this book), in part because of the new means of consumption. Furthermore, these settings are important beyond their role in the consumption process. Many of the settings considered here—for example, McDonald's, Wal-Mart, IKEA, Disney—have become some of America's and the world's most powerful popular icons. My net is cast even more widely than the reach of Disney's extensive empire of means of consumption to include discount malls, superstores, warehouse stores, Las Vegas casinos (which are increasingly Disneyesque with their theming and goal of attracting families), and so on.

CATHEDRALS OF CONSUMPTION

The new means of consumption can be seen as "cathedrals of consumption"— that is, they are structured, often successfully, to have an enchanted, sometimes even sacred, religious character.[35] To attract consumers, such cathedrals of consumption need to offer, or at least appear to offer, increasingly magical, fantastic, and enchanted settings in which to consume. (Sometimes this magic is produced quite intentionally, whereas in other cases, it is a result of a series of largely unforeseen developments.) A worker involved in the opening of McDonald's in Moscow spoke of it "as if it were the Cathedral in Chartres . . . a place to experience 'celestial joy.'"[36] A visit to Disney World has been depicted as "the middle-class hajj, the compulsory visit to the sunbaked city,"[37] and analogies have been drawn between a trip to Disney World and pilgrimages to religious sites such as Lourdes.[38]

Shopping malls have been described as places where people go to practice their "consumer religion."[39] It has been contended that shopping malls are more than commercial and financial enterprises; they have much in common with the religious centers of traditional civilizations.[40] Like such religious centers, malls are seen as fulfilling people's need to connect with each other and with nature (trees, plants, flowers), as well as their need to participate in festivals. Malls provide the kind of centeredness traditionally provided by religious temples, and they are constructed to have similar balance, symmetry, and order. Their atriums usually offer connection to nature through water and vegetation.[41] People gain a sense of community as well as more specific community services. Play is almost universally part of religious practice, and malls provide a place (the food court) for people to frolic. Similarly, malls offer a setting in which people can partake in ceremonial meals. Malls clearly qualify for the label of cathedrals of consumption.[42]

As is the case with religious cathedrals,[43] the cathedrals of consumption are not only enchanted but also highly rationalized. As they attract more consumers, their enchantment must be reproduced over and over on demand. Furthermore, branches of the successful enchanted settings are opened across the nation and even the world with the result that essentially the same magic must be reproduced in a wide range of locations. To accomplish this, the magic has to be systematized so that it can be easily re-created from one time or place to another. However, it is difficult to reduce magic to corporate formulas that can be routinely employed at any time, in any place, and by anybody.[44] Yet, if these corporations are to continue to attract consumers who will spend money on goods and services, that is just what they must be able to do. Although such rational, machine-like structures can have their enchanting qualities (food appears almost instantaneously, goods exist in unbelievable profusion), they are, in the main, disenchanting; they often end up *not* being very magical. There is a tendency for people to become bored and to be put off by too much machine-like efficiency in the settings in which they consume. The challenge for today's cathedrals of consumption (as for religious cathedrals) is how to maintain enchantment in the face of increasing rationalization.

Although the new means of consumption will be described in terms of rationalization and enchantment (as well as disenchantment), it is important to recognize that they are not all equally rationalized or enchanting. Some are able to operate in a more machine-like manner than others. Similarly, some are able to take on a more enchanted quality than others. Disney World, a Las Vegas casino, or a huge cruise ship seems far more enchanted than the local McDonald's, Wal-Mart, or strip mall. In addition, specific settings may enchant some consumers and not others. For example, fast-food restaurants and theme parks may enchant children far more than adults, although adults may be led by their children or grandchildren to participate—and to pay the bills. Furthermore, enchantment tends to be something that declines over time for consumers as the novelty wears off. After over a half century of existence in the United States and proliferation into seemingly every nook and cranny of the nation, modern fast-food restaurants offer very little enchantment to most adult American consumers. However, we should not forget that many adults found (and young children continue to find) such restaurants quite enchanting when they first opened in the United States, and they still do in other nations and cultures to which fast-food outlets are relatively new arrivals. In sum, although we will describe the new means of consumption in terms of rationalization and enchantment, there is considerable variation among them, and over time, in their degree of rationalization and enchantment.

The terms *new means of consumption* and *cathedrals of consumption* will be used interchangeably in this book to refer to the new settings in and through which we obtain goods and services. The idea of the new means of consumption emphasizes both that these settings are new and that they allow and encourage (and sometimes compel) us to consume. The idea of cathedrals of consumption emphasizes that these settings are characterized by the enchantment needed to lure consumers, although disenchantment is an ever-present possibility as a result of the process of rationalization.

Two theories (a third will be added later) lie at the base of these conceptualizations of the new means of consumption. The first is the work of Karl Marx and his extension of his ideas on the means of production to the lesser known, but central to us, conceptualization of the "means of consumption." The second is the theorizing of Max Weber, who gave us the ideas—rationalization, enchantment, and disenchantment—that are fundamental to the conceptualization of the "cathedrals of consumption." I will offer a more detailed discussion of these and other theoretical ideas in Chapter 3, but before that, I need to delineate more fully the major cathedrals of consumption.

OVERVIEW OF THE CATHEDRALS OF CONSUMPTION

We will review the cathedrals of consumption, beginning with fast-food restaurants and other franchise systems.

Franchises and Fast-Food Restaurants

A large proportion of fast-food restaurants are franchises. Franchising is a system in which "one large firm . . . grants or sells the right to distribute its products or use its trade name and processes to a number of smaller firms . . . franchise holders, although legally independent, must conform to detailed standards of operation designed and enforced by the parent company."[45] Franchising began in the mid-1800s,[46] and today, 1 out of 12 businesses in the United States is a franchise.[47] Nearly half of all retail sales come from franchises.[48] On business days, a new franchise opens once every 8 minutes; more than 8 million people work in the franchise industry.[49]

A&W was the first food service franchise, beginning operations in 1924; Dairy Queen opened in 1944 and, by 1948, had a nationwide chain of 2,500 outlets. Bob's Big Boy started in the late 1930s, and Burger King (then InstaBurger) and Kentucky Fried Chicken (now called KFC) began in 1955. McDonald's was a successful hamburger stand in San Bernardino, California, owned by Mac and Dick McDonald before it was discovered by Ray Kroc; the first of the McDonald's chain opened in 1955. By the end of 2007, McDonald's had in excess of 31,300 restaurants.[50] In addition to its expansion within the United States, McDonald's has become a significant international presence in recent years with restaurants in almost 120 nations.

The other big player in the fast-food business is Yum! Brands, which owns three of the largest franchises—Pizza Hut, Taco Bell, and KFC, as well as A&W All-American Food Restaurants and Long John Silver's. Overall, Yum! Brands has almost 36,000 restaurant units in more than 110 countries and operates the largest fast-food system in the world.[51] There are, of course, other important players in the industry, including Subway, Hardee's, Wendy's, Domino's Pizza, and Starbucks.

It is worth noting that the fast-food industry and franchises are not coterminous. Franchises represent only 70% of McDonald's restaurants, and Starbucks does not offer franchises; most of its coffee shops are company owned.

Chain Stores

The chain store is closely related to the franchise. The main difference is that chain stores have a single owner (thus Starbucks is a chain), whereas individual franchises are owned by independent entrepreneurs. The first true chain store was the supermarket chain A&P (the Great Atlantic and Pacific Tea Company), which by 1880 encompassed 95 stores. Others were J.C. Penney (begun in 1902) in the dry goods area and among the variety stores the five-and-dime store opened by Frank Woolworth in 1879 in Lancaster, Pennsylvania. Although many of these early chains have declined or disappeared, the chain store is still an important presence in American retailing. Examples include chains of supermarkets (Giant, Kroger, Safeway, Whole Foods, Harris Teeter) and the multipurpose Wal-Mart (see "Discounters"), which, among other things, is now the largest supermarket chain in the United States (as it is in Mexico), doing much more business that its nearest competitors[52]; drug stores (Rite Aid, Walgreens, CVS); and department stores (Sears, Macy's) as well as elite shops such as Valentino, Ralph Lauren, Calvin Klein, and Dolce & Gabbana.[53]

Shopping Malls

The first planned outdoor shopping center in the United States, Market Square, was built in the Chicago suburb of Lake Forest in 1916.[54] It was followed in 1924 by Country Club Plaza on the then-outskirts of Kansas City. The Highland Park Shopping Village in Dallas, built in 1931, represented the first time that storefronts were turned away from the public streets inward to a central area. Virtually all of the early malls, and most of what we still think of as malls, are so-called strip malls. There was a hiatus in the building of malls until the post–World War II suburban boom gave it new impetus. The first "dumbbell" mall, Northgate in Seattle, was built in 1947. It included "two department stores anchoring the ends of an open-air pedestrian mall, set in the middle of acres of parking."[55] More important, the first modern, fully enclosed shopping mall was Southdale Center in Edina, Minnesota, which opened in 1956. Enclosing the mall gave it a vertical dimension and served to make it more spectacular. Enclosed malls were also cheaper in many ways to build and created a synergy that increased business for all occupants. Many shopping malls have since been built on the Southdale model, and they are considered one of the new means of consumption. One of the largest is the 1.7-million-square foot Ontario Mills outside of Los Angeles with 200 stores and a 30-screen movie house.[56]

However, the formulaic pattern of shopping malls and the competition from newer means of consumption have caused the conventional outdoor mall, especially the strip mall, considerable difficulty. One observer went so far as to argue that we are moving into a "postmall world,"[57] and this was *before* the onset of the current recession. Shopping time per trip to the mall has been declining since the early 1980s. The number of trips to the mall has declined dramatically as well.[58] A significant number of existing regional malls either will be forced to close or will be converted to other purposes. While the current economic downturn is one source of the malls' problems, another is the fact that they all look very much alike. "There is too much sameness in retailing. If you dropped a person into most malls, they would not know what part of the country they were in."[59] The result is a shift toward entertainment in shopping malls[60] (more generally, the "entertainmentization" of retailing[61]), as well as the development of different kinds of malls.

Of tremendous importance itself as a cathedral of consumption, the shopping mall has been of perhaps even greater importance in providing the groundwork for a variety of related developments. There is, for example, the development of increasingly large malls culminating in so-called megamalls such as the West Edmonton Mall (opened in 1981) in Alberta, Canada, and the Mall of America in Minneapolis, Minnesota (opened in 1992). The newest mega-mall is Xanadu, scheduled to open in late 2010 (for more on Xanadu and its likely problems resulting from opening in the Great Recession, see Chapter 8).

In recent years, the epicenter of the growth in malls and mega-malls has shifted from the United States to other parts of the world, especially China. A majority of the world's largest indoor shopping malls already exist in China; most of the largest mega-malls now exist in Asia.[62] The largest, by far, is the South China Mall in Dongguan, China,[63] which is much larger than the Canadian and American mega-malls (see Chapter 8).

There is also the profusion in the United States of various kinds of specialty malls, especially the discount outlet malls that have been so popular in resorts or as tourist destinations. The first outlets appeared in the 1920s attached to the mills of New England fabric companies. Later, the outlets took hold in association with the sewing factories in the Southeast. The first outlet centers are traceable to the opening of the Reading (Pennsylvania) Outlet Center in 1970. Larger outlet malls began to appear in the 1980s. The largest is Sawgrass Mills in Florida, which encompasses 2 million square feet, attracts millions of customers a year, and is one of the state's most popular tourist attraction (trailing Disney World and Universal Studios).[64] The outlet mall in tiny Manchester, Vermont (population 3,600), is a large contributor of sales tax revenue to the state.[65] While they have suffered a decline in numbers in recent years,[66] outlet malls have become a cultural phenomenon, destinations in their own right. People even take vacations or trips to go to outlet malls. For example, on a typical fall weekend with the changing foliage at its peak, one is likely to find long lines at Manchester's factory stores, but the nearby Appalachian Trail is apt to be comparatively empty.[67] Outlet malls and their seemingly discounted prices are likely to be particularly attractive in hard economic times.

Also of interest is the spread of shopping malls into other settings such as Las Vegas casinos, cruise ships, airports, train stations, and college campuses (especially in student unions). And we can think of various sites on the Internet—eBay.com, Amazon.com, and Overstock.com, for example—as virtual shopping malls (see "Electronic Shopping Centers").

Finally, mention should be made of a more recent type of mall—Easton Town Center in Columbus, Ohio—to be discussed at length in Chapter 7. Easton is, as we will see, a shopping mall that is also a town with apartments and substantial office space. Once part of larger towns or in distinct and separable (often suburban) locations, the mall of the future may be, like Easton Center, a town unto itself. While it has an indoor mall, Easton Town Center is primarily an open-air mall. As such, it is part of a very recent trend away from indoor malls and back to those that are outdoors.[68] As one architect put it, "There's something magical about being able to look up and see the sky."[69]

Overall, in an average month, hundreds of millions of people shop in U.S. malls, the vast majority of the adult population. Malls employ millions of people and a significant percentage of nonfarm employees in the United States.[70] Malls are now so diverse and ubiquitous that one scholar describes the United States as "the world's biggest shopping mall."[71]

Electronic Shopping Centers

Worthy of special treatment is the advent of the "dematerialized" new means of consumption. One variant is the television home-shopping networks such as HSN (Home Shopping Network) or QVC (Quality, Value, Convenience).

Round-the-clock television retailing has grown enormously in the years since it was first broadcast on HSN in 1985; QVC followed a year later.[72]

Another variant is the infomercial, which is estimated to have done almost $200 billion in business in 2007.[73] These are ordinarily half-hour "shows" (typically broadcast late at night or on weekends) that are really extended advertisements for a particular product. They are included as a means of consumption because they usually offer telephone numbers that allow viewers to purchase the product by telephone and credit card.[74]

Internet shopping, or more generally e-commerce, is still relatively new. The Internet was founded in 1988, based on earlier technologies such as Arpanet (created in 1969 by the Pentagon for messages between defense labs and universities) and NSFNET.[75] Although fewer than 10 million households had online computer access in 1995, by early 2008, 77% of American homes had such access.[76] Wal-Mart opened its online Internet center in 1996 with 2,500 items; it now offers over a million items online.[77] Big attractions are sites that offer stocks, computer equipment, music, movies, books, and flowers.[78] Worth special notice is Netflix, which began renting DVDs through the mail in 1999 and now has 7.5 million subscribers.[79] However, Netflix is now moving away from movie delivery by mail and to the streaming of movies to one's PC, TV, TiVo, Xbox 360, and Blu-Ray DVD player.[80] This is likely to be its big growth area in the coming years. Then there are sites such as ebay.com and craigslist.com where one can find virtually everything one could ever want. While indications are that Internet sales will continue to boom (e.g., even during the otherwise disastrous Christmas season of 2008, Amazon.com claimed that 2008 was its "best ever" holiday season[81]), the biggest growth is likely still some years away, and additional future major expansion may be in business-to-business commerce and finance.[82] In the long term, it is likely that online shopping will outstrip the shopping mall, especially as more and more people use their PDAs (e.g., iPhones, Blackberries) to shop.

Amazon.com is an interesting case study in this realm. In 1994, the company's founder, Jeff Bezos, then on Wall Street, noticed that the new World Wide Web was growing at 2,300% a year. He decided he wanted to do business on the Web and thought through a list of products that could be sold. He decided on books because of the large variety, the fact that no single merchandiser controlled the market, and because computers could help customers find what they wanted. He quit his job and headed for Seattle because it was a high-tech town and provided him access to an important book distribution center. Thus, a new means for consuming books was founded. Amazon.com moved well beyond simply selling books and sells such a diverse array of products that it is now thought of as a virtual shopping mall. By the late 1990s, Jeff Bezos had become a multibillionaire.[83]

Also worth noting is the dramatic and controversial growth of gambling through online casinos such as World Sports Exchange.[84] Already a multibillion dollar a year business,[85] it is expected to continue to grow. Like all of the cybersites discussed, it is a threat to the more conventional means of consumption, in this case the casino (to be discussed shortly). The reason is clear from the following statement by a person who plays almost every day for 2 or 3 hours: "It's great. I don't have to leave the house. . . . It's very private. There are no distractions, no dirty looks from the casino people if you win."[86] Much the same thing could be said by consumers of perhaps the most important online business, pornography, and Web sites devoted to consuming it are expanding at a dramatic rate (although they are losing ground to free amateur sites).[87]

Discounters

Discount merchandising began to boom in the 1950s. Although such stores had predecessors (e.g., Korvette's, Kmart), discount department stores have undergone enormous expansion.[88] Of great note is the Wal-Mart chain. It and its major competitor, Target, were both founded in 1962. For the fiscal year ending January 31, 2008, Wal-Mart's total sales were almost $374 billion, and it had more than 176 million customers per week.[89] As of 2008, there were 971 Wal-Mart stores, 2,447 supercenters, and 132 neighborhood markets.[90] In addition, Wal-Mart spawned Sam's Club—a chain of warehouse stores— that began operations in 1983 and now has 591 outlets. (Warehouse clubs are very basic retail operations with merchandise displayed in huge, bare settings, and they offer opportunities to buy in bulk. They advertise little and offer few services. Membership requirements are very loose, and the annual cost for an individual is usually between $40 and $50.[91])

Another warehouse club, Costco, was created out of a merger of Price Club (founded in 1976 by Sol Price) and Costco (created in 1983). As of the end of 2008, the company operated 403 warehouse stores in the United States (a total of 550 throughout the world), averaging more than 130,000 square feet in size, in 40 states (and Puerto Rico). In 2008, it had 57 million cardholders and employed more than 142,000 people in the United States. In fiscal year 2008, its revenues exceeded $71 billion.[92] Like Sam's Club, Costco is characterized by simple, warehouse-like settings. A limited range of low-priced and discount goods, including food, are sold. Costco offers discounted goods, especially in large sizes and in multiple-item packages, so that consumers often end up purchasing more of a given commodity than they intended to purchase. Demonstrations and samples are abundant. Goods are laid out in such a way that customers often end up buying many things on a whim that they may not need or ever finish.

Also worth mentioning are supercenters that combine a grocery store, a drug store, and a mass merchandiser in one enormous setting. For example, a 200,000–square foot Wal-Mart Supercenter is twice as large as a normal Wal-Mart and six or seven times the size of a typical supermarket.[93] Wal-Mart opened its first supercenter in 1988 and, as mentioned above, now has almost 2,500 of them. Other important operators of supercenters are Fred Meyer in the West, Meijer in the Midwest, Target, and BJ's.

It is worth noting that because of their emphasis on low price, discounters and supercenters continue to succeed even in the current recession. The same cannot be said of the cathedral of consumption to be discussed next—the superstore.

Superstores

Not to be confused with the supercenter is the superstore (or "big box" store), which is arguably traceable to a 1957 ancestor of the current Toys 'R Us.[94] The distinguishing characteristic of a superstore is that it carries an extraordinary number and range of goods within a specific retail category.[95] Toys 'R Us has all the toys one can imagine (and it controls 16% of the U.S. toy market, although it long ago lost its leadership position in this area to Wal-Mart, which now accounts for over 25% of toy sales,[96] largely because it sells many toys close to or below wholesale prices); Home Depot is the giant in home improvement building supplies (a major competitor is Lowe's); Best Buy offers a wide range of electronic gear; books are the specialty at Barnes & Noble and Borders; office supplies are abundant at Staples, and the specialties of many of the rest—Sports Authority, Babies R Us, PetSmart, and so on—are obvious from the names. Superstores have evolved in a number of incredible, even bizarre, directions with, for example, Garden Ridge at one time offering 4,000 varieties of candles. Many of these superstores overspecialized (in candles, canes, or thousands of varieties of recreational shoes) and have since disappeared.

Superstores are sometimes called "category killers" because their enormous variety and low price tended to drive an earlier means of consumption, the small specialty shop, out of business.[97] They account for a large proportion of retail revenue in the United States, up from virtually nothing a few decades ago. However, like much else in the economy, the superstores overexpanded in the boom years of the 1990s and early 21st century. A number of them have gone bankrupt or have reduced their number of stores.[98] While such closings are likely to continue (see Chapter 8), this can be seen as a weeding out of weaker chains and stores in a domain that saw great overexpansion. After the dust settles, the stronger superstores (e.g., Best Buy; Bed Bath & Beyond) will remain as the dominant players in this type of cathedral of consumption.

The new means of consumption discussed to this point are the kinds of settings that most of us frequent on a regular basis. There is a whole other set of new means of consumption that are more unusual. They relate more to tourism, or extraordinary vacations, than to day-to-day activities; they involve attempts to escape the mundane.[99] In fact, they are part of a general trend toward viewing tourism as a type of consumption.[100] Disney World and other theme parks are one example, but there are several others.

Cruise Ships

Cruise ships have a long history. The great ocean liners of the late 1800s and early 1900s are certainly important predecessors. However, the modern cruise ship can be traced to the maiden voyage of the cruise ship *Sunward* in Florida on December 19, 1966.[101] A major boon to the cruise business occurred in 1977, when the television series *Love Boat* made its debut. The show took place on ships of the Princess Line and made that line famous. It also served to popularize the cruise. The Carnival line began operations in 1972 and soon thereafter came to emphasize the "Fun Ship."

In recent years, both cruise ships and the idea of a cruise have been revolutionized. In the early years of the industry, people took ships to get from one location to another; the ship was seen as a novel way of getting to interesting locales. Now the experience of the ships themselves, as well as the entertaining experience onboard, is the main reason for taking a cruise. There are significantly more cruise ships, and cruises are far more frequent. Although the cruise lines carried only about one-half million passengers in 1970, by 1995, that number had increased tenfold to 5 million passengers[102] and has since increased to about 12.6 million passengers.[103] Through most of the 1980s and 1990s, the number of cruise passengers grew at a rate of 7.6% per year,[104] and despite a lull due to the terrorist attacks of September 11, 2001, by 2007, the number has grown by 4.7% a year.[105] With the beginning of the recession in late 2007, cruise ships began to experience declines. While problems will continue, cruise ships will survive because they are so spectacular *and* because they are perceived by many as offering an inexpensive type of vacation (cruise lines are now even offering customers the option of financing their voyages) for such a spectacular experience (the largest cruise ship by far, the Royal Caribbean *Oasis of the Seas,* which can handle well over 6,000 passengers,[106] is currently under construction and scheduled to launch in December 2009 [see Chapter 6]). There are now many more cruise destinations and a much wider variety of types of cruises (gay, family, nature, etc.).

The cruise ship itself has been transformed. Ships of the 1970s tended to be small, uncomfortable in inclement weather, with tiny cabins, no television, and limited menus. Although there are a wide variety of cruise ships, the most popular have become much larger and more spectacular. They also have come to encompass a number of other means of consumption such as casinos, night clubs, health spas, shopping malls, bars, and so on. Each of these plays a role in making the modern cruise ship a highly effective means for getting people to spend large sums of money and consume an array of services and goods.

Casino-Hotels

Like amusement parks and cruise ships, casinos (often coupled with hotels as casino-hotels) have a lengthy history. The modern casino-hotel can be traced to the founding of the Flamingo by gangster Bugsy Siegel in Las Vegas in 1946.[107] There had been casinos in Las Vegas prior to this time, but the Flamingo was the first of what was to be the development of increasingly spectacular casino-hotels. In its early years, Las Vegas relied on income from gambling, and other potential money makers (hotel rooms, food, shows, etc.) either were loss leaders or marginal producers of income. Later, Las Vegas reinvented itself and became more oriented to family entertainment. Although gambling was still an important source of revenue, the other facets of the business of casino-hotels were also designed to make lots of money. The casino-hotel became a highly effective means of promoting gambling, the Las Vegas experience, and the activities, souvenirs, and other products that go with them.

More recently, Las Vegas has begun to rethink its emphasis on family entertainment. With business beginning to flag in the early 21st century, there was some return to the basics of Las Vegas's early success—gambling and sex. However, it seems likely that to maximize its number of visitors, Las Vegas will try to combine the latter with more family-oriented venues and activities.

Modern Las Vegas hotels make money by offering thousands of rooms with high operating margins. The city as a whole has well over 100,000 hotel rooms, and new casino-hotels have opened (Wynn Encore in late 2008) and are under construction (e.g., the Cosmopolitan and City Place [see Chapter 8]). The casinos are enormous and spectacular, offering an increasingly large number of ways to gamble. And these casinos are huge money makers for the house with operating margins on table games (e.g., blackjack) of roughly 25% and of more than 50% on slot machines, the true cornerstones of the modern casino.[108] Whatever last small bills and coins a departing visitor might not yet have lost or spent are apt to be taken by the slot machines at Las Vegas's McCarran Airport or in state-line casinos for those who are leaving by automobile (if they haven't lost it, as well).

Las Vegas casinos have also, in one way or another, been transported to much of the rest of the United States. The most notable examples are the casinos in Atlantic City, on Native American reservations, and in many other settings. Tunica County, Mississippi, "long known as one of America's most wretched backwaters," almost overnight became a gambling mecca with nine casinos (several of them branches of Las Vegas casinos) and by the late 1990s was averaging 50,000 visitors a day.[109] In just 5 years, it went from the poorest to the richest county in Mississippi. Other examples of the spread of the casino influence include the previously discussed online casinos as well as racetracks, many of which are managing to survive only because of their poker rooms and slot machines. Las Vegas hotels have also expanded overseas with perhaps the most notable example being in Macau, just off the coast of China (see Chapter 7).

Yet, the ongoing recession has been difficult for casino-hotels in Las Vegas, Macau, and many other locales throughout the United States and the world. There may be some closings because of excessive expansion, but it is likely that in the long run, most major casino-hotels will survive and at least some will prosper.

Entertainment Aimed at Adults

The Las Vegas casino model has had other kinds of influences. For example, there is a chain of adult-oriented entertainment centers known as Dave and Buster's (the first one opened in 1982; there are now 48 complexes throughout the United States[110]), which look like miniature casinos; the chain was at one time seen as a possible harbinger of "the Las Vegasification of America."[111] In fact, one of the co-owners said, "By virtue of its scale and the adult concept . . . yes, we're like Las Vegas."[112] They are large (in one case, 50,000 square feet) and have bars, restaurants, pool tables, and many modern (video and virtual reality games such as virtual skiing and car racing) and traditional (e.g., skee ball) arcade games. One can win tickets redeemable for prizes. Servers deliver food and drink to the play areas from the restaurant and bars.

Reflective of the Vegas influence, Dave and Buster's is itself also representative of the growing number of new means of consuming adult-oriented entertainment (now sometimes called "shoppertainment"). Many shopping malls offer entertainment like that found at Dave and Buster's.

Eatertainment

Another contemporaneous example of the trend toward emphasizing entertainment is chains of themed restaurants (often called "eatertainment"). Theme restaurants "typically combine lackluster food, designs that resemble theater sets and entertainment ranging from costumed waiters to museums of memorabilia."[113] The pioneer in this realm, Hard Rock Cafe, was founded in London in 1971. Although a British creation, it took as its mission the introduction of "good, wholesome American food" to the English. Today, there are 124 Hard Rock Cafes in 48 countries.[114] It is interesting to note that it is not the food but products with the Hard Rock Cafe logo that are generally coveted by visitors and tourists. According to one observer, "Most people who wear the T-shirts never even sit down to have a meal there; they simply walk into the apparel stores to look at and purchase Hard Rock buttons, caps and sweatshirts. What in the world compels these people to buy memorabilia from a restaurant in which they have never eaten?"[115] In fact, with the wide array of merchandise (including $295 leather jackets) now available sporting the Hard Rock Cafe logo,[116] the wearing of anything with that logo gives the wearer almost instant international recognition. As Thorstein Veblen argued long ago, "Esteem is awarded only on evidence," and for many today that evidence is the Hard Rock logo on a T-shirt.[117]

A similar chain (albeit one that has had financial difficulty and been through bankruptcy) is Planet Hollywood, which openly admits that it "operates movie-themed restaurants in the Hard Rock Cafe 'eatertainment' vein."[118] Instead of rock memorabilia, Planet Hollywood offers movie memorabilia. It does not try to conceal the fact that its hamburgers are "high-priced." And it proudly states that the sale of T-shirts and other souvenirs accounts for 40% of all of its sales. Planet Hollywood has 16 restaurants throughout the world, as well as a casino-hotel in Las Vegas. Hard Rock also operates a casino-hotel in Las Vegas, as well as at a number of other locations throughout the United States.

The leader in children's eatertainment is Chuck E. Cheese's restaurants, which in late 2007 had 490 company-owned and 11 franchise restaurants in 48 states and five countries. In addition to food, Chuck E. Cheese's offers games and entertainment of various kinds. It is best known for its "musical and comic entertainment by life-size, computer-controlled robotic characters."[119] Rainforest Cafe is another player in this area with 35 locations in eight nations.[120] However, this is a tough market and many entrants have failed, with others having difficulty getting established, let alone expanding to any great extent.

OTHER MEANS OF CONSUMPTION

The cathedrals of consumption are important not only in themselves but also for their influence on other parts of society. A surprising number of settings are emulating the new means of consumption in one way or another.

A variety of modern athletic facilities such as golf clubs, tennis clubs, ski resorts, and fitness centers can all be seen as new means for consuming athletic activities. The newer professional athletic stadiums can be described in a similar fashion. In baseball, early innovators were Baltimore's Oriole Park at Camden Yards, the Cleveland Indians's Jacobs Field, and the Atlanta Braves's Turner Field. A number of others have been built in recent years, with the most notable and expensive being the new Yankee Stadium that opened in New York City in 2009 (it will end up costing well over $1 billion). Although these stadiums often resemble earlier versions and even seek to copy them in many ways, they also have a number of innovations. For example, they all feature spectacular computerized scoreboards; they have all become more adept at extracting money from those who use their services (e.g., high-priced suites at baseball and football games; food courts that resemble those found in shopping malls; elaborate souvenir shops). The new Yankee Stadium features a "Great Hall" with over a million square feet of retail space (as well as, among other things, a Hard Rock Cafe). As a stock prospectus for the Cleveland Indians Baseball Company put it, "Fans at Jacobs Field are offered a customer-focused experience in an attractive, comfortable environment featuring a variety of amenities, concessions and merchandise options."[121] Although these athletic facilities have a long history, the more modern forms are far more oriented to, and effective at, serving as means for the consumption of athletic services (and related goods and services). Not only have new stadiums been built with these amenities, but older ones (such as Boston's Fenway Park[122]) have been altered to include a number of them.

Many of these things have now found their way to the college level in football stadiums and basketball arenas (e.g., the renovated Byrd Stadium [football] and the relatively new Comcast Center [basketball] on the campus of the University of Maryland). In minor league baseball, there is a miniature version of Oriole Park (Ripken Stadium) built in the small town of Aberdeen, Maryland, by former Oriole Star Cal Ripken Jr. for his team, the Aberdeen IronBirds.[123] In addition to many other similarities with Oriole Park, Ripken Stadium offers a scaled-down version of the old-fashioned warehouse beyond right field in Oriole Park (which was left standing and renovated to help give the Oriole Park the aura of an old-time stadium). On the Aberdeen complex, of which Ripken Stadium is part, there are other fields for youngsters. Besides those "themed" to resemble Oriole Park, one is reminiscent of Memorial Stadium that preceded it as the home of the Baltimore Orioles.

Like the new athletic stadiums, luxury gated communities often seek to resemble, and even to copy, traditional communities. Unlike the majority of these early communities, these new communities have opted to wall themselves off from the outside and to privatize their streets.[124] Consumed in these spectacular settings are expensive homes and a rich and luxurious lifestyle, including golf courses, tennis clubs, fitness facilities, and so on. Almost de rigueur in these communities are expensive home furnishings, landscaping, and automobiles. (In the exclusive and expensive gated communities of Boca Raton, Florida, the high-priced Lexus is known as the "Boca Chevy.")

Administrators are coming to recognize that in order to thrive, their educational campuses need to grow more like the other new means of consumption. The high school has been described as resembling a shopping mall.[125] The university, too, can be seen as a means of educational consumption. These days, most campuses are dated, stodgy, and ineffective compared to shopping malls, cruise ships, casinos, and fast-food restaurants. To compete, universities are trying to satisfy their students by offering, in addition to state-of-the art athletic facilities that have many of the characteristics of professional stadiums, food courts and "themed housing"—dorms devoted to students with shared special interests.[126] As universities learn more and more from the new means of consumption, it will be increasingly possible and accurate to refer to them as "McUniversities."[127] A related and important trend is the growth of the online university, especially the Western Governors University put together at the initiative of the governors of 19 states (as well as 20 U.S. corporations)[128] and University of Phoenix online.[129] It will be increasingly difficult to distinguish such dematerialized universities from e-commerce.

A similar point can be made about medicine and hospitals.[130] We already have "McDoctors" (drive-in, quick service medical facilities), and there are many indications that we are moving in the direction of "McHospitals." Examples of the latter trend include expensive suites that look more like hotel than hospital accommodations, more and more "in-and-out" procedures, and so on.

Even museums are coming to look more like shopping malls.[131] The Metropolitan Museum of Art houses what amounts to a small department store and has 17 satellite stores in six states as well as 17 international stores in seven countries, selling books and museum-made products. The "MetStore" is even online.[132] The Louvre has 55 shops in France (with 14 others licensed to carry its products), an underground shopping mall with high-end boutiques such as Chanel and Yves Saint-Laurent,[133] and an online store.[134] The National Gallery of Art in Washington, D.C., has been described in the following terms:

The huge skylighted atrium is surrounded by promenades connected by bridges and escalators; individual galleries open off this space, placed exactly where shops would be in the mall. Potted plants, lavish use of marble and brass, and, in the neon-lit basement concourse, fountains, shops, and fast-food counters make the resemblance even more striking.[135]

The former chair of Neiman Marcus said, "I was in the Metropolitan [Museum of Art] recently, and I was flabbergasted when I saw the size of their store. They are selling everything from rugs to jewelry."[136] He might have been less flabbergasted had he known that the roots of the modern museum are, in part, in the World's Fairs and Expositions.

We can bring this discussion full-circle by pointing out that although the cathedrals of consumption have a quasi-religious character, religion has begun to emulate those cathedrals[137] and, more generally, to become more oriented to "Christotainment."[138] Here is one description of the result:

Megachurches are huge steel and glass structures with acres of parking . . . at their fanciest [they] feature aerobics classes, bowling alleys, counseling centers, and multimedia bible classes where the presentation rivals that of MTV. On Sunday morning, big screens project Scripture verses and the lyrics to pop-style religious songs so that everyone in the congregation can see and follow along.[139]

Said one expert, "They're the biggest movement going in the Protestant Church."[140] Another commented, "They are what I call the Wal-Martization of American Religion."[141] Similarly, the pastor of a large Baptist church has sought to make his services "fun" and to that end urged his staff to study Disney World.[142]

CONCLUSION

This chapter has been devoted to introducing the twin concepts of new means of consumption and cathedrals of consumption. I have also introduced the reader to the major types and examples of such means. Chapter 2 offers insight into the wider context and implications of the cathedrals of consumption, as well as their impact on the way Americans and, increasingly, much of the world consumes.

2

The Revolution in Consumption and the Larger Society

This chapter is devoted to several interrelated issues. First, we will examine why we witnessed, at least until very recently, a steady rise in the new means of consumption. Second, we will analyze the role that the cathedrals of consumption play in generating hyperconsumption. Third, we will discuss the fact that the new means are affecting not only how much we consume but also the ways in which we consume. Fourth, we will see that the new means of consumption are having similar effects in many other parts of the world.

WHY DID THE REVOLUTION OCCUR?

The creation of means of consumption is nothing new. However, the pace accelerated dramatically after the end of World War II, and expansion continued until the beginning of the recession in late 2007. Following the war, and until very recently, people wanted and could afford (or at least thought they could) ever more goods and services. The means of consumption proliferated to give people what they wanted, to create new wants, and, in the process, to allow those who satisfied those desires to profit. But why did so many people come to want so much more? One reason is that many people had more resources, and they were eager to spend much of it on personal consumption. There was (and is) also an enormous amount of money invested in advertising designed to create those wants and to induce people to consume. Stuart Ewen traces the development of modern advertising to the 1920s and to the realization on the part of owners and managers that it was no longer enough to control only workers.[1] Consumers had come to play too important a role in capitalism to allow them to make decisions solely on their own. The result was the growth of modern advertising designed to "help" people make those decisions. This represented an early step in the movement from a production to a consumption society.

It is clear that over the years, we moved much further in that direction; in fact, American society is still far better characterized by consumption than production (70% of gross domestic product [GDP] is attributable to consumption, or at least it was before the Great Recession). That is, as more and more basic production was moving to other nations, especially developing nations, consumption assumed center stage in American society. Although advertising has certainly proliferated enormously, other mechanisms for controlling consumers can be identified. The new means of consumption are the most important of these other controls.[2] Their development after World War II supplemented the efforts, begun in the 1920s in advertising, to control consumers. People are lured to the cathedrals of consumption by the fantasies they promise to fulfill and then kept there by a variety of rewards and constraints. The idea is to keep people at the business of consumption. This is nowhere clearer than in the case of credit cards,[3] which lured people into consumption by easy credit and then enticed them into still further consumption by offers of "payment holidays," new cards, and increased credit limits. The beauty of all of this, at least from the point of view of those who profited from the system, is that people were (and are) kept in the workplace and on the job by the need to pay the monthly minimums on their credit card accounts (and their home equity loans) and, more generally, to support their consumption habits.

The Economy

Many other factors were involved in the growth of the new means of consumption. The booming economy—especially the dramatic expansion in the 1990s and through late 2007, as reflected in the startling upturn in the stock market and a minuscule unemployment rate—left large numbers of people with unprecedented amounts of disposable income. The economic downturn associated with the aftermath of the terrorist attacks of September 11, 2001, slowed consumption for a time, but it quickly returned, or exceeded, its previous high levels, at least for a large proportion of the population. It helped that the mayor of New York City and the president of the United States urged people to respond to the crisis by going shopping. Of course, as I write, it is far less clear what the impact, both short and long term, will be of the current deep recession (we will have much more to say about this issue in Chapter 8). For those with disposable income (and even many without it), consumption, especially shopping,[4] became (and for many still is) a major form of recreation. Increasingly, many people had the time to spend their large incomes. For example, many were retiring earlier even as their life expectancy was increasing. The result was many years of the life cycle in which the focus, to a large extent, was on consumption. And because of the strong economy, an increasing number of retirees had the wherewithal to be active consumers.

The growth of the new means of consumption was also fueled by the increasing reality that corporations, including those that owned the new means of consumption, were driven by the stock market in which it was not good enough to maintain a high level of profitability; profits had to show a substantial increase from one year (or even quarter) to the next. This created a continually expanding need to lure people into the marketplace more frequently and more actively and to keep them there longer. Old customers needed to be retained and new customers recruited. The new means of consumption offered more new goods and services, sometimes at bargain prices,[5] in increasingly fantastic settings, an irresistible combination to many people. Good examples were (and are) outlets of electronics chains such as Best Buy where huge stores, impressive and often interactive displays of a wide array of the latest gear, and very low prices attract legions of shoppers and many buyers. The new means of consumption both lured more people out of their homes to consume *and* allowed them to consume more even while they were at home. The fantastic settings represented, or at least did until recently, key sites where more of people's resources were extracted *and* more of their future income was captured in the form of credit card or other consumer debt.

There was a confluence of interests here: People wanted, or at least were led to think they wanted, all of those goods and services. The new means of consumption required consumers to want those things and in increasing quantities. The same was true of manufacturers. Bank loan officers and the executives of credit card companies also had vested interests in increased consumption because that meant rising debt and growing income from servicing that debt. Politicians wanted (and still want) to see an increasingly robust economy—their positions often depended on it—so they adopted policies that helped to pump it up (e.g., making it easier for people to obtain mortgage loans), although the dilemma now is how to rebuild the economy without the disastrous debt levels that wrecked it during the recession.

The Youth Market

More teenagers and young children than ever before were and are involved in the economy as consumers.[6] As Ellen Goodman put it, "The marketplace has turned kids into short consumers."[7] Young people have much more money and play a larger role in family decisions about consumption, with the result that many of the new means of consumption cater to them directly (fast-food restaurants and theme parks) or indirectly (amusement parks in mega-malls, superstores such as Toys 'R Us, Blockbuster Video, online consumption sites offering games, music, and movies).

Take the role that McDonald's and Disney, alone and in concert, play in hooking children on consumption.[8] Both clearly recognize that their success depends on attracting young children.[9] Of course, children grow up to be adult consumers, many of whom eventually will have children of their own and begin the cycle anew.

In recent years, children and adolescents have become increasingly important consumers in their own right (e.g., lines of cosmetics and iPods and their associated iTunes targeted at children and adolescents), and they play a central role in bringing adults into a number of the new means of consumption (e.g., Apple Store). In the past, toys were play versions of adult tools (the toy hammer), taught adult skills (erector sets, dollhouses), or involved shared interests in gadgets (electric trains).[10] The 1930s witnessed the first toys that were not play versions of adult objects and that appealed directly to children, among them toys derived from the early Disney characters. By the 1950s, toys such as Barbie and G. I. Joe were being marketed directly to children through television advertisements. Today, adults know little or nothing of many toys—Leapfrog Leapster 2 or Guitar Hero World Tour, for example— "because they are part of a distinct children's culture that is marketed directly to children on television and at the movies."[11] Children must make their toy interests known to adults so that adults can make the purchase. Or adults can surrender completely, give the children money, and allow the children to make purchases on their own.

Technological Change

The chasm between children and their toys and adults has led to online toy registries (kidsreg.com, walmart.com/catalog/catalog.gsp?cat=4171, www9 .toysrus.com/index.cfm?lb=1, and other Web sites). Children (parents can assist very young children) can create an online wish list that can be accessed by relatives and friends anywhere in the world. Such online wish lists are great aids to adults ignorant of the world of children's toys, but they put even more power in the hands of children in determining consumption, and they bolster the position of any means of consuming toys (and everything else) using such a system.

It is probable that technological change is the most important factor in the ascendancy of the new means of consumption. Automobiles and superhighways enabled us to use shopping malls, superstores, fast-food restaurants, and so on. The national highway system was developed in the 1950s, expediting the development of Disneyland and Disney World, Las Vegas, Atlantic City, and, more recently, Tunica County, Mississippi. The commercial jet airplane arrived in 1952; its development through the 1950s and beyond allowed resorts and cruise lines, to say nothing of airports and their attendant malls, to prosper. Television, first nationally broadcast in 1946, was necessary for the emergence of home-shopping networks and infomercials. The explosive growth of express package deliverers such as UPS, FedEx, DHL, and the like revolutionized the ability of consumers to obtain commodities. By increasing the speed and efficiency of package delivery, these carriers played a major role in making possible a number of the new means of consumption. E-commerce, home television shopping, and catalog shopping all depend on such delivery services for quick, low-cost delivery.

No technological change was more important in this context than the building of the first high-speed computer in 1946. Virtually all of the new means of consumption would be impossible, at least in their present forms, without the computer. Far-flung chains and franchises could not operate without computers to keep track of sales, inventories, shipments of goods, and so on. The toy wish lists described previously depend on the computer. Modern amusement parks, cruise ships, and gambling casinos depend on computers for a variety of tasks. Online malls and other consumption sites could have come into existence only with the development and widespread use of powerful home computers.

And technological change is important in bringing a steady stream of new and alluring products to the market. In recent years, for example, DVD players/recorders have replaced videocassette players/recorders and are themselves now being replaced by videos streaming to home computer or TV screens, and high-definition television receivers are replacing traditional analog receivers (which, as of mid-2009, no longer function unless one has a converter box or is associated with a cable provider).

New Facilitating Means

Many of the technological changes discussed in the preceding section (the computer, highways, etc.) facilitate the operation of the new means of consumption but are not themselves such means. The recent development of new facilitating means contributed greatly to the rise of the new means of consumption.

A major example is the credit card.[12] The credit card is *not* itself a means of consumption. It is not a setting or a place of consumption, of course. The goods or services that we desire are not to be found in the credit card. But the credit card is a mechanism that facilitates our ability to use various means of consumption. It is possible to bring large sums of cash or, for that matter, even gold ingots to the shopping mall, but consuming at a mall is expedited if we use a credit (or debit) card. In the case of more recent means of consumption such as home-shopping television and online shopping, we are unable to use other facilitating means such as cash; the use of the credit card is mandatory. Indeed, much of the success of online shopping has been based on the ability of vendors and credit card companies to reassure consumers of the safety of disseminating credit card numbers through the Internet. The key point is that the credit card is a *facilitating means* that makes it possible for people to obtain what they want and need from the cathedrals of consumption.

Although most of the new means of consumption could exist without credit cards (visitors could bring wads of cash with them to Best Buy, Disney World, or Las Vegas), it could be argued that their explosive growth depended on the credit card. The arrival of the modern credit card beginning in the 1950s is more or less simultaneous with the appearance of many of the new means of consumption. As the use of the credit card expanded in ensuing decades, so did the new means of consumption. More recently, the arrival of massive home equity loans came to far outstrip credit cards as a source of money for consumers.

There are, of course, other types of facilitating means. Within the financial realm, cash, installment loans, personal checks, and traveler's checks preceded credit cards (and home equity loans) as important facilitators and continue to be important today because we are still a long way from a cashless and checkless society. Among the newer facilitating means of this type are debit cards, smart cards, and ATM (automatic teller machine) cards and ATMs themselves.

The Internet, itself a facilitator, is giving rise to other new facilitating means such as PayPal for online payments.[13] Apple has created the iPod to facilitate the purchase and downloading of music (as well as videos and photos) from the Internet. And there is the online iTunes Music Store (a new means of consumption), which permits the downloading of hundreds of thousands of tunes at a cost of 99 cents each.[14] Parents can even create refillable allowance accounts for their children, or accounts that automatically refill each month. Payment is made through the use of credit cards.

Even more important facilitators of consumption are the media and their ever-present advertisements. The new means of consumption, indeed almost all aspects of consumption, could not function were it not for the advertisements that are the lifeblood of the traditional media and are fast becoming central to the Internet as well. Although the facilitators of consumption are clearly of great and increasing importance, I will have little more to say about them in this book since the focus here is mainly on the new means of consumption themselves.

In any case, we should acknowledge that the distinction between means of consumption and facilitating means is not as clear-cut as it first appears. Although there are some pure facilitating means (e.g., money and credit cards), some phenomena can be simultaneously facilitators and means of consumption. For example, the contemporary airport facilitates the consumer's ability to fly to such places as Disney World and Las Vegas, but it is simultaneously a means for consuming airline tickets and, as it has grown more and more like a shopping mall,[15] many other goods and services (such as massages) as well. In fact, with airlines in most cases no longer offering food onboard, the airport restaurant and carryout business has boomed. Rather than get into these complexities, I will largely ignore pure facilitating means and, in those cases where a setting performs a dual function, focus on it as a means of consumption.

CHANGES IN HOW MUCH WE CONSUME

American consumerism is not a new phenomenon. Concern about it dates back nearly 200 years.[16] By the end of the 19th century,[17] according to William Leach, the "cardinal features of this culture were acquisition and consumption as the means of achieving happiness; the cult of the new; the democratization of desire; and money value as the predominant measure of all value in society."[18] The means of consumption of the day—large department stores, mail-order houses, dry goods shops, chain stores, banks, hotels and restaurants, dance halls, theaters, and amusement parks—played a key role in generating and supporting mass consumption.[19] Many of these have since declined in importance.[20] Others are still important and have been joined by the new cast of characters that are the subject of this book.

Leach discusses the concept of *consumptionism,* coined in 1925 by the journalist and political philosopher Samuel Strauss. According to Strauss, consumptionism involved a commitment to produce (and consume) more things from one year to the next. All other values were subordinated to emphasize one's standard of living. The concept of consumptionism involved an emphasis on the pressure that business interests placed on people to consume. Previously, business had sought to give consumers what they wanted. Now business shifted to an emphasis on seeking to compel consumers to want and to "need" the things that business was producing and selling. Traditions were being abandoned in the search for the new in goods and services. Business was interested only in "standardization, mass production, and mass distribution," and consumers were seen as little more than "'units in mass' or as 'mass consumers.'"[21]

There is little question that throughout the last half of the 20th century and the first 7 years of the 21st century, the United States was increasingly characterized by what has come to be termed *hyperconsumption*[22] and that most Americans grew increasingly obsessed by consumption.[23] Calling consumption America's "all-consuming passion," one journalist wrote near the peak of this obsession in early 2003, "Consumerism was the triumphant winner of the ideological wars of the 20th century, beating out both religion and politics as the path millions of Americans follow to find purpose, meaning and order and transcendent exaltation in their lives."[24] In a book that appeared just before the collapse of hyperconsumption caused by the beginning of the recession in 2007, Benjamin Barber argued that Americans had become "consumed" by consumption.[25] According to Juliet B. Schor, Americans spent three or four times as much time shopping as Western Europeans.[26] Of the total land area of the United States, about 4 billion square feet was devoted to shopping centers, which worked out to 16 square feet of shopping area per capita. And most important, "The average American [was] consuming, in toto, more than twice as much as he or she did forty years ago."[27] On a per capita basis, Americans were apt to consume more of virtually everything than people in most, if not all, other nations of the world. Examples included high-definition television sets, laptop computers, smartphones (which function like mini-computers), iPods, iPhones, automobiles, and the energy needed to keep them all running. In the realm of services, Americans became the world leaders in the consumption of medical, psychiatric, legal, and accounting services. It is not just that they consumed more of everything, but more varieties of most things were available to, and used by, American consumers than those of most other nations. (As we will see, Americans were eager to see the rest of the world join them in hyperconsumption, and many were eager to act just like Americans.)

At its broadest level, hyperconsumption[28] is a highly democratic form of consumption involving the vast majority of the population. The amount of money available to individuals for consumption varies enormously, but virtually everyone today, even at the depths of the current recession, is a consumer to some degree. The poor have fewer resources than the rich, most ethnic and racial minority groups have much less to spend than members of the majority, children have fewer means than adults, and so on, but all are enmeshed in the consumer culture. Even those who live on the streets survive off the discards and charity of that culture.[29] This is not to deny the immense impact of factors such as race, class, gender, and so forth on consumption, but it is virtually impossible for anyone in the United States to avoid being deeply involved in, or at least touched by, the culture of consumption.

Those with lots of resources may buy high-priced originals, and those with modest means may buy inexpensive imitations, but all are, or were until recently, buying. Beyond the purchase of luxury goods (or cheap simulations of them), everyone must consume the basics (e.g., food) needed to survive, although here, too, there is likely to be great variation in the prices paid for, and the quality of, the goods obtained. America has been characterized by mass consumption because all but a handful of the population is actively involved in one way or another as consumers. The mass character of consumption also means that the occupations of large numbers of people have been implicated in the culture of consumption (although millions of those jobs were lost as consumption declined precipitously in the recession). Many millions of people continue to work in fast-food restaurants, shopping malls, superstores, gambling casinos, cruise ships, and the like.[30]

There is yet another sense that mass consumption was (and may once again be) characteristic of American society: People were apt to spend most, if not all, of their available resources on consumer goods and services. In fact, in many cases, it became no longer enough to spend all available resources; one was enticed to go deeply and increasingly into debt.[31] Various data support this contention. For example, the rate of personal savings as a percentage of disposable income dropped from 6.2% in 1992 to 3.8% in 1997[32] and plummeted further to 1% in 2004 (however, in the current economic crisis, that rate has been rising, perhaps quite dramatically).[33] About half of all American households had no savings at all. Those in the world's other advanced economies were managing to save two to three times what Americans saved (although that did not protect many of them from the ravages of the global recession).[34] Conversely, Americans were far more likely to be in debt, and the average level of indebtedness was much greater. Huge and ever-increasing sums of money were owed on home mortgages, car loans, and credit card balances.[35] Total American credit card debt translated into $8,700 per household.[36] Many found themselves unable to repay their debts, as reflected, for example, in the increases in credit card and mortgage delinquencies, foreclosures, and bankruptcies.[37]

In the 20th century, the United States went from a society that emphasized personal savings to one that focused on debt. Banks had, to a large degree, shifted from the business of inducing people to save to luring them into debt. Americans received about 5 billion mail solicitations in 2007,[38] up from about 3 billion in 1997, imploring them to sign up for a credit card. (Another dimension of the recession is that this number declined to 4.2 billion in 2008 and is expected to decline even more precipitously in the coming years as banks and consumers rein in credit.[39]) The profits from servicing debt, especially credit card debt, were much higher than those derived from savings. Easy and extensive credit played a key role in making America's mass consumer society possible and that, especially in the form of credit cards, was exported to many parts of the world.

Schor adds to the idea that there were problems associated with hyperconsumption by contending that

> the new consumerism has led to a kind of mass "overspending" within the middle class . . . large numbers of Americans spend more than they say they would like to, and more than they have. That they spend more than they realize they are spending, and more than is fiscally prudent. And that they spend in ways that are collectively, if not individually, self-defeating. Overspending [was] how ordinary Americans cope with the everyday pressures of the new consumerism.[40]

However, Schor argues that public opinion polls demonstrated that despite the increase in consumption and in material possessions, Americans seemed no happier than previous generations. According to one who gave up the rat race, "The more you have, the more you spend, and the more you go into debt."[41] The increased demand for consumer goods forced people to devote long hours to work in order to pay for those goods, what Schor calls the work-and-spend syndrome. This focus on consumption meant that many people had to forgo the option of exchanging less work and more leisure time for fewer goods and services.[42]

The Role of the Cathedrals of Consumption

Advertising, credit card companies, and the consumers themselves (among others) played important roles in hyperconsumption, but our main focus is on the part played by the new means of consumption in this phenomenon. In addition to contributing to the general atmosphere of consumptionism, the cathedrals of consumption helped in various ways to lead to higher levels of consumption.[43] Most important, they were, and still are, designed artistically and scientifically to lure people into consumption.[44] For example:

- In Las Vegas casinos, the few remaining nickel slot machines are usually placed in hard-to-get-to corners where gamblers in search of them are forced to pass by—if they are able to resist—the lure of far greater payoffs from higher cost machines.

- In airports, wherever possible, gift shops are located on departing passengers' right as they head to the gate with fast-food restaurants on the left. The reasoning is that passengers are more likely to cross the aisle in order to get food; they might pass up the gift shop if it is not conveniently placed on the right.

- At the Gap, the much sought-after denims are positioned at the back of the store, forcing customers to pass by all of the other goods in order to get to them.

- In Disneyland and Disney World, the visitor enters and exits through a mini-mall, Main Street, so that purchases can be made both on entering and leaving.

- In shopping malls, the number of exits is often deliberately limited to keep people in the mall; escalators tend to be placed at the end of corridors to force people to walk their length; "fountains and benches are carefully positioned to entice shoppers into stores."[45]

- At the cathedral in Canterbury, England, visitors must leave through the gift shop, which sells a wide variety of souvenirs and *not* just those related to the cathedral specifically and religion in general.

• At warehouse stores such as Sam's Club and Costco, goods are sold in large quantities or multipacks so that people often end up buying more than they intended. Said one customer, "Look, you just see it and then you use it. I don't need 24 batteries, but, oh well, it's here and it's cheap and I'll use it—eventually."[46] In addition, consumers are channeled past long rows of seemingly bargain-priced nonfood items before even getting to the food area. Many of these items find their way into customers' carts.

• Direct-mail marketers seek to prevent us from throwing their junk mail directly into the trash by, for example, making it look like government mail, like it was delivered by a courier service, or by personalizing it by making it look as if it were handwritten.[47]

Although an older means of consumption, the supermarket continues to be important and is especially revealing in terms of the techniques used to lead customers to do what is desired of them:[48]

• The flower (or bakery) section is often the first one encountered in a supermarket. It is designed to tickle consumers' sensations, produce a positive image for the market and weaken consumers' resolve.

• The best place to display food is at the head and foot of each aisle. Food displayed in those places ("end caps") can easily double or triple in sales. More generally, sales increase for items displayed at eye level or at the beginning of an aisle.

• Foods oriented to children are usually placed lower on shelves. This allows children not only to see the products but also to pick them up and plead with a parent to purchase them.

• Dairy is generally on one side, produce on the other, with meat in the back. To get all the basics, customers must work their way through much of the store and its array of merchandise.

• Stacking cartons of merchandise in the aisles can slow shoppers down and cause them to peruse the shelves more. They also present a warehouse image that conveys a sense of bargain pricing.

There are many such examples, but the central point is that the means of consumption (both new and old) were, and continue to be, structured in such a way as to induce people to buy more than they intended.[49]

The novelist Émile Zola saw the department store as a "selling machine."[50] It is clear that the new means of consumption are far more sophisticated and effective selling machines than their predecessors were. In addition to the devices described, innovations such as drive-through windows, computerized inventory control and cash registers, adjacent and enormous parking lots, shop at home, and credit cards have all served to greatly enhance the ability of the "machines" to sell. However, the new means of consumption have done more than simply sell more things better.

CHANGES IN THE WAY WE CONSUME

The new means of consumption have also greatly altered the *way* we consume.

One-Stop Shopping

Many innovations aim at one-stop shopping. For those who want a wide range of goods at discount prices, Wal-Mart and its supercenters combine the discount store with a supermarket so that a shopper can get his or her food and other goods on one trip. For shoppers who want an even wider range of discounted merchandise, one stop at the discount mall should work. If, instead, consumers want a huge variety of a particular product (such as sneakers, electronics, etc.), a single trip to a superstore should do the trick. For those desiring a huge number of shops and department stores in one place, there is the shopping mall. For consumers who want all those shops as well as a wide range of entertainment, the mega-mall is the place for them. Then there are mall/towns such as Easton Town Center (see Chapter 7) where one can live amid, and in close proximity to, many new means of consumption. For all those who want to have a world of goods and services at their fingertips without leaving home, all they need do is open their catalogs (or check them online), turn the channel to the Home Shopping Network, or switch on the computer and enter cyberspace and its online malls. For vacationers who want to go to just one place and have a complete vacation experience, a cruise, a trip to Disney World, or a visit to Las Vegas will work quite well. At IKEA, parents shop for furniture while the children play at supervised play centers or on numerous displays throughout the mammoth store, and then all can have a low-priced lunch of Swedish meatballs at the in-store cafeteria. By offering a wide range of things under one roof or in one setting, the new means of consumption have altered the nature of the experience of shopping and vacationing by making them more efficient.

Destinations

As noted earlier, many of the new means of consumption are so all-encompassing, or more generally so attractive and appealing, that consumers set out with the specific intention of going to them and spending hours, or days, or even weeks there. For example, while in the past, vacationers may have set out for the warmth of Florida, many now head directly for Disney World. Clearly, not only Disney World but also Las Vegas and cruises have become such vacation destinations. All of the other new means of consumption have become destinations for more mundane outings—Best Buy when we want electronics, Wal-Mart and Toys 'R Us when we are desirous of toys, Costco and BJ's when in search of a bargain, IKEA for low-cost furniture, and so on. Not all of the new means of consumption seek to be all-encompassing, but they do seek to be destinations.

Do-It-Yourself and the Rise of the Prosumer

Doing more things ourselves is another major change in the way we consume, brought about by the new means of consumption. Many cathedrals of consumption require that the consumer do many tasks that in the older means of consumption were done for them. In traditional shops, clerks fetched goods for us, but we now spend a great deal of time retrieving what we want in supermarkets, superstores, mega-malls, and so on. In fast-food restaurants, we are asked not only to wait on our tables but also to clean up after ourselves. At IKEA, we are expected to pick up most of what we want ourselves as we circle the store and then to assemble much of it when we get home. In using the ATM, we are doing work formerly performed by bank tellers.

Recently, this phenomenon has come to be called *prosumption,* and those who engage in it are called *prosumers.*[51] This underscores the fact that in the new means of consumption—and elsewhere, as well—people are not either consumers or producers but in many cases consumers and producers simultaneously. Thus, in the fast-food restaurant, we not only consume our meal but also produce it in various ways (putting condiments on our burgers, waiting on our own tables). Much of what we do online, especially in association with Web 2.0 (e.g., blogs, Facebook, MySpace), involves prosumption as we usually both produce and consume things like a blog or a Facebook page. This is also the case with the online cathedrals of consumption such as Amazon.com and eBay. Thus, on Amazon.com, people not only do virtually all of the work associated with their orders but may also write reviews posted in association with book listings.[52]

Altered Social Relations

The new means of consumption profoundly altered the nature of social relations. In earlier means of consumption, there tended to be more in-depth, face-to-face relationships among and between consumers and those who served them. They tended to get to know one another quite well, and the social character of consumption could be as important as, if not more important than, that which was consumed. In the new means of consumption, face-to-face relationships have been reduced (e.g., at the drive-in window of a fast-food restaurant) or eliminated completely (e.g., in online shopping, on home-shopping networks, and at self-service storage centers). With the advent of the current recession, personnel have been reduced at many cathedrals of consumption, making personal interaction even less likely. The interaction that remains tends to be superficial. Few people today go to the new means of consumption for the social relationships offered by those who work there. Rather, they go to get what they want as quickly and impersonally as possible.

In fact, the new means of consumption are better characterized by interaction with things than with people. In that sense, they are part of what has been termed the *postsocial* world.[53] On one hand, the new means seek to maximize the unmediated contact between consumers and goods and services. On the other hand, a significant part of the success of the new means is the fact that they are constructed so that people will interact with and gaze on them and derive satisfaction from that relationship. This is especially true of the more extraordinary cathedrals such as cruise ships, Las Vegas casinos, and Disney World. Interaction with people, at least in the realm of consumption, is gradually being replaced by interaction with things, both great and small.

Consumers are supposed to be involved in actively consuming the means of consumption and their goods and services, and most of the time they are. But other kinds of behaviors are encouraged by the cathedrals such as sitting, gazing at the setting, watching other people, and wandering about. All of these can be done in the company of other people, but they also lend themselves well to being done alone. Consuming alone is just about the only way to consume online.

Speed, efficiency, self-service, and limited interaction get to the heart of many of the new means of consumption. This should come as no surprise because these are largely American innovations and therefore reflect American values.

CHANGES IN THE WAY OTHERS CONSUME

The new means of consumption were rapidly and aggressively exported by the United States. However, that flood all but ceased as the recession gained in force. Nevertheless, America's new means of consumption were already well entrenched in many parts of the world.

In many places around the world, the characteristics of these means of consumption—for example, speed, efficiency, a do-it-yourself mentality, and limited interaction—were (and are) devalued. However, those in other nations were led increasingly to consume more and more like Americans. In many countries, this posed a threat to indigenous culture. At the minimum, it posed the danger of greater global standardization and homogenization as more people around the world consumed in the primarily American new means of consumption (or ones modeled after them) and obtained goods in much the same way Americans did. It also involved, at least until recently, increased consumption around the world and threats derived from that to global resources, the environment, and so on.

Although we will focus on the exportation of the new American means of consumption to the rest of the world, it goes without saying that there has been a simultaneous exportation of American-style products and the lifestyle they bring with them. Even if they are manufactured elsewhere, these products (Nike shoes is a good example) reflect American culture and have American logos. Mattel offered a line of clothing (e.g., a rhinestone denim jacket) in Japan fashioned after the attire of its iconic Barbie doll.[54] The company relied on the fact that the Barbie doll itself was already beloved in Japan. Said one young Japanese woman, "I'm incredibly happy that the Barbie brand is coming . . . I will buy some for sure."[55]

How America consumes has, until recently, been likely to have a profound impact (often quite quickly) on most other developed nations. This has been the case in part because American-based corporations have been intent on, and aggressive about, exporting American consumer goods and the American way of consuming them. In most of the world's developed nations (and in many less developed ones), potential customers were (and still are, although not as frequently) bombarded by American products and advertisements. Many of those being assailed in these ways were far from hostile to the blitz. Indeed, all indications were that, at least in the realm of consumption, the days of the "ugly American" were long past in many parts of the world. Judging by their popularity and proliferation, virtually every new incursion of American goods and services and the American way of consumption was quite welcome in those areas, at least until the onset of the recession.[56]

In fact, many relatively well-to-do people from around the world have been traveling to the United States to shop in the new means of consumption and to purchase American goods:

> Strolling past the Saks Off Fifth outlet, Dress Barn and a camera store in the vast corridors of the Potomac Mills discount mall in Dale City, Va., three college students from France smiled with anticipation as they spotted a shop that sold athletic wear.

When they emerged with their purchases, including the New York Yankees baseball caps that were high on their list, one student . . . said, "Now that we've seen the tourist sights, we can go home."[57]

It is little wonder that the American cathedrals of consumption have been so eager to export the American way of consuming.

The acceptance and popularity of American cathedrals of consumption in the past half century or so in much of the world stands in stark contrast to, for example, the situation in the 1940s, when a major commotion took place in France over the threat posed by the exportation of Coca-Cola to the wine-loving French café culture. Quite a bit of heat was generated over what came to be known as "Coca-colonization."[58] In the end, Coca-Cola gained a foothold in France, and that led neither to the disappearance of that nation's beloved cafés nor of the wines consumed in them and virtually everywhere else in France. Nevertheless, the initial reaction was telling.

Although much of the world came to be enamored of the American way of consuming, that is not to say that controversy ever completely disappeared. For example, a similar, albeit less heated, version of the "Coca-colonization" debate occurred over the 1992 opening of Euro Disney outside Paris (although as we saw in Chapter 1, Disney is now well established there and is even expanding). As a result of adverse publicity stemming from the "McLibel" trial in London,[59] McDonald's became a prime target of a number of health, environmental, and other groups.[60] There have also been periodic objections to the opening of McDonald's in, for example, the older parts of the world's great cities.[61] Although such protests continue to occur, in the main they are quite muted and are overwhelmed, at least until very recently, by the evidence of wide-scale acceptance of, indeed excitement over, American consumer exports.

Although the aggressive exporting of American consumer culture has been one factor in its worldwide acceptance, another key is the absence, with the fall of communism, of any viable worldwide alternative to the American model. Whatever its problems in practice, communism served as an alternative world-historical model around which people could rally against American capitalism and its model of consumption.[62] Today, the major opposition to these things is based on cultural and local considerations. While culture is a serious barrier in many places (especially Islamic nations), there is evidence that a surface opposition is coupled with covert acceptance (e.g., Saudi women wearing Victoria's Secret lingerie under their burqas). Local forms of resistance to the American mode of consumption are apt to be manifest in various locations, but they are not likely to offer as serious an impediment as that associated with culture. More serious resistance may arise if the global recession deepens and becomes prolonged. Of course, in that case, less of American consumerism will be exported, and fewer people elsewhere in the world will be able to afford its products and cathedrals of consumption.

Much of the worldwide opposition to American economic practices has focused in the past on the exportation of American production theories and methods. Although the exportation of the American mode of production certainly continues, it has been increasingly supplanted in importance by the exportation of the American way of consuming. This paralleled a similar shift within the United States.

A Growing International Presence

There are much data to support the idea that the new means of consumption have been a growing international presence. Take the case of McDonald's. In 1991, a little more than a quarter of its restaurants were outside the United States; by 1996, more than 40% of its sites were overseas; by late 2007, nearly 56% of them were overseas.[63] As was mentioned in Chapter 1, by 2007, McDonald's was in almost 120 nations.[64] The percentage of overseas outlets is likely to continue to grow (the vast majority of new restaurants have been built outside the United States). Systemwide sales increased from $12.4 billion in 1986 to $25.5 billion in 1997, to $30.2 billion by the end of 2002, and to almost $47 billion in 2007.[65] Less than a third of systemwide sales came from outside the United States in 1986, but in 1996, that proportion had grown to nearly one half, with sales in the United States (approximately $16 billion) exceeding international sales by less than $1 billion.[66] By 2007, international sales exceeded American sales by almost $15 billion.[67] One observer offered a broader perspective on the exportation of the American means of consumption:

> Tool around Australia: the regional malls sprouting along its highways look more than a bit familiar. Walk Brazil's streets: a sign says Chocolate, but the store feels like Ann Taylor, the R. L. Polo store mimics Ralph Lauren and Bill Brothers bears a strong resemblance to Brooks Brothers. Tour Bangkok: the Big C Superstores are the image of Wal-Marts.[68]

Examples of the influence of the American means of consumption on other cultures are legion:

- Canada has been invaded by superstores and almost all other new means of consumption.[69]

- Israel has been "McDonaldized"[70] and now has numerous fast-food restaurants[71] and many other chains with American roots.

- Among many other American new means of consumption, home-shopping TV invaded Russia.[72]

- American-style shopping centers came to Budapest, Hungary,[73] more than a decade ago, and they have become increasingly common throughout central and eastern Europe—Czech Republic, Poland, Slovakia, Romania, Ukraine, and Croatia. Said a teenager working in his family's clothing store in a shopping center in Budapest soon after it opened, "Finally, we have something really Western in this boring country."[74]

- Wal-Mart and Sam's Club arrived in China in late 1996. They have had to adapt to a variety of differences between China and the United States. For example, the Chinese typically live in small apartments, which "means that huge American-sized packages and cases are out; smaller, compact sizes are in."[75] Customers usually walk or bike to the store, which limits what they can carry home with them.

- The shopping mall has, as we've seen, exploded in China, which now has not only the largest mall in the world but also a disproportionate number of the world's largest malls.

- Vietnam has been Americanized and populated by Baskin-Robbins, T.G.I. Friday's, and Kentucky Fried Chicken, among many others.[76] There are also bowling alleys, huge video arcades, food courts featuring burgers and fries, and shopping malls.[77] The mall came to Ho Chi Minh City even before McDonald's, which opened in 1998.

- Argentina and Brazil have their water parks and amusement parks. Large cities are being surrounded by shopping malls complete with multiplex movie theaters and game centers of various types. Theme restaurants are expanding, including indigenous varieties such as Rock in Rio Cafe. Said one developer, "Entertainment has graduated from a secondary theme to a central one in Latin America. . . . We've learned you can make money from showing people a good time."[78] These developers are drawing on American models and American expertise.

- For their part, American developers are eager for new Latin American markets. Already, a major amusement park is within a 2½-hour drive of every major American city. There is fear of a shakeout in the overdeveloped theme restaurant market, and similar problems confront other types of entertainment centers—hence the attraction of the underserved Latin American market.[79]

- In Paris, "The Champs-Elysees is now an American mall, complete with Disney Store and Planet Hollywood."[80] And that grand boulevard has long had McDonald's. More shocking is what has happened to the neighborhood of Saint Germain des Pres. Once known for its bookshops and cafés, it is now being invaded by international shops such as Louis Vuitton,

Giorgio Armani, Dior, and Cartier. "It didn't matter that these companies were French (or Italian), they're still mega-corporations that are proud to have the same exact product on shopping streets in Hong Kong, Beverly Hills, Monte Carlo, Tokyo, London, New York, Bal Harbour and the other side of the Seine."[81] They are joining other less elegant chains, either American or inspired by the American model, such as Benetton, Body Shop, and the Gap, which are already there. Although locals are generally opposed to the luxury shops, they quietly whisper, "It's better than McDonald's."[82]

• England already looks increasingly like the United States, at least as far as its means of consumption are concerned:

West Thurrock is probably the greatest bastion of American shopping culture in Great Britain. There are familiar names, now recognizable to most Brits, such as Burger King and Toys 'R Us. There's a giant American-style supermarket. And farther along the service road is something more unusual for Britain: a gargantuan, thoroughly American mall called Lakeside Shopping Centre, which offers a range of department stores, scores of smaller shops, parking for 12,000 cars, and the requisite food court with quick-service cuisine from many lands. But it is the latest American-bred addition to this shopping tract that has brought national attention to modest West Thurrock: "Costco . . . arrived . . . opening the first warehouse membership club in Britain amid an onslaught of media fanfare."[83]

Not satisfied, a large factory outlet developer has been looking into various sites in England, largely because its American tenants such as Nike and the Gap saw European expansion as key to their continued growth.[84] For their part, the English have been attracted to the American discounters for a very good reason—the high cost of American products in English shops.[85]

Many in other parts of the world not only are accepting of the new means of consumption but also are producing their own variants that they are eager to export to the United States. For example, in Latin America, the Rock in Rio Cafe has clearly taken a lead from American theme restaurants with its "entry by monorail, walls with projected imagery that changes the decor, and an indoor fireworks show every night."[86] Its developer eventually plans to turn the tables and export his theme restaurant to the United States: "Why import something American when we can do it better ourselves. . . . After all, you can export as much as you import in today's world."[87]

There was a time when American production was the envy of the world, and others were eager to emulate its structures and methods. More recently, it is more America's new means of consumption, as well as what is offered in them, that virtually every nation around the world has coveted. Although there are certainly foreign precursors of many of these means, there is something quintessentially American about McDonald's, Disney, Wal-Mart, and the Flamingo Hotel and also about their respective founders Ray Kroc, Walt Disney, Sam Walton, and Bugsy Siegel.

However, although the largely American cathedrals of consumption have made inroads in many parts of the world, it is important to remember that other nations retain means of consumption that are distinctly their own. Tokyo has fast-food restaurants, large discount stores, and department stores, but it also has a profusion of small shops and innumerable automatic vending machines "that dispense not only soft drinks and cigarettes, but also beer and liquor, socks, ties, women's stockings, coffee, hot noodles, magazines and . . . unbelievably, flowers and engagement rings."[88]

Pilgrimages to America

Merchants from many nations have been making pilgrimages to the United States to study the means of consumption and to see how they can be adapted to their cultures:

> The Mall of America is our Uffizi, Home Depot our Forum. The Gap, Nordstrom, Disney Stores, Sears, Crate and Barrel, Niketown, Barnes & Noble and Wal-Mart—these are our cathedrals. . . . Heading for shopping centers of all kinds—malls, strip centers, outlet malls, downtown stores and designer boutiques—travelers from overseas board buses, trains, planes and taxicabs for days at a time.[89]

There are regular tours of the new means of consumption organized for interested parties from many nations. Innumerable other foreign retailers have come on their own in an effort to learn the secrets of America's new means of consumption.

Critics of the Trend

It is abundantly clear that many welcomed the invasion of the largely American new means of consumption, but there have long been critics of this trend (and those criticisms, especially of the role of the means of consumption in hyperconsumption and excessive indebtedness, have mounted as the recession gained steam) and especially its homogenizing impact, its creation of "generica"[90]:

> This view that the culture of consumerism is a type of generic culture . . . is buttressed by the spread of huge shopping centers. Remarkably alike in design

and in content, these free-market temples sell the same clothes (Levis, Nike), serve the same food (Pizza Hut, McDonald's, Taco Bell) and show the same movies. From Santiago to Rio de Janeiro, Bogota and Mexico City, these centers in effect allow people to travel without leaving home and to feel at home even when traveling.[91]

The area around Kruger National Park in South Africa has a casino linked to a shopping mall. Considerable attention has been devoted to developing this area to attract more tourists, but the head of the tourist agency is obviously aware of the dangers of American-style development:

> The most successful or enduring cultural happenings internationally are not staged Disney-type events, with tourists as a spectator audience and with locals as actors. . . . They are living festivals such as the running of the bulls in Pamplona, the Carnival in Rio and Easter in Jerusalem. . . .
>
> What better way . . . than to assist in the creation of ways for tourists to actually engage with living cultures by bringing travellers into our townships, villages and kraals. Why give them Disney when you can give them authentic Africa?[92]

There is no question that this exportation of the American means of consumption to the rest of the world has involved a process of Americanization. There have been many examples of backlash here, but McDonald's among others has sought to be "glocal"—that is, integrate the global with the local.[93] (This is also true of the Disney parks in Tokyo and Hong Kong and outside Paris.[94]) McDonald's does this by using many local owners and by adapting its products to each local environment.[95] A good example is the McDonald's in Delhi, India. Given the Hindu deification of the cow, this McDonald's sells the "Maharaja Mac" made from 100% chicken. Also on the menu because of the large number of vegetarians in India are "Vegetable McNuggets." Nonetheless, McDonald's has had opposition, especially from Indian animal rights activists, one of whom said, "I am against McDonald's because they are the chief killers of cows in the world. . . . We don't need cow killers in India."[96]

In sum, there has been an explosion of the largely American new means of consumption not only in United States but in many other parts of the world as well. They have brought with them lower prices and a cornucopia of consumer goods unheard of in human history. They have also brought a series of potential drawbacks, not the least of which is the fact that people throughout the United States, and increasingly throughout the rest of the world, became voracious consumers. That level of consumption proved unsustainable and crashed as the Great Recession gained momentum.

It remains to be seen how the American cathedrals of consumption will, in light of that recession, fare in the coming years. It seems clear that they, like virtually everything else associated with the economy in general, and consumption in particular, will experience declines in the short run and, perhaps, in the longer term. It is also likely that hard times will, especially if they persist, lead to disorder and protests in many parts of the world. It also seems like a safe guess that at least some of these protests will focus their wrath on the cathedrals of consumption with roots in, and associated with, the United States. In the longer term, however, people will continue to consume, and their level of consumption will pick up as the global economy recovers. While at least some of the cathedrals of consumption may be forced to change in various ways (some have closed and still others will be forced to close), they will continue to exist, and revivified consumers will find their way back to them in increasing numbers. However, it does seem clear that a return to the kind of consumer society that existed in the past 60 years is not likely anytime soon. We will deal with this general issue in much more detail in Chapter 8.

CONCLUSION

In addition to discussing why it is that we witnessed the creation of so many new and important means of consumption, this chapter has dealt with the ways in which these means altered the amount and way that Americans, as well as much of the rest of the world, consumed. In the next chapter, I will present a set of theoretical tools that will help to analyze the cathedrals of consumption.

3

Social Theory and the
New Means of Consumption

This chapter is devoted to the three basic and interrelated theoretical perspectives that inform this book. The first is the approach of Karl Marx and neo-Marxian theory (including the early work of Jean Baudrillard, a theorist whose ideas will play a prominent role in this analysis). Marxian and neo-Marxian theory is the origin of the concept "means of consumption." In addition, that theory highlights the fact that the success of modern capitalism and the cathedrals of consumption is highly dependent on the control and exploitation of the consumer. (It also highlights the boom and bust nature of capitalism and allows us to better understand, and put in historical context, the Great Recession.)

The second perspective is Max Weber's work on rationalization, enchantment, and disenchantment. Rationalization helps to transform the cathedrals of consumption into highly efficient selling machines, thereby enhancing their ability to control and exploit consumers. However, rationalization tends to lead to disenchantment and, therefore, to cold, inhuman settings that are increasingly less likely to attract consumers. Weber saw little possibility of enchantment in the modern world, but the neo-Weberian, Colin Campbell, extended Weber's ideas to include the possibility of such enchantment. Walter Benjamin's neo-Marxist work on the Parisian arcades is discussed in this context, especially his view that they are "phantasmagoric." The work of Rosalind Williams and Michael Miller demonstrates that the early French department stores were *both* highly rationalized and enchanted "fantasy worlds." The theory of the relationship among rationalization, enchantment, and disenchantment highlights the difficulties faced by the cathedrals of consumption in attracting and keeping large numbers of consumers. This is related to Marxian theory in the sense that to be controlled and exploited, consumers must be attracted, and continually return, to the cathedrals. Enchantment and rationalization help to bring large numbers of consumers to these settings, but their attractiveness to consumers is continually threatened by the prospects of disenchantment.

Marxian and Weberian theories are modern perspectives; the third theoretical orientation is postmodern social theory, especially ideas drawn from the later theories of Baudrillard. The ideas of the postmodern theorists are especially helpful in explaining how the new means of consumption overcome the problems associated with disenchantment and attain the reenchantment needed to continue to lure, control, and exploit ever-increasing numbers of consumers. We will see that, paradoxically, at least one of the postmodern processes leading to reenchantment ("implosion" into the home) is posing a profound threat to the nature, if not existence, of most of the new means of consumption. Consistent with the contradictory character of postmodern society, the new means of consumption are both bolstered *and* threatened by postmodern developments.

MARXIAN THEORY AND
THE MEANS OF CONSUMPTION

The German social theorist Karl Marx (1818–1883) developed his ideas in the 1800s in reaction to the Industrial Revolution and the early, highly exploitative days of capitalism. Marx wanted to understand better the workings of capitalism, but he was most concerned with explaining the source of what he perceived to be its evils and with helping to bring about the downfall of capitalism. In the nearly 130 years since Marx's death, capitalism has undergone many changes, and Marx's disciples have sought to use his theories as a base to analyze and criticize these changes. However, such theorizing had little long-term effect on capitalism, which is triumphant (even with the Great Recession) on the world stage. Furthermore, most of the Communist regimes that were erected, at least in part on a base of Marxian ideas, have collapsed. Given capitalism's unparalleled position of preeminence today, some think it is more important than ever to analyze it from a Marxian perspective.

Animating Marx's original interest was his distress over the fact that the capitalists' ownership of the means of production allowed them to control and exploit the proletariat (the worker). To work, the proletariat had to have access to the means of production such as tools, machines, factories, and raw materials. Knowing this, at least subconsciously, the capitalists were able to pay them far less than they should have, given the value of what the workers produced. In fact, in the Marxian view, the proletariat deserved just about all of the money earned by the capitalists because all value is derived from labor.

Like most other modern theorists, Marx focused mainly on production—that is, he had a productivist bias. Given the realities that he was dealing with (the early days of the Industrial Revolution and capitalism), a focus on production in general, and the means of production in particular, was sensible. However, in recent years, to the degree that production and consumption can be clearly separated,[1] production has grown increasingly less important (e.g., fewer workers are involved in goods production), especially in the United States, whereas consumption has grown in importance. In such a society, it makes sense to shift our focus from the means of production to the means of consumption. However, this is not to say that production, the means of production, and those who work in them are unimportant. Among the issues of concern in production are the following: What is the source of wealth in a society that produces less and less? What is the fate of a society (such as the United States and Dubai) in which far more is invested in the means of consumption than the means of production? And what is the likely fate of already exploited workers when production grows increasingly less important to the society as a whole?

Within the general framework of production, Marx actually had a great deal to say about consumption, especially in his well-known work on commodities. Much less well known and visible is the fact that Marx (following Adam Smith, as he often did[2]) employed the concept "means of consumption."

Marx defined the *means of production* as "commodities that possess a form in which they . . . enter productive consumption."[3] That is, the means of production—labor-time, tools, machines, and so on—are used and used up, in the process of production. To Marx, the *means of consumption* are "commodities that possess a form in which they enter individual consumption of the capitalist and working class."[4] Thus, here we are in the realm of the kind of consumption—"individual" as opposed to "productive"—that will be discussed in this book. Under the heading of individual consumption, Marx differentiates between subsistence and luxury consumption (Adam Smith made a similar distinction). On one hand are the "necessary means of consumption," or those "that enter the consumption of the working class."[5] On the other are the "luxury means of consumption, which enter the consumption only of the capitalist class, i.e., can be exchanged only for the expenditure of surplus-value, which does not accrue to the workers."[6] Basic foodstuffs would be subsistence means of consumption, whereas elegant automobiles would be luxury means of consumption.

However, there is a logical problem in the way Marx uses the concept of the means of consumption, especially in comparison to the paired notion of means of production. The means of production occupy an intermediate position between workers and products; they are the means that make possible both the production of commodities and the control and exploitation of the workers. In contrast, the way Marx uses the idea, the means of consumption are not means but rather the end products in his model of consumption; they are those things (either subsistence or luxury) that are consumed. In other words, there is *no* distinction in Marx's work between consumer goods and what I see as the means of consumption (e.g., shopping malls and cruise ships).[7] To put it another way, in his work there is no parallel in the realm of consumption to the mediating and expediting role played by the means of production.

In this book, I distinguish the means of consumption from that which is consumed. Fast-food restaurants are decidedly not the same as the hamburgers we eat in them.[8] The means of consumption will be seen as playing the same mediating role in consumption that the means of production play in Marx's theory of production. That is, just as the means of production are those entities that make it possible for the proletariat to produce commodities and to be controlled and exploited as workers, the means of consumption are defined as those things that make it possible for people to acquire goods and services and for the same people to be controlled and exploited as consumers.[9]

The concept of the means of consumption appears, at least in passing, in various other works,[10] most notably in one of Baudrillard's early books, *The Consumer Society*.[11] At this early point in his career, Baudrillard was still heavily influenced by Marxian theory, although he was to break with that approach a few years later en route to becoming the preeminent postmodern social theorist. Baudrillard does not define the concept, but the way he uses it makes it clear that (unlike Marx) he is not conflating the means of consumption with the commodities to be consumed but is using a definition similar to mine. Baudrillard's paradigm of the means of consumption is the Parisian "drugstore":

> Any resemblance to an American pharmacy is tucked into one small corner. The rest of this amazing establishment is more like a mini-department store with everything from books to cameras, toys, French and foreign newspapers and magazines, clothing, and a booming takeout business in carved-on-the-spot sandwiches, salads, and soft drinks as well as caviar, pate de foie gras, and elaborate picnic hampers. Le Drugstore's outdoor cafe offers what it claims is an "authentic" American menu.[12]

The Parisian "drugstore" is clearly a means of consumption in that it is a social and economic structure that enables consumers to acquire an array of commodities. Baudrillard goes on to talk about an entire community as the "drugstore writ large." In this context, he describes a community, Parly 2, with its shopping center, swimming pool, clubhouse, and housing developments. The shopping center and at least a version of the kind of community described by Baudrillard (the elite gated community) are, as noted in Chapter 1, examples of the new means of consumption. Other examples discussed by Baudrillard are holiday resorts and airport terminals.[13]

Baudrillard was prescient in writing about the significance of these new means of consumption in the late 1960s. However, he did little with the idea and related phenomena. Furthermore, he erred in focusing on the Parisian drugstore because of its limited impact on the rest of the world. In fact, today that drugstore has been swamped by the importation of the kinds of means of consumption that occupy our attention: fast-food restaurants, chains of all sorts, Euro Disney, and so on. Nonetheless, Baudrillard's sense of the means of consumption is the closest in the literature to the way the concept is employed in this book.

Exploiting and Controlling the Consumer

As discussed previously, Marx's theory, especially as it relates to the means of production, focuses on the control and exploitation of workers (the proletariat).

In 20th-century capitalism, the focus shifted increasingly from production to consumption, resulting in a parallel shift from control and exploitation of workers to that of consumers. Consumers could no longer be allowed to decide on their own whether to consume, how much or what to consume, and how much to spend on consumption. Capitalists felt that they had to devote more time, energy, and money to influence, if not to control, those decisions. This idea is explicit in Baudrillard's early work. He views consumption as "social labor" (thereby implying the idea of the prosumer) and compares its control and exploitation to that of productive labor in the workplace. Capitalism has created a controllable and exploitable "consuming mass" to complement the control and exploitation of the "producing mass."[14]

The Marxian theory of the exploitation of workers was clear-cut because all value came from the workers. If they got anything less than everything, they were being exploited (when in fact they received barely enough to subsist).

In what sense can the consumer be said to be exploited? There are many ways to respond to this question. For example, advertisements are designed to lure people into buying things they might not otherwise consume. And it is the consumers who must ultimately pay for the cost of the advertisements as part of the purchase price of goods or services. In fact, as neo-Marxists Paul Baran and Paul Sweezy showed long ago, capitalists prefer competition on the basis of advertising campaigns (and other sorts of sales competition) to price competition because it enables them to keep prices high and to pass the costs of advertising campaigns on to consumers (for more on this, see Chapter 8).[15] However, our focus is not on the way advertisements are used to exploit consumers but on how the new means of consumption perform a very similar function.

At one level, the new means of consumption are set up to lead people to consume more than they intend and perhaps more than they can afford.[16] At another level, the sometimes astronomical cost of constructing and maintaining the cathedrals of consumption leads to high prices that are driven even higher by the desire of those involved in the cathedrals to reap large profits. Credit cards aid the ability of the new means of consumption to exploit consumers by leading them to buy more. Furthermore, credit cards are exploitative in themselves in the sense that people are lured into debt that many find difficult to extricate themselves from and into paying usurious interest rates on balances that serve to stretch indebtedness out for years, if not decades. Consumers can be said to be exploited by the new means of consumption by being led to buy more than they need, to pay higher prices than need be, and to spend more than they should.[17]

It is true that it is far harder to argue that the consumer is exploited than it was for Marx to contend that the proletariat was exploited. The proletariat had no choice. If they wanted to work, they had to sell their labor-time to the capitalists in exchange for access to the means of production and ultimately a subsistence wage. In contrast, the consumer appears to have the option of avoiding the new means of consumption and obtaining goods and services in other ways (e.g., making products themselves or using older means of consumption). However, the fact is that the proliferation of the new means of consumption made it more difficult and less attractive for consumers to obtain goods and services in other ways. It was increasingly the case that if consumers wanted to consume, they had to use ("labor" in) one of the new means of consumption. In a sense, consumers must give the capitalists their "consumption time" in exchange for access to the means of consumption. Consumers are then able to get goods and services only by placing themselves in a context in which they are likely to buy more, to pay higher prices, and to spend more money than they intended.

In a similar way, consumers are not *forced* to use credit cards. They could pay in cash and avoid many of the problems associated with credit cards. However, in the case of an increasing number of transactions through, for example, cybermalls or home-shopping television networks, it is almost impossible to consume without credit cards. Furthermore, the need to create a credit record to obtain other kinds of credit (e.g., mortgage loans) serves to force people into credit card use. Even in the many cases that consumption can be accomplished in other ways, the credit card proves to be an irresistible lure.

So although the analogy between workers and consumers is far from perfect, there is a sense in which both have become "exploitable masses." With the proliferation of the new means of consumption, the choices open to consumers have, at least in some senses, declined. Although they may not be subject to much, if any, overt coercion, consumers are the objects of a variety of softer, more seductive controlling techniques. And such techniques are one of the defining characteristics of a postmodern society. Consumers can still choose venues other than the new means of consumption; they can opt not to pay exorbitant prices and not to buy things that are not absolutely needed, but at the same time, we must not forget that enormous sums of money have been spent on advertising and on the new means of consumption (among other sales mechanisms) to get people to buy and pay more. On balance, the evidence seems clear that this money has been well spent and people have often done what is expected of them.

Take the case of the lottery, a new means of consuming gambling that, while traceable to Colonial America, boomed in the 1970s and 1980s as a result of state government efforts to raise money.[18] Jackpots have reached astronomical levels, and a wide array of new games have proliferated, most notably the multistate Powerball where one can win $100 million or more.

Outlets that sell lottery tickets tend to be concentrated in poor areas and to target those with lower incomes and education. Heavy players may gamble as much as 10% or more of their annual income on the lottery. A great deal of money is spent in advertising lotteries and in luring people into playing for the first time or to continue being regular players. Advertisements are clever and target specific groups such as low-income players who tend to prefer specific types of games such as Keno, the superstitious with the Lucky Numbers game, and the more affluent players with games based on constantly changing themes, such as "Star Trek." Players are often ill informed about payout percentages and the incredibly slim chances of winning. For all of these reasons and more, it could be argued that the lottery is an exploitative means of consuming gambling.

Nevertheless, the analogy between the exploitation of workers and consumers is far from ideal. However, various neo-Marxists have offered us a different way of looking at the analogy between the capitalist's treatment of workers and consumers. They contend that the real focus in contemporary capitalism is no longer the *exploitation* of workers but rather their *control*.[19] If control is the central concern as far as contemporary workers are concerned, then that must certainly be the case for consumers. We are on far firmer footing simply arguing that the new means of consumption concentrate on the control of consumers to get them to spend as much as possible. This allows us to skirt the bothersome issue of exploitation without losing any of the focus and power of our argument. And we can retain at least a partial theoretical footing in (neo-) Marxian theory.

WEBERIAN THEORY AND ENCHANTMENT, RATIONALIZATION, AND DISENCHANTMENT

German-born Max Weber (1864–1920) did his most important work in the three or four decades after the death of Marx. Although Weber shared Marx's interest in capitalism, he came to see it as just one of a number of developments that were unique to the Occident. Just as Marx believed that capitalism created a number of social advances, Weber noted the positive contributions of the Western institutions of interest to him. And like Marx, Weber was deeply concerned with the problems created by these changes. However, whereas Marx was a radical hoping for a revolution that would overturn capitalist society, Weber was much more pessimistic about doing anything significant about the problems associated with the distinctive set of Occidental institutions.

The key factors in Weber's theorizing are enchantment, rationalization, and disenchantment. His argument is that the modern process of rationalization in the Occident, as exemplified in capitalism and in the bureaucracy, has served to undermine what was once an enchanted (i.e., magical, mysterious, mystical) world. Rational systems in general, and the bureaucracy in particular, have no room for enchantment. It is systematically rooted out by rational systems, leaving them largely devoid of magic or mystery.

Rationalization

Weber delineated four different types of rationality and argued that rationality takes different forms in different social settings. *Practical rationality* is a mundane form in which people in their day-to-day activities look for the best means to whatever end they seek. *Theoretical rationality* is cognitive rather than practical and involves an effort to master reality through increasingly abstract concepts. *Substantive rationality* involves a choice of means to ends guided by, and in the context of, larger social values. *Formal rationality* involves a similar choice of means to ends, but this time guided by universally applied rules, laws, and regulations. It is formal rationality that is the distinctive product of the West.

Despite Weber's effort to distinguish among these types of rationality and to see them operating differently in various institutions, one emerges from a reading of his work with a clear sense that there is an overall trend in the West in the direction of the increasing domination of formal rationality—rationality as an "iron cage." This idea is clear, for example, in Weber's conclusion that socialism would not eliminate or reduce the possibility of such a future: "Not summer's bloom lies ahead of us, but rather a polar night of icy darkness and hardness, no matter which group may triumph externally now."[20] It is phrases like "polar night," "icy darkness," and "hardness" that convey such a disenchanted, frigid, nightmarish image when the new means of consumption are thought of in terms of Weber's theory of rationalization.

Authority Structures

The trend toward increasing formal rationalization is found in Weber's work on authority. Here, Weber differentiated among three types of authority by specifying the way in which each is legitimated. *Traditional authority* exists when the leader rules on the basis of a claim to, and a resulting belief on the part of the followers in, the sanctity of age-old rules and powers. In the case of *rational-legal authority,* the leader rules and has the ability to issue commands on the basis of legally enacted regulations. Followers accept that right and those rules and therefore follow the leader's dictates. Finally, *charismatic authority* is based on the devotion of followers to, and their belief in, the exceptional sanctity, exemplary character, heroism, or special powers (e.g., the ability to work miracles) of the leader, as well as to the normative order sanctioned by the leader.

All three types have existed throughout history, but Weber argued that in the modern West, we are witnessing the triumph of rational-legal authority and the progressive elimination of the other two types as legitimate bases of authority. For one thing, fewer people are inclined to accept the authority of someone (say, a king or queen) who rules on the basis of tradition. For another, as rational-legal authority becomes more firmly entrenched, it is less and less vulnerable to overthrow by charismatic leaders and their followers. As is the case for rationality in general, formal rationality eventually comes to reign supreme in the realm of authority.

The demise of tradition and especially charisma as ways of legitimating authority is of particular interest. Both traditional and charismatic authority can be seen as involving an enchanted relationship between leader and followers. In one case, the enchantment comes from a belief in the way things have always been done, and in the other, it comes from a belief in the leader's extraordinary qualities. Their demise implies the end of enchantment, at least in such a relationship. It is clear that the relationship between rational-legal leaders and followers is not enchanted; there is no mystery in such a system about why some lead and others follow.[21]

It is also the case that Weber sometimes uses *charisma* in a broader sense to denote not just leaders but anyone with extraordinary abilities (many see Barack Obama as such a person). Such individuals can be seen as enchanted, certainly in comparison to those who staff such rational-legal systems as the bureaucracy. There is less and less room for such individual charisma in a rationalized world and therefore less room for enchantment.

Bureaucracy

The bureaucracy embodies Weber's thinking on rationality, authority, and the iron cage. First, bureaucracy is the epitome of formal rationality. As Weber put it, "From a purely technical point of view, a bureaucracy is capable of attaining the highest degree of efficiency, and is in this sense formally the most rational known means of exercising authority over human beings."[22] Second, bureaucracy is the organizational structure that is associated with rational-legal authority and its triumph over other forms of authority. Indeed, one of the key reasons that rational-legal authority wins out over the others is the superiority of its characteristic bureaucratic form in comparison to the organizations associated with traditional and charismatic authority. There really is no other option if the objective is mass administration. Third, the bureaucracy is itself an iron cage in terms of those who function in it. More generally, as more and more sectors of society come to be characterized by bureaucracies, they tend to form one enormous iron cage.

Although Weber praised the bureaucracy on a variety of grounds, he was also critical of its constraints on people. He described bureaucracies as "escape proof," "practically unshatterable," and among the hardest institutions to destroy once they are established. Along the same lines, he felt that individual bureaucrats could not squirm out of the bureaucracy once they were "harnessed" in it. Weber concluded,

> This whole process of rationalization in the factory as elsewhere, and especially in the bureaucratic state machine, parallels the centralization of the material implements of organization in the hands of the master. Discipline inexorably takes over ever larger areas as the satisfaction of political and economic needs is increasingly rationalized. This universal phenomenon more and more restricts the importance of charisma and of individually differentiated conduct.[23]

The bureaucracy, and formally rational structures in general, must be seen as objective structures that constrain people in very material ways. Rules, offices, hierarchies, and the like constrain people so that although they are enabled to do certain things, they are forced into doing others.

Capitalism

Weber conceived of capitalism as another formally rational system, and he offered an extraordinarily clear image of its material, cage-like character:

> Capitalism is today an immense cosmos into which the individual is born, and which presents itself to him, at least as an individual, as an unalterable order of things in which he must live. It forces the individual, in so far as he is involved in the system of market relationships, to conform to capitalist rules of action.[24]

The coercive image that is being conveyed is well reflected in the fiction of Franz Kafka, especially *The Trial*.

To greater or lesser degrees, most of the new means of consumption are objective structures[25] (often themselves bureaucratic structures or a part of larger bureaucracies) that exert constraint on those people who are lured into them. This constraint is important in itself, for its relationship to exploitation, and also because it makes possible the systematic extraction of enchantment from these structures.[26]

Disenchantment

It is from Friedrich Schiller that Weber derived the notion that as a result of rationalization, the Western world has grown increasingly disenchanted,[27] involving a displacement of "magical elements of thought."[28] As Mark Schneider puts it, "Max Weber saw history as having departed a deeply enchanted past en route to a disenchanted future—a journey that would gradually strip the natural world both of its magical properties and of its capacity for meaning."[29] Or,

> In the face of the seemingly relentless advance of science and bureaucratic social organization, he believed, enchantment would be hounded further and further from the institutional centers of our culture. Carried to an extreme, this process would turn life into a tale which, whether told by an idiot or not, would certainly signify nothing, having been evacuated of meaning.[30]

The theme of disenchantment recurs in many places in Weber's work but especially in his sociology of that most enchanted of domains: religion.[31] For example, he saw a historical process of rationally and professionally trained (and, therefore, disenchanted) priests gaining ascendancy over magicians who acquired their positions through irrational means and who clearly have a more enchanted view of, and relationship to, the world than priests. Weber argued that in the modern world, "One need no longer have recourse to magical means in order to master or implore the spirits, as did the savage, for whom such mysterious powers existed."[32]

Prophets, who as a group are more enchanted than the priests, receive a personal calling and engage in emotional preaching. They are either the founders, or the renewers, of religion. Weber differentiated between ethical (e.g., Muhammed and Christ) and exemplary (e.g., Buddha) prophets. Ethical prophets believe that they have received a commission directly from God, and they demand obedience from followers as an ethical duty. Exemplary prophets demonstrate the way to salvation to others by way of example. Both types are useful in creating a group of followers, but once they have succeeded in creating such a group, they tend to be replaced by the disenchanted priests who are far better than either type of prophet at the pastoral, day-to-day affairs of managing such a group. In the process, religion begins to lose its enchanted character and comes under the sway of the rationalized church that houses the priests. The priests derive their authority from their position within the church, whereas prophets derive theirs from their service to a sacred (and enchanted) tradition.

Weber also argued that the Protestants, especially the Calvinists, developed an idea system, the "Protestant ethic," that helped give birth to the spirit of capitalism. Weber is here working at the level of ideas rather than material structures. Weber depicted a world that is, at least initially, enchanted. The Protestant ethic sprang from the Calvinist belief in predestination. Believing that whether or not they were saved was preordained, the Calvinists looked for particular signs as a way of indicating whether or not they were among the saved. The most important of those signs became economic success. The Calvinists came to work hard and to reinvest profits in their businesses, to help ensure that they would, in fact, see the signs of their salvation. This was clearly an enchanted world. That is, the Calvinist was making decisions on the basis of mystical ideas ("signs," "salvation") rather than rational, matter-of-fact principles and procedures.

The capitalist economic system eventually lost all vestiges of enchantment and came to be a highly disenchanted world without room for ideas such as predestination and salvation. In fact, it became inhospitable to the Calvinists, indeed to all religions, because of the tie between religion and enchantment. There was little patience in the rationalized and disenchanted world of capitalism for such enchanted worlds as religion.

Enchantment

Weber's thinking on magicians, prophets, the Protestant ethic, and charismatic and traditional leaders had a great deal to do with enchantment. However, his thinking on more recent developments, especially in the West, had much more to do with rationalization and *dis*enchantment, enchantment having been largely driven out by the machine-like bureaucracy and rational-legal authority. A formally rational world is a disenchanted world. In a modern context, it is not unusual to associate Weber with the imagery of disenchanted and rationalized iron cages, but it is unusual to link him to the idea of enchantment. However, such a connection has been made by Colin Campbell, who has extended Weberian theory, at least as it relates to the Protestant ethic thesis, in such a way that it is able to encompass the ideas of enchantment, dreams, and fantasies.[33]

The Romantic Ethic

In *The Romantic Ethic and the Spirit of Modern Consumerism*,[34] Campbell does not contest Weber's basic argument about the central role of early Calvinism in the rise of capitalism but merely contends that Weber did not take his analysis far enough. That is, Weber analyzed the Protestant ethic up to approximately 1700, but it continued to evolve after that point and began to move in a very different direction. Although Campbell pointed out that there was more emotion[35] in early Calvinism than Weber recognized, he argued that later Calvinism became even more accepting of emotion. In other words, there were elements of enchantment in later Calvinism.

Although the early Calvinists required signs of success to help them to determine whether they were to be saved, later Calvinists sought evidence of their good taste. Good taste was linked to beauty and beauty to goodness. The Calvinist who demonstrated good taste simultaneously displayed goodness. In other words, pleasure seeking came to be linked with the ideals of character. An easy mechanism for demonstrating that one had good taste was to show that one was in fashion. The later Calvinists grew "eager to 'follow fashion' and hence to consume 'luxury' goods with avidity."[36]

The later Protestant ethic led, albeit unintentionally, to the spirit of modern *consumerism*. Defining this spirit was what Campbell called "autonomous, self-illusory hedonism." This hedonistic spirit stood in stark contrast to the asceticism of the early Protestants as well as of the spirit of modern capitalism. It also was individualistic and involved illusions, daydreams, and fantasies; in other words, it was a world of enchantment. The key is individual fantasies because, as Campbell pointed out, fantasies can be far more important and rewarding than reality. In fact, he argued that disappointment inevitably occurs when people are able to fulfill their fantasies, especially with a variety of consumer goods and services. Each time they venture forth into the marketplace, people delude themselves into believing that this time it is going to be different; the material reality is going to live up to the fantasy. These fantasies, rather than material realities, are crucial to an understanding of modern consumerism because they can never be fulfilled and are continually generating new "needs," especially for consumer goods and services.

Although Weber saw the spirit of modern capitalism leading to rationalized, disenchanted capitalism, for Campbell, the spirit of modern consumerism leads to romantic, enchanted capitalism. Weber's capitalism is a coldly efficient world virtually devoid of magic, and Campbell's "romantic capitalism" is a world of dreams and fantasies. Although production is accorded central importance in rational capitalism, it is of secondary importance in romantic capitalism, taking the form, for example, of the production of arts and crafts by bohemians. What is of central importance for romantic capitalism (and for Campbell) is consumption. And, within the realm of consumption, Campbell accorded great importance to fantasies, especially the fantasizing of consumers. However, Campbell focused on the fantasies of individual consumers.

In this book, I extend Campbell's work by focusing on the enchanted aspects of the new means of consumption. We will see that these not only are increasingly fantastic in themselves but also are involved in generating fantasies about consumption among consumers.[37] Despite Weber's pessimism, enchantment persists. As Schneider puts it, "Enchantment . . . is part of our normal condition, and far from having fled . . . it continues to exist."[38]

I draw on both Weber and Campbell in my conceptualization of the cathedrals of consumption as not only rationalized and disenchanted but also enchanted. Much the same thing could be said of the cathedrals associated with organized religions.

Perhaps religious structures seem rather removed from our concrete concern with the enchanted and disenchanted aspects of the new means of consumption. Much closer is work on the major precursors of the new means of consumption, such as the Parisian arcade[39] of the late 1700s and early 1800s and the French department store of the mid-1800s.

The Parisian Arcade

Walter Benjamin's *The Arcades Project* (*Der Passagen-Werk*) is a major resource for thinking about the enchantment of the new means of consumption. This fragmentary, unfinished undertaking focuses on the 19th-century Parisian arcades,[40] which were, in their time, seemingly as little grist for the scholarly mill as fast-food restaurants or discount department stores are today. However, Benjamin used the arcades as a lens to gain greater insight not only into the era in which they flourished but also into the time in which he wrote (late 1920s through the 1930s). Benjamin's work on the arcades not only serves as a model for this work, but the arcades themselves were forerunners to many of the means of consumption discussed in this book.

One key difference between the two works is that Benjamin was looking back to phenomena (the arcades) that, by the time Benjamin wrote, had lost their central place in the process of consumption in France to later developments such as the department store. In contrast, in this work, we are examining phenomena that have only recently attained center stage in the world of consumption in recent years or, in some cases (e.g., e-commerce) are only beginning to acquire centrality. However, we should keep in mind that the newer means of consumption, like the arcades and even the department stores that eventually triumphed over them, will eventually recede (perhaps sooner than expected given the current recession; see Chapter 8) and be replaced by as yet unknown, even newer means of consumption.

The arcades were essentially privately owned covered city streets lined on both sides with shops of various sorts. The streets were closed to vehicular traffic, allowing consumers to wander from shop to shop in order to buy or merely window shop. (Fremont Street in downtown Las Vegas has a canopy that has made it into a kind of arcade except that it is lined more with casinos than shops.) Here is a description of the arcades used by Benjamin himself:

These arcades, a recent invention of industrial luxury, are glass-roofed, marble-walled passages cut through whole blocks of houses, whose owners have combined in this speculation. On either side of the passages, which draw their light from above, run the most elegant shops, so that an arcade of this kind is a city, indeed, a world in miniature.[41]

The arcades had their origin in Paris of the late 1700s. While London had broad streets with sidewalks that came to be lined with shops, Paris had narrow streets that lacked sidewalks and therefore could not easily accommodate shoppers. Hence there was a need in Paris for arcades that provided a public area for strolling and shopping. The first arcade, the Palais Royalem, developed in the 1780s; between 1800 and 1830, Paris witnessed the creation of 17 arcades. Additional Parisian arcades were built in subsequent years, and the arcade spread to other cities, including London, Brussels, Milan (Galleria Vittorio Emanuele; see Chapter 7), Berlin (Kaisergalerie), Moscow (GUM), and even Cleveland in the United States. Toward the end of the 19th century, the arcade disseminated still further to places such as Melbourne, Johannesburg, and Singapore.

As a neo-Marxian social theorist, Benjamin is not satisfied with merely describing the arcades as a new social phenomenon. Benjamin is critical of the arcades and what they represent, and a critical perspective, while not mainly animated by a Marxian perspective, also informs this book, at least in part. The following excerpt from a 1929 book (*A Walk in Berlin* by Franz Hessel) offers a critical, even nightmarish, view of Berlin's Kaisergalerie, which was modeled after the Parisian arcades:

I cannot enter it without a damp chill coming over me, without the fear that I might never find an exit. I am hardly past the shoeshine and newspaper stands under the lofty arches of the entrance, and I feel a mild confusion. A window promises me dancing daily and that Meyer without whom no party would be complete. But where is the entrance? Next to the ladies' hairdresser there is another display: stamps and those curiously named tools of the collector: adhesive pockets with guaranteed acid-free rubber, a perforation gauge made of celluloid. "Be sensible! Wear wool!" demands the next window of me . . . I . . . almost stumbled over the peep shows, where one poor schoolboy stands, his school bag under his arm, wretched, immersed in the "scene in the Bedroom."

I linger over . . . Knipp-Knapp cufflinks, which are certainly the best, and over the Diana air rifles, truly an honor to the goddess of the hunt. I shrink back before grinning skulls, the fierce liqueur glasses of a white bone cocktail set. The clowning face of a jockey, a handsome wooden nutcracker graces the end of the musical toilet paper holder.

The whole center of the arcade is empty. I rush quickly to the exit; I feel ghostly, hidden crowds of people from days gone by, who hug the walls with lustful glances at the tawdry jewelry, the clothing, the pictures. . . . At the exit, at the windows of the great travel agency, I breathe more easily; the street, freedom, the present![42]

While the goods and services might be different today, a critic might offer a very similar description of more modern means of consumption such as the shopping mall or the casino. Such a critique might focus on such issues as the difficulty in getting out once one wanders in, the proliferation of useless commodities, and the orgy of consumerism to which today's means of consumption contribute.

Putting it in its broader Marxian context (and picking up on the theme of enchantment), Benjamin sees the arcade as "the original temple of commodity capitalism."[43] It was the immediate precursor of other temples for the consumption of commodities—the department store and the international Exposition. (The arcades themselves, of course, had predecessors such as the church—arcades were often shaped like a cross—and Oriental bazaars.) More important, they were the precursors of even later means of consumption, the modern temples (or cathedrals) of commodity capital that concern us here. Also anticipating later developments, the arcades were not just about buying goods. They also offered food, drink, gambling, entertainment in the form of vaudeville, and even prostitution.

What were originally confined to the arcades later burst out of those confines and flooded Paris "where commodity displays achieved even grander, even more pretentious forms."[44] Benjamin accords an important role here to the architect Baron Georges-Eugene Haussmann, who created in Paris

the new urban phantasmagoria . . . railroad stations, museums, wintergardens, sport palaces, department stores, exhibition halls, boulevards—[that] dwarfed the original arcades and eclipsed them. These once magical "fairy grottoes" that had spawned phantasmagoria went into eclipse.[45]

Still later, of course, commodity displays came to inundate the rest of France and much of the developed world.

In focusing on the arcades, Benjamin was examining the debris or residue of the mass culture of the 1800s; these leftovers were the most mundane, the most banal of everyday sites. But he specifically chose such sites because they permitted him to relate an interest in the everyday world with more academic and political concerns. Benjamin believed that the study of such phenomena would permit the "dialectics of seeing" and lead to "both metaphysical and political illumination."[46] And the latter, given Benjamin's Marxist orientation, would lead to historical awakening, social change, and perhaps social revolution. In effect, Benjamin sought to do for consumers in the world of consumption what Marx had hoped to do for the proletariat in the world of production. Involved in this is an implicit recognition by Benjamin of the fact that the essence of capitalism was already beginning to shift from production to consumption. Therefore, if a revolution was to be mounted, it had to be in the world of consumption and the consumer and not, as Marx believed, in the realm of production among the proletariat.

Paralleling Benjamin's work on the arcades, at least in part, this book seeks not only to illuminate the nature of the means of consumption themselves, as well as the ways in which they interrelate and interpenetrate, but also to elucidate the nature of consumerism (the "fetishization of commodities"). It is easy to accept Benjamin's goal of illumination and even of social change, although we must bear in mind that the modern world produced, at least until recently, temples of consumption and a cornucopia of consumer goods and services that have been the envy of the denizens of every other era in human history. Yet the means of consumption, as well as the consumerism that they help fuel, have more than their share of problems. Thus, at the minimum, one might want to offer changes that retained the best of the consumer society while coping with some of its worst excesses. One thing, though, that is almost impossible to accept, in this postmodern era following the death of communism, is Benjamin's Marxist-inspired hope for social revolution.[47]

However, Benjamin's major attraction to us in this context is the fact that he sees the arcades not only as disenchanted, reified structures but also as enchanted storehouses of dreams and fantasies. The arcades and their goods are seen as commodity fetishes, but ones that are used to evoke dreams, especially the "collective dream of the commodity phantasmagoria."[48] In general, in the process of commodification, the "wish image congeals into fetish."[49] These wish images can also be said to petrify or solidify into "fossils" or, in this case, commodities and the structures in which they are sold. More specifically, the arcades are seen as "houses without exteriors," themselves "just like dreams."[50] The arcades can be seen as having "housed the first consumer dream worlds." And more generally, Benjamin was interested in the "mass marketing of dreams within a class system."[51]

The idea of a phantasmagoria is crucial to understanding the new means of consumption as enchanted worlds. On one hand, it implies a cornucopia of goods and services that offers the possibility of exciting and satisfying people's wildest fantasies. The dream here, and one that is played to by most of the new means of consumption, is to be immersed in a world filled with everything one could ever imagine, with all of these things there for the taking. It is akin to the childhood dream of finding oneself in a land in which everything is made of candy and all of it is within easy reach.

On the other hand, phantasmagoria also implies a negative side of enchantment—a nightmare world filled with specters, ghosts, and a profusion of things that seem simultaneously to be within one's grasp and impossible to obtain. William Leach describes the turn-of-the-20th-century means of consumption as "the sometimes dreamlike, sometimes nightmarish world of modern merchandising."[52] More contemporaneously, the modern mall, for example, is both a dream world filled with a cornucopia of goods and services and, especially today in the midst of recession, a modern nightmare for many. While we might be able to afford to buy a few of those offerings, most of them are increasingly beyond our reach. Of course, this is far from the only nightmare associated with the mall. Another might be one in which we come to the realization that all of our needs and abilities have atrophied because of our single-minded effort to acquire what the mall has to offer. Thus, just as we are destined to live out some of our dreams within the mall, we are also simultaneously doomed to nightmares involving frustration and failure (this is also the case in Campbell's notion of self-illusory hedonism). The same can be said of our involvement in all of the new means of consumption.

In integrating a concern with enchanted dreams (and nightmares), Benjamin was influenced by the surrealists (e.g., the art of Salvador Dali) and their "fascination with urban phenomena," which they experienced both as something *objective* and as something *dreamt.*[53] The surrealists questioned the prioritization of material reality by the realists and sought instead to focus on the subconscious, unconscious, irrational, and dreamlike.[54] The vantage point of the surrealists also allows us another way of seeing that what are described as dreams can just as easily turn into nightmares. While the surrealists offered an attractive theoretical orientation, and one that is helpful in this book as well, Benjamin was critical of them for their lack of a practical interest in awakening people from the reverie that is being created for them by these structures.

This leads us to the point that while dreams are usually thought of in positive terms, they also can be interpreted negatively not only as nightmares but also in the sense that they tend to lull people into a reverie that blinds them to the material realities that surround them. In other words, they can be conceived of as a kind of "opiate" of the masses. Williams (see below) uses such notions as "numbered hypnosis" to describe consumers.[55] Thus, the dreams created by the new means of consumption can be seen as creating a "false consciousness" among consumers in much the same way that such a consciousness was created among the proletariat in the heyday of producer capitalism. Adrift in a dream world of consumption, people are unable to see what is happening to them as well as the realities of the economic system in which they are immersed.

There is much else in Benjamin's work of great relevance and interest to contemporary work on consumption and the cathedrals of consumption. In fact, this book will close with a discussion in Chapter 8 of the possibility that at least some of the cathedrals of consumption may be following the arcades and are in the process of decline, if not disappearance. Further, over time, the other cathedrals discussed in this book will experience the same fate. When Benjamin wrote about them (1920–1940), the arcades, with their roots in the early 19th century, had long since past their prime. As a result, he dealt with them as "monuments," or the "detritus," of an earlier age. He focused on them because of what they told us about both the past and the present. It could be argued that at least some of the new means of consumption (e.g., strip malls) are already monuments and that the others will be, sooner or later. Nevertheless, studying them can perform the same functions as Benjamin's work on the arcades.

The French Department Store

Rosalind Williams sees settings like the early French department store (arguably today a "monument" in Benjamin's terms given its roots in the mid-19th century) as enchanted "dream worlds."[56] She focuses on such things as the use of decor to lure customers to the stores and to "imbue the store's merchandise with glamour, romance, and, therefore consumer appeal."[57] The stores were in the business of enchanting and seducing their customers. In these settings, consumers could live out many of their fantasies by either purchasing goods or merely imagining what it would be like to own them. In other words, the early French department stores strove mightily to be enchanted worlds.

Although Williams did relatively little with the rationalized, and therefore disenchanted, characteristics of the early French department stores, that issue gets much more attention in Michael Miller's study of Bon Marché.[58] The early Bon Marché was a fusion of the emerging rationalized world with more traditional elements of French bourgeois culture; over the years, it moved increasingly in the direction of becoming a rationalized, bureaucratized structure. That is, it encountered "an incessant push towards greater efficiency."[59] Among the rationalized elements of the store were its division into departments; its partitioning of Paris for the purposes of making deliveries; its files and statistics, records, and data; its telephone lines, sliding chutes, conveyor belts, and escalators; and its *blanc,* or great white sale, "the most organized week of the store."[60]

Taken together, the work of Williams and Miller indicates that the early French department store, like contemporary cathedrals of consumption, was both enchanted and disenchanted. Perhaps the most general conclusion to be drawn from this discussion is that enchantment and disenchantment are not easily distinguished from one another; one does not necessarily preclude the other. There is a reciprocal relationship between them. Fantasies draw people into the new means of consumption, and those fantasies can be rationalized to further draw people in and to reinforce the cage. The cage-like quality of the new means of consumption can itself be a fantasy—the fantasy of being locked into one of those cages with ready access to all of its goods and services. In fact, Campbell concluded his work with just such an image: "Modern individuals inhabit not just an 'iron cage' of economic necessity, but a castle of romantic dreams, striving through their conduct to turn the one into the other."[61]

Marxian theory leads us to see the new means of consumption as oriented to, and based on, the control (and exploitation) of the consumer. Weberian theory points us toward some of the problems involved in being able to control consumers. Enchanted settings would seem to be well suited to controlling consumers by luring them into a dreamlike state so that it is easier to part them from their money. However, in the long run, to service and control large numbers of consumers, the cathedrals of consumption are forced to rationalize, and rationalization leads to disenchantment and the decline in the capacity to continue luring consumers or to create the dreamlike states needed for hyperconsumption. The cathedrals of consumption, therefore, are faced with a seemingly unresolvable dilemma. However, a third, very contemporary resource—postmodern social theory—suggests a way out of this dilemma.

POSTMODERN SOCIAL THEORY AND REENCHANTMENT

It is almost impossible to summarize postmodern social theory in a section of a book devoted to so many other matters, but I can offer a brief introduction to the theory as well as its role in this analysis.[62] Postmodern social theory is premised on the idea that in various ways, we have moved beyond the modern world into a new, postmodern world that is very different socially and culturally from its predecessor. New, postmodern theories and ideas are required to analyze this new world.

Both modern social theory and modernity itself were closely tied to the idea of rationality. Theorists (including Marx and Weber) were led to think rationally about that world, and when they did, they discovered that it was a world that was best characterized as being rational. Although acknowledging the advantages of rationality, they were also highly critical of it on various grounds.

Postmodern social theory rejects the idea of the centrality of rationality and is associated more with the ideas of nonrationality or even irrationality. This means that postmodern social theorists reject the careful, reasoned style of modern academic discourse. The author's objective is often more to shock and startle readers than to win them over with logical, reasoned argument. Postmodern social theory also tends to be more literary than academic in style. In fact, thinkers associated with this perspective reject not only the idea of drawing a clear line between academic scholarship and literature but also, as part of a modern way of thinking, most or all efforts to draw boundaries.

Postmodern theory is of obvious relevance to this work because of its association with consumption and the idea that the postmodern world is defined by consumption (rather than production).[63] As Eva Illouz put it, we are dealing with a world "in which economy has been transmuted into culture and culture into the transient and disposable world of goods."[64] One of the leading postmodern thinkers is Baudrillard, whose contribution to our conceptualization of the means of consumption we have already encountered.[65]

More important, postmodern thinkers also reject the idea that society is highly rational. Although postmodern society may have some rational elements, it is even more likely to be characterized by "emotions, feelings, intuition, reflection, speculation, personal experience, custom, violence, metaphysics, tradition, cosmology, magic, myth, religious sentiment, and mystical experience."[66] Rather than discuss this in general terms, I will focus on an idea, "symbolic exchange," associated with the work of Baudrillard.

To Baudrillard, symbolic exchange involves "taking and returning, giving and receiving . . . [the] cycle of gifts and countergifts."[67] Baudrillard developed his notion of nonrational symbolic exchange as a contrast, and alternative, to the highly rational economic exchange that characterizes modern capitalist society.[68] For example, although economic exchange produces such things as goods and services, as well as profit, symbolic exchange is nonproductive. Economic exchanges tend to be limited to a specific exchange of, for example, goods and services for money, and symbolic exchanges occur continually and without limitation. In societies characterized by symbolic exchange, economic exchanges (considered to be of preeminent importance in modern societies) tend to be only a small portion of all exchanges.[69] Baudrillard privileges nonrational symbolic exchange and associates it with primitive societies. He uses the idea of nonrational symbolic exchange to criticize modern societies, which are dominated by rational economic exchange. Baudrillard argued that contemporary society was on the verge, or in the midst, of the transition to the postmodern. However, this newly emerging society offers powerful barriers to symbolic exchange. Although he develops a postmodern theory, Baudrillard ends up being a critic of both modern and postmodern society.

Two of Baudrillard's specific ideas—implosion and simulations—will play a prominent role in this book, as will other ideas closely associated with postmodern social theory such as spectacles, time, and space. Later, I will define and deal with these concepts. However, we must not forget that the greatest significance of postmodern social theory is its emphasis on enchantment, the lack thereof in the modern world, and the continuing need for it. For Baudrillard, the enchanted world of symbolic exchange continually haunts, and poses a threat to, the modern disenchanted world of economic exchange. There is no possibility of returning to the primitive society dominated by symbolic exchange, but there is the possibility of such exchange reasserting itself. In other words, postmodernists hold out the possibility of the *reenchantment* of the world.

Zygmunt Bauman accords great centrality to this process of reenchantment:

Postmodernity . . . brings "re-enchantment" of the world after the protracted and earnest, though in the end inconclusive, modern struggle to dis-enchant it (or, more exactly, the resistance to dis-enchantment, hardly ever put to sleep, was all along the "postmodern thorn" in the body of modernity). The mistrust of human spontaneity, of drives, impulses, and inclinations resistant to prediction and rational justification, has been all but replaced by the mistrust of unemotional, calculating reason. Dignity has been returned to emotions; legitimacy to the "inexplicable," nay *irrational*. . . .[70] The postmodern world is one in which *mystery* is no more a barely tolerated alien awaiting a deportation order. . . . We learn to live with events and acts that are not only not-yet-explained, but (for all we know about what we will ever know) inexplicable. We learn again to respect ambiguity, to feel regard for human emotions, to appreciate actions without purpose and calculable rewards.[71]

To take a specific example, Baudrillard argued that "seduction" offers the possibility of reenchanting our lives. Rather than the complete clarity and visibility associated with modernity, seduction offers "the play and power of illusion."[72]

The introduction of the concept of reenchantment allows us to expand on Weber's theory. Weber offers a theory of the relationship among enchantment, rationalization, and disenchantment. We have seen that some neo-Weberians (Campbell, especially) allow for the possibility of enchantment in the contemporary world, but the postmodernists offer a stronger thesis. Postmodern thinkers such as Baudrillard tend to think of reenchantment as either a possibility within modern society or the basis of a future alternative to modern society and its numbing disenchantment. However, in this work, reenchantment will be viewed as an ongoing and very real development (albeit often existing as a simulation, a fake; see below) within the contemporary cathedrals of consumption. It constitutes the way out of the dilemma posed by the disenchantment of the world in general and of the means of consumption in particular. To continue to attract, control, and exploit consumers, the cathedrals of consumption undergo a continual process of reenchantment. Of course, those efforts at reenchantment may, themselves, be rationalized from the beginning. Even if they are not, with reenchantment the stage is set for the entire process to recur.

One of Baudrillard's best-known concepts is *simulation,* by which he means a copy, perhaps of something for which there is no original (for more on simulations, see Chapter 5). As such, a simulation is a fake, and Baudrillard sees the contemporary world as increasingly characterized by simulations, fakes. This is especially true in consumption in general (e.g., McDonald's Chicken McNuggets for which there is no original) and the cathedrals of consumption (the many Las Vegas hotel-casinos that simulate Paris, Venice, New York, or Mandalay Bay). These casino-hotels are copies of the original cities, but in some cases, the copies have been copied (there is now a copy of the Venetian casino-hotel in Macau). Indeed, this is another way in which Baudrillard thinks about simulations—as copies of copies (sometimes without an original, as in the case of the endless procession of Chicken McNuggets).

Postmodern theory offers us three other perspectives that are crucial to this analysis. First, postmodern theorists tend to see the contemporary world as both exhilarating and threatening. Most of the processes associated with the reenchantment of the cathedrals of consumption can easily be seen as quite exhilarating in reviving and reinvigorating those cathedrals. And many of those same processes (especially simulations) are also quite threatening, even to the very existence of those cathedrals.

Second, postmodern theory offers a useful corrective on the idea that the means of consumption control and exploit consumers. Although there is control and exploitation in the sense that people are led to buy and to spend too much, the fact is that people have not, in the main, been coerced into doing so but have been quite eager to behave in these ways. As we have seen, this has not only been true of American consumers; much of the rest of the world has seemed intent on consuming like Americans. Most consumers do not see themselves as being controlled and exploited and would vehemently reject the idea that this is what is taking place. Whatever the objective realities (if one can even speak of such realities in a postmodern world) of prices paid and quantities purchased, most consumers have seemed willing, at least before the recession, to pay the prices and would, if anything, consume even more if they could.

There is an even stronger point to be made about postmodern consumers. Rather than having their consumption orchestrated by people such as advertising executives and directors of cathedrals of consumption, it may be that it is consumers who are in control. It is the consumers who demand reenchanted cathedrals of consumption, and those demands must be met if their business is to be retained. Moreover, once one setting has been reenchanted, competitors must follow suit or risk the permanent loss of business.

The means of consumption have been in constant competition with one another to see which one could be most responsive to, or even ahead of, the demands of consumers for (re)enchanted settings in which to consume. In fact, it could be argued that consumers forced the means of consumption into a reckless and potentially destructive war to see which one could offer the most (re)enchanted setting. This is nowhere clearer than in contemporary Las Vegas, where old hotels have been torn down and enormously expensive new ones constructed with ever more enchanted themes and settings. Furthermore, it is the casino-hotels (and other cathedrals of consumption) that have been the most excessively reenchanted that are most threatened in the Great Recession.

Third, modern social theory tends to focus on agents and their intentions. Postmodern social theory, however, seeks to decenter the analysis by abandoning such a focus. This is one of the reasons why this book does not focus on consumers as agents but rather on the settings in which consumption occurs. In addition, this postmodern perspective leads us to the view that the processes involved in the reenchantment of the means of consumption are only in part a result of the intentions of the agents operating on behalf of the cathedrals of consumption (see Chapters 5 and 6).

CONCLUSION

In the end, this is not a work in postmodern theory or any other theory for that matter. The goal is to gain a greater understanding of the new means of consumption, and to that end, theoretical tools that work will be employed, whatever their origin.[73] To create the theoretical framework for this book, I have borrowed the ideas of exploitation, control, rationalization, phantasmagoria, and disenchantment from modern social theory and the notion of reenchantment (as well as implosion and simulation) from postmodern social theory. This book offers what the postmodernists call a "pastiche" (a mixture of sometimes seemingly contradictory ideas) of modern and postmodern ideas in order to analyze the cathedrals of consumption. The latter, of course, are themselves combinations of modern, postmodern, and even premodern elements. Both the subject matter and the theoretical perspective of this book stand with one foot in some of social theory's oldest ideas and the other in some of its most contemporary thinking.

4

Rationalization, Enchantment, and Disenchantment

This chapter expands on the Weberian and neo-Weberian theories outlined in the preceding chapter and applies ideas derived from them to the cathedrals of consumption. The discussion is divided into three sections. First, I will examine the several dimensions of the rationalization of the new means of consumption. Second, I will link rationalization to the disenchantment of these settings. Third, I will deal with the degree to which rationalized systems can, themselves, be enchanting. Overarching all of this is the problem of continuing to attract, control, and exploit customers. Rationalization is needed to accomplish these objectives on a large scale, but the resultant disenchantment can have the opposite effect. It is this that leads to the necessity for reenchantment, which is the subject of Chapters 5 and 6. Though always at risk of new disenchantment, reenchanted settings, especially in concert with rationalized procedures, can continue to attract, control, and exploit consumers.

THE RATIONALIZATION OF
THE NEW MEANS OF CONSUMPTION

Rationalization (or, what I have more contemporaneously called "McDonaldization"[1]) has five basic elements: efficiency, calculability, predictability, control through the replacement of human by nonhuman technology, and the irrationality of rationality. I examine each in turn in this section using illustrations from a variety of the new means of consumption.

Efficiency

Efficiency involves the choice of the optimal means to an end. Since they sometimes overlap and at other times stand in opposition to one another, it is important to distinguish between efficiency that is in the interest of the customer and efficiency for the sake of the organization.

For the Customer

As we have seen, the shopping mall has been described as "an extremely efficient and effective selling machine."[2] This, in turn, makes it a highly efficient "buying machine" from the customer's perspective. Consumption is obviously made far more efficient for the consumer by having virtually all shops in one location that also has a large adjacent parking lot. Similar efficiencies are provided by enormous discounters such as Wal-Mart and Costco. Superstores (e.g., Bed Bath & Beyond) offer efficiencies of another kind for customers in search of a specific type of product.

Catalogs, especially those available online, have grown in number and popularity because they represent a highly efficient means of consumption: "Lifestyles have changed dramatically and people are busier than ever. . . . Both parents often work and people don't have time to go shopping. Catalog people realized they were serving a purpose for consumers."[3] Basically, the efficiency of catalog shopping stems from the fact that the customer does not have to leave home to shop. The same, of course, is true of shopping through home-shopping networks and online malls; all the steps involved in getting to, through, and home from the shopping mall are eliminated. Because of this efficiency (and for other reasons), consuming through online malls and other Internet sites (including online catalogs) is on the increase. Not only are the large companies that one might expect involved, but many small businesses (e.g., those in the hobby and office supply business) are as well. Local flower shops are associated with Internet sites (e.g., ftd.com), and they quickly and efficiently deliver standardized bouquets to local customers, who do not need to trek to the shops to pick up their flowers.

The huge Las Vegas casino-hotels bring with them many fairly obvious efficiencies, most notably that a person can stay in a hotel room that is only an elevator ride away from the gaming tables and slot machines. Disney's hotels offer similar efficiencies for visitors to the theme park. On cruise ships, as many as 3,000 (and soon over 5,000) people can quickly and easily consume a large number of goods and services, including gambling in the ship's casino. In Chapter 7, we will discuss Easton Town Center, which offers the efficiencies of literally living in a shopping mall.

For the Organization

The mall creates many efficiencies for shop owners, including collective security and maintenance services, a large pool of customers, the synergy provided by the existence of many shops, and so on. And, of course, these efficiencies (for both customers and merchants) are that much greater in the case of the mega-malls.

Many of these efficiencies do not exist in the case of the superstore, but there are various other kinds of efficiencies involved in selling only one type of product. For example, the only customers who pass through the doors of Bed Bath & Beyond are those in search of what it has to offer.

Slot machines are the most profitable of undertakings from the point of view of the casino operators, and the machines are efficient in that they do not require employees to operate them—an example of the increasing tendency to put the customer to work at no pay; the gambler (as a prosumer) both produces and consumes each play on the machine.

As an Internet provider of books (and now many other things), Amazon.com (and other consumption sites on the Internet) presents an interesting case of efficiency through putting the consumer to work. The most obvious point is that the customer (again, really, the prosumer; see Chapter 2) does all the work involved in placing an order and in reviewing books. Many other sites on the Internet invite comments from people (e.g., cruise lines), and those who write positive statements are serving as unpaid public relations people.

At Wal-Mart, the emphasis is on efficient internal operations. "In its quest for finding more efficient ways to meet consumer needs, Wal-Mart significantly altered for years to come the ways in which Americans would shop."[4] For example, rather than having suppliers ship goods to each individual store, Wal-Mart created its own distribution centers. Suppliers deliver to these centers, and Wal-Mart then uses its own trucks to make deliveries to individual outlets. This efficiency allows suppliers to ship in bulk and therefore to charge Wal-Mart less for goods. Such distribution centers also permit the development of centralized procedures for receiving and processing goods. This is far more efficient than leaving it to each and every Wal-Mart to develop its own procedures.

Another efficiency at Wal-Mart involves distribution centers where the goods are not stored but simply transferred from incoming trucks and railroad cars to outbound trucks (the procedure is known as "cross-docking"). Wal-Mart employs its own fleet of trucks. More often than not, those trucks are used not only to deliver goods to stores but also to pick up products from manufacturers and wholesalers on their way back to the distribution centers.

Sam's Club increased efficiency still further. For example, the limited variety of merchandise sold at these warehouse stores permits truckloads of items to be delivered directly to them. Mechanical means of moving merchandise are employed throughout the process with forklift trucks even being used inside the clubs. Merchandise is often sold prewrapped and preticketed in, for example, three- or six-packs.

Catalog operations, home-shopping networks, and online malls are even more efficient than Wal-Mart or Sam's Club in that they do not need retail outlets and can operate directly out of distribution centers.

Disney World is efficient in many ways, especially in processing the large numbers of people who would easily overwhelm a less rationalized theme park. The basic issue at Disney World is how to keep so many people moving rapidly through the park, or at least to give them the illusion that they are moving quickly. Even though people often find themselves in long lines, they usually feel as if they are moving and that they are getting closer to the attractions. Once in an attraction, conveyances of one kind or another—cars, boats, submarines, planes, rockets, moving walkways—often keep people moving through them far more efficiently than they would were they on foot; no dawdling is permitted.

Trash removal at Disney World is similarly efficient. Were this not the case, Disney World would quickly be swamped with debris. Crews are employed to sweep, collect, and dispose of trash. There is also an elaborate underground tube system into which trash is emptied and whisked away at 60 miles per hour to a central trash disposal plant far from the view of visitors. The trash seems to disappear magically; Disney World is surrealistically clean, especially when one considers how many people use the park each day.

The leader in the funeral business, Service Corporation International, has made the preparation and consumption of a funeral far more efficient. Take, for example, the preparation of corpses for burial:

> It [the corpse] will be sprayed with disinfectant, and his throat and anus will be packed with gauze to prevent fluids from leaking. His mouth will be closed with glue or sewn shut by a thread run through his septum and lower gum. His eyes will be closed with plastic eyecaps or glue. Then an incision will be made in his throat, upper arm, or pelvis, and embalming fluid . . . will be pumped into his body, forcing all the blood out. . . . Upon completion another worker will dab a bit of makeup on his face and hands.[5]

It is impossible to resist noting that one would be hard-pressed to find a better illustration of the disenchantment associated with rationalization than this description of routine procedures for handling human corpses in an assembly-line fashion.

Calculability

The second dimension of rationalization is *calculability*. Rationalization involves an emphasis on things that can be calculated, counted, and quantified. It often results in an emphasis on quantity rather than quality. This leads to a sense that quality is equal to certain, usually (but not always) large, quantities of things.

McDonald's emphasis on quantity—as reflected, for example, in the "Big Mac"—is mirrored by the other fast-food restaurants. The most notable is Burger King, which stresses the quantity of the meat in its hamburger called the "Whopper" and of the fish in its sandwich called the "Whaler" (renamed, a few years ago, not surprisingly, "Big Fish"). Not long ago, Wendy's touted a variety of "biggie" and even "super biggie" offerings. However, in an attempt to appear to be offering less unhealthy food, these products were dropped. Ironically, despite dropping these products, the size of the offerings at Wendy's actually *increased*. Jack-in-the-Box has its "Jumbo Jack" and KFC offers us a "Variety Big Box" meal. Not to be outdone, Pizza Hut has its "Panormous" pizza and Domino's touts its "Dominator." CiCi's offers an "endless" pizza buffet. A few years ago, Little Caesars offered a "Big! Big!" pizza. When it announced even bigger "Big! Big!" pizzas with no increase in price, this was pronounced "a stroke of genius" (clearly, the term *genius* is dispensed quite easily in the fast-food business) by an industry consultant.[6] Similarly, 7-Eleven offers its customers a hot dog called the "Big Bite," a large soft drink called the "Big Gulp," the even larger "Super Big gulp," as well as the "Double Gulp." Starbucks offers the "big gulp" of coffees (the 20-ounce Venti size) and makes it clear how many espresso shots are in various drinks.

In fact, the general tendency has been for fast-food restaurants to push ever-larger servings. For example, McDonald's offered, at least until super-sizing was phased out in 2005, "Super-Size" meals and invited customers to "super size it."[7] Then there was the advent of the "Double Quarter Pounder" and the "Double Cheeseburger" as well as the reintroduction of the "Big N' Tasty" Burger.[8] Wendy's allows customers to add patties (a dollar each) to their hamburger order; there is no upper limit on the number that can be added. Although Hardee's no longer has its "Monster Burger" (it included *two* quarter-pound hamburgers, *three* slices of cheese and no less than *eight* (!) slices of bacon on a seeded bun with mayonnaise) or the "Monster Omelet Biscuit," it does offer "Big Chicken Fillet," "Big Hot Ham & Cheese," and "Big Shef" sandwiches. Hardee's also offers burgers by weight—one-half lb. sourdough burger, one-third lb. thick-burger, and the two-thirds lb. monster double thick-burger. Of course, in using the term *thick-burger,* Hardee's is doubling the quantitative message by telling the consumer not only that it weighs a lot but also that it is thick.

What is particularly interesting about all this emphasis on quantity is the seeming absence of interest in communicating anything about quality. The result is a growing concern about the decline of quality, not only in the fast-food business but in society as a whole. Were fast-food restaurants interested in emphasizing quality, they might give their products such names as the "Delicious Mac," or the "Prime McBeef," or the "All Beef McFrank." But typical McDonald's customers, or more generally those who patronize ratio-nalized systems, know they are *not* getting the highest quality products in general and food in particular (it isn't called "junk food" for nothing!).

Las Vegas hotels compete to see which one can offer the most hotel rooms, the largest casino, the "loosest slots,"[9] and the biggest entertainment attraction. A similar competition takes place among the largest cruise lines, which boast about how many people their ships can carry, how long and wide the ships are, how many tons they weigh, how many different kinds of attractions they offer, and so on. In discount department stores, including Wal-Mart, customers are led to believe they can rely on three things that are easily quantified—low prices,[10] a large number of goods, and a wide variety of them. The same belief prevails in discount malls. The set prices for a daily or weekly pass at Disney World, as well as the abundant signs indicating how long a wait one can expect at a given attraction, illustrate similar calculability in the means of consuming tourism.[11]

The book superstores compete with one another and with small, local bookstores on the basis of how many books they stock. They must also compete with Internet booksellers such as Amazon.com. The book superstores emphasize quantity rather than quality by devoting a disproportionate share of their marketing budget and shelf space to what they perceive to be potential blockbusters. Publishers must print hundreds of thousands of copies of a book for it to be taken seriously by the superstores. Books that do not achieve best-seller status are often quickly returned to the publishers, who reimburse the bookstores for unsold books. Independent booksellers sell about 80% of the books they order, superstores less than 70%, and discount chains such as Sam's Club about 60%. Books are increasingly like movies; the emphasis is on blockbusters that open big.[12] As mentioned previously, Disney is in the book publishing business (under the Hyperion imprint) and not too long ago announced that, to be taken seriously by the superstores, it would print 300,000 copies of a book by a first-time novelist and spend $750,000 promoting it.

Indeed, being a "blockbuster" is what has animated not only the super bookstores but all of the new means of consumption. Blockbuster, a chain of video stores, is only the most blatant about it. The goal is to be big; no, huge—to straddle the nation—no, the world. The goal is defined quantitatively rather than qualitatively. However, with the Great Recession, many of these blockbusters (including the Blockbuster chain) are in trouble. Furthermore, various changes, especially those associated with the Internet (Amazon, Netflix), have led to the increasing ability to profit from products with lesser sales, those that have a "long tail."[13] That is, they can profit by stocking and selling small amounts of a large number of relatively unique and/or niche market products (i.e., selling less of more).

Perhaps the best example of the emphasis on large quantity is found in warehouse stores such as Costco and Sam's Club. Everything about them is big. The stores are cavernous; goods are piled high; enormous sizes of individual products are offered for sale (a gallon of pickles that is unlikely ever to be finished; 200 ounces of laundry detergent that one can barely lift); other products are offered in multiple packages. The following case for the attractiveness of bigness at Price Club also applies to many other new means of consumption: "Big has intrinsic value, especially to Americans. Price Club is the kind of big that's just right for difficult times . . . if Price Club entertains us by tucking the mammoth-sized jars of Tabasco sauce down one of its shadowy aisles, we will say thank you and bring home the big game."[14]

Las Vegas casinos offer an interesting example of calculability. Free perks used to be doled out to gamblers largely on the whim of casino officials, but now it is all reduced to numbers. On average, regular gamblers are likely to receive about $1 worth of "comped" rooms, meals, or other perks for every $3 they can be expected to lose. One high roller was told that in exchange for a free $650 a night suite and other perks, he had to play blackjack for 4 hours at roughly $150 per hand. To gamble for the required number of hours, this visitor slept for only an hour and played blackjack into the wee hours of the morning. He commented, "If you went out and just paid for your room and your food, you'd probably be better off."[15] Whether or not this is true, the fact is that the modern casino has reduced comping to a highly calculable phenomenon. This is aided by the fact that casinos increasingly rely on electronic cards rather than cash, and these cards allow the casino to quantify all sorts of things.

Despite all of this emphasis on quantity, there are examples of new means of consumption that do emphasize quality (or, at least purport to). Starbucks is the best known of these. In the realm of what is called the "home-meal replacement" business, Trader Joe's specializes in gourmet-quality food.[16] Another example is the pizza chain Papa John's, which is growing dramatically (the number of stores grew from 878 in 1995 to 3,208 in 2007 in 50 states and 28 international markets[17]) on the basis of the contention that its pizzas taste better than the others; its slogan is "better ingredients, better pizza."[18] Among other things, Papa John's claims to use vine-ripened tomatoes rather than sauce from concentrate, premium mozzarella, purified water in its dough, and so on. Competitors that focus on quantitative factors such as speed are working to come up with campaigns that emphasize quality. However, to maintain quality, Papa John's has had to rationalize its procedures by offering a stripped-down menu to "ensure that even the newest employee can make a top-notch pizza. A 'keep it simple, stupid' approach pervades operations, from a goof-proof kitchen layout to dough mix that comes to regional commissaries pre-blended."[19] In other words, not only the food but also the jobs at Papa John's have been rationalized; they are McJobs.[20]

Predictability

Rationalization involves the increasing effort to ensure predictability from one time or place to another. In a rational society, consumers want to know what to expect in all settings and at all times. They neither want nor expect surprises. They want to know that the "Big Mac" they order today is going to be identical to the one they ate yesterday and to the one they will eat tomorrow.

The fast-food industry perfected such things as replicated settings, scripted interactions with customers, predictable employee behavior, and predictable products. As Robin Leidner put it, "The heart of McDonald's success is its uniformity and predictability . . . [its] relentless standardization."[21] Such predictability is evident even in more upscale chains such as Hard Rock Cafe:

> It is not as if the Hard Rock Cafe gained its fame from its food or even its association with any one place. Like McDonald's, its menu is identical all over the world, the Caesar salad tastes the same in Las Vegas as it does in Osaka, and the same Eric Clapton guitars grace the walls of the Berlin and San Francisco restaurants.[22]

Nor is it much different in various types of chain stores such as Pottery Barn, Crate and Barrel, the Gap, and J. Crew, which "have raised standardization to a high art." These chains have brought high design to the mass market, but "the cost of this achievement is that while everything may be better, it is also increasingly the same. The khakis and sweat-shirts the Gap sells in Dallas shopping malls are the same as the ones it purveys along Columbus Avenue in Manhattan—in nearly identical stores."[23] Ironically, although these chains offer uniformity and predictability, they tout themselves as offering individuality.

There are many advantages to the homogenization of products and their display—even high-style, high-quality products—but there are liabilities associated with all of this. Some of these liabilities can be linked to the influence of McDonald's:

> But there's a downside, connected to the global homogenization of products and culture and shared with McDonald's, *USA Today* and Starbucks: the stuff may be good but it ain't special. . . . Everything seems more and more the same, wherever you are. Eccentric and idiosyncratic things fill the shelves of these mass stores, but they have been devalued by their very accessibility. The truly special and inventive is harder and harder to find, unless you are very, very rich or have lots of time to look . . . we pay the price in a gradual but very real loss of individual variation: our houses and our wardrobes, like our entertainment, become part of mass culture, wherein we all increasingly consume and display the same thing. . . . That's the sad thing: that as uniformity becomes more and more what stores are selling—uniformity of presentation as well as uniformity of merchandise—a kind of high-level blandness begins to take over. . . . You begin to yearn for some off-note, something wrong, something even a bit vulgar, just to show individual sensibility.[24]

This passage reflects a feeling shared by many and one that is at the heart of this chapter and this book: Although not without enchanting qualities, the homogeneity of rationalized settings and their products (although this may be reduced by businesses that rely on a "long tail") seems to diminish our lives and leaves us craving some form of enchantment.

Control Through the Substitution
of Nonhuman for Human Technology

Because they are so closely linked, I combine the discussion of two elements of rationalization—increased control and the replacement of human
by nonhuman technology. Replacement of human by nonhuman technology
is often oriented toward greater control. The principal source of uncertainty
and unpredictability in any rationalizing system is people—both the people
who work within those systems and those who are served by them.

McDonald's seeks to exert increasing control over both its employees and
its customers. It is most likely to do this by steadily replacing people with
nonhuman technologies. After all, technologies such as robots and computers are far easier to control. In addition to eliminating some people by
replacing them, these nonhuman technologies also exert increasing control
over the remaining human laborers and the people served by the system.

Wal-Mart's central distribution centers (there are now more than 100 of
them) are fully automated. For example, enormous conveyor belts move
goods at 200 feet per second and allocate them to the proper location. Such
technology removes control from the hands of human workers.[25]

Wal-Mart dove deeply into computer technology very early. Electronic
cash registers were employed, and they generated point-of-sale data that
could be used as the basis for automated decisions on replenishing store supplies. The computer system "logged every item sold at checkout counters,
automatically kept warehouses informed of merchandise to be ordered, and
directed the flow of goods not only to the stores but also even to the proper
shelves."[26] When people were involved, it was most often to carry out the
dictates of the technologies.

Wal-Mart also was an early user of bar codes and the Uniform Product
Code (UPC) that, having been developed for supermarkets, was quickly seen
as greatly relevant to Wal-Mart's business. By the end of the 1980s, UPC
scanners were used throughout the Wal-Mart system, including its distribution centers. Scanners took the need to read certain information away from
human beings and built it into the technology. The UPC also increased the
efficiency with which customers could be processed through checkout lines
and products reordered.

Laser scanners are used in the distribution centers, in the automated
receiving in the stores themselves, and by stocking crews who use handheld
lasers to get the goods to the sales floor more quickly and efficiently.
Similarly, employees use laptop computers to automatically record relevant
information on each product (e.g., inventory levels) and as an aid in the
reordering process. Suppliers are able to respond quickly and accurately

because they are directly supplied with relevant information as well as documents such as purchase orders and invoices. The company also has its own satellite system that facilitates communication within the Wal-Mart empire.

Borders Books employs a sophisticated computer inventory system and artificial intelligence technology to keep track of inventory. These technologies constantly adjust inventory on the basis of sales, eliminating certain titles and increasing the supply of others. There is, again, no longer any need for humans to make these decisions; the technologies do it for them.

The shopping mall can be seen as a technologically controlled kingdom with a variety of advanced technologies that control all aspects of its operation. Tight control is exercised over temperature, lighting, events, and merchandise. Time and space are controlled by making the malls windowless; there are few doors to beckon one outside; the uniformity of malls means they could be anywhere; in many cases, there are no clocks; the maintenance and periodic remodeling make it seem as if the malls do not age; there is overall an unreal perfection about the malls.

Control is also exercised over customers. In this context, William Kowinski discusses what he calls the "zombie effect,"[27] floating for hours in malls without an awareness of the passing of time. By inducing this state, malls make it likely that consumers will encounter many shops, see more goods and services, and purchase more of them. Malls control what we purchase not only by deciding what is included and excluded but also by employing the principle of "adjacent attraction."[28] Through the latter, for example, mundane objects are made to seem more desirable by being surrounded with different and more exotic objects. Malls also manage the emotions of consumers by offering bright, cheery, and upbeat environments. "Controlling the emotions of customers is another natural aspect of the mall's basic control apparatus, which treats the consumer as an object to be lulled and manipulated."[29] Children are singled out for special attention on this count and are described as "growing up controlled."[30] Overall, Kowinski concluded, "Big Brother is managing you."[31] Even greater control is exerted over employees, who are described as "prisoners of the mall."[32]

The surveillance of consumers in the new means of consumption is integrally related to the ability to exercise control over them.[33] These settings are awash with surveillance cameras (and, increasingly, audio devices) and personnel on the alert for shoplifting and other crimes. However, all customers are watched, not just those deemed to be "suspicious." The people and machines that observe us are generally unseen and anonymous. Many settings are structured to maximize surveillance over our activities. The existence of electronic tags on many items allows us to be "frisked" electronically every time we leave a consumption site. Most of our dealings with these settings involve computers that yield data on us that can be used in various ways, especially to sell us other things. Transactions are frequently accomplished with credit (or debit) cards, leaving other sorts of information about us that can be viewed and used by many others.

Luxury gated communities are also interesting from the point of view of surveillance and control over people.[34] Such structures have many of the trappings not only of a Weberian iron cage but also of "total institutions" (see below) such as prisons and asylums. Among the similarities are the rules and regulations governing individual behavior,[35] walls surrounding the communities, the guards at the gates around the clock, guard patrols, surveillance cameras, intruder alarms, and limitations on ingress and egress. Visitors are sometimes videotaped on arrival at the gates. The goal is to create "a nearly crime free bubble."[36] Although the barriers are there to prevent unwanted outsiders from gaining entry, they do place constraints on the "inmates" as well, the consumers of this way of life, who often find themselves on the video screen or the object of the gaze of security personnel.

In a sense, not only the gated community but also many of the new means of consumption can be seen as elegant minimum security, albeit voluntary, prisons. Las Vegas casinos are heavily policed, and security cameras give personnel the ability to observe closely the activities of visitors to the casinos and guests in the hotels. The latter may be asked to show their room keys to guards at the elevators in order to get to their rooms. Malls and mega-malls have similar means of observing and controlling consumers. Theme parks such as Disney World are notorious not only for their security efforts but also for their attempts to control both employees and visitors. Controls over employees tend to be blatant, but controls over visitors, though more subtle, are present nonetheless. For example, the parks and the attractions are structured to lead people to do certain kinds of things and not to do others. The paths are set up in such a way that people think they are making free choices when in fact they are generally moving in directions preordained by the designers. Another device to control visitors is the use of what Walt Disney called "wienies" to lead visitors in certain directions. Wienies are highly visible attractions (mountains, castles, and the like) to which virtually all visitors will find themselves drawn.

Disney parks, like the malls, are "preplanned, enclosed, protected, and controlled." Disney World is a triumph of nonhuman over human technology. The following description of the way most theme parks operate fits Disney World especially well:

> Thought and decisions are rarely necessary, because visitors are essentially batched through the various attractions. Each attraction is designed much like

an assembly line, with long, regimented waiting lines leading to fixed cars or boats, which carry guests on an undeviating path through the event in a set period of time. Guests go in one end and out the other, having engaged in exactly the same sensual program as thousands or millions of other people.[37]

Nonhuman technology dominates not only the visitors but also the human employees, whose performances (e.g., through lip-synching) and work (following scripts) are similarly controlled.

A major theoretical resource for those interested in surveillance and con-straint on consumers (and many others) is the work of Michel Foucault. One of his well-known foci is the Panopticon, a structure that allows the complete observation of individuals. The most obvious example is a tower in the center of a circular prison from which guards can see into cells but are themselves invisible to inmates. The Panopticon is a tremendous source of power because it gives prison officials the possibility of total surveillance. In such cases, officials need not always be present; the mere existence of the structure (and the possibility that officials might be there) constrains criminals. More important, its power is enhanced because prisoners come to control themselves; they stop themselves from doing various things because they fear that they *might* be seen by the guards. Foucault's ideas can be extended to the new means of consumption with his argument that the Panopticon becomes the base of "a whole type of society," the disciplinary society.[38] Although there may be no Panopticons per se in any of the new means of consumption, there are certainly many points (the video security room of a casino, the closed-circuit video surveillance at shopping malls[39]) at which both employees and customers may be observed, and that possibility of observation makes for control over both.

We can think of the new means of consumption as part of the "carceral archipelago" that has come to encompass the "entire social body."[40] Taken collectively and individually, the sites of these new means possess the ability to exert control over people throughout society. Although Foucault recognizes that there are forces operating against the carceral system (e.g., inter-national processes that are beyond the control of any agency), his work leaves us with a sense that the carceral system has some of the characteristics of a Weberian iron cage.[41] Foucault focuses more on what he calls a micropolitics of power, which leads to a view that is more like an enormous number of mini-cages in which our lives are more controlled and even more insufferable than they would be in a Weberian, society-wide iron cage. I have described these mini-cages as "islands of the living dead."[42]

At the most extreme end of the continuum of constraint is what Erving Goffman calls a "total institution"—that is, one that exerts near complete control over the people in it. Although Goffman has prisons and mental asylums in mind, his definition of a total institution could be applied to several new means of consumption, especially the cruise ship. A total institution is "a place of residence and work where a large number of like-situated individuals, cut off from the wider society for an appreciable period of time, together lead an enclosed, formally administered round of life."[43] Although sailors have already been examined from this perspective,[44] it also is possible to look at cruise passengers in this way. Passengers are not nearly as constrained as members of the crew, to say nothing of inmates of prisons or mental institutions, but there is nonetheless significant constraint on them. They cannot leave the ship while at sea, they can do only what is available to them on board, and they can consume only when and what the ship offers.

Nonhuman technology not only controls people but also serves to eliminate them in many cases. Typically, this occurs as employees are rendered redundant by technological innovations that do their jobs more quickly and cheaply. For example, one of the home-shopping networks uses a voice-response android to screen and process incoming calls; its studio cameras are electronically controlled and require no human personnel.[45] Technological change may also eliminate the physical presence of consumers. Peapod is a service that allows customers to do their supermarket shopping online. They can cruise virtual aisles comparing per unit costs, assessing the nutritional value of various foods, and using virtual coupons. Once an order is placed, Peapod's "personal" shoppers pick out the food. If goods are not in stock or up to quality standards (e.g., the bananas are too ripe), the personal shoppers confer by telephone with the customers.[46]

Irrationality of Rationality

We can conceive of the irrationality of rationality in several ways. At the most general level, it is simply the overarching label for all of the negative aspects and effects of rationalization. More specifically, it can be seen as the paradoxical outcome of efforts to be highly rational. That is, rationalization can be viewed as leading to inefficiency, unpredictability, incalculability, and loss of control. The irrationality of rationality also means that rational systems are *unreasonable* systems.[47] That is, they serve to deny the basic humanity, the human reason, of the people who work within or are served by them. In other words, they are dehumanizing. This dehumanizing effect is related to another aspect of the irrationality of rationality and the one of most concern in this context—the disenchantment of rational systems and, more generally, the society they come to dominate.

There are a number of ways in which the health and perhaps the lives of people have been threatened by progressive rationalization. One example is the high-calorie, -fat, -cholesterol, -salt, and -sugar content of the food served in fast-food restaurants. Such meals are the last things the vast majority of Americans (and Western Europeans) need. Many Americans already suffer from obesity, high cholesterol levels, high blood pressure, and diabetes. The kinds of meals typically offered at fast-food restaurants only serve to heighten these problems. Even more worrisome, they help to create eating habits in children that contribute to the development of these and other health problems later in life. It can be argued that fast-food restaurants are turning children into lifelong devotees of fast food, "addicted" to diets high in salt, sugar, and fat. In fact, there have been several lawsuits, thus far unsuccessful, claiming that fast food causes obesity.

The fast-food industry generates an enormous amount of trash, some of which is nonbiodegradable. Many people have been critical of the public eyesore created by litter from innumerable fast-food meals strewn across the countryside. Even greater criticism has been leveled at the widespread production by the fast-food industry of debris that piles up into mountainous landfills.

Rationalized institutions have a negative effect not only on our health and on the environment but also on some of our most cherished institutions, most notably the family. For example, instead of preparing a meal at home and sitting around the dinner table and eating it, a family may obtain its evening meal from the drive-through window and eat it in the car.

Another irrationality associated with rationalization is the possibility that we could lose control over a system that comes to control us. Already, many aspects of our lives are controlled by these rational systems, but at least it appears as though these systems are ultimately controlled by people. However, these rational systems can spin beyond the control of even the people at the top. Or these interlocking rational systems could fall into the hands of a small number of leaders who through them could exercise enormous control over all of society. There are authoritarian and totalitarian possibilities associated with the process of rationalization (as is clear, in among other places, the literature of Franz Kafka and George Orwell).

Virtually all of the means of consumption discussed in this book contribute to hyperconsumption. For example, our supermarkets and supercenters are crammed with all sorts of foods that have disastrous effects on the health of many. Similarly, the stands throughout Disney World purvey a wide range of junk food, Las Vegas casinos offer all-you-can-eat buffets, and cruise ships compete to see which one can offer vacationers the most food. In terms of family life, the best that can be said about the new means of consumption is that they give family members a chance to consume a great deal together.

There is no lack of irrationalities of rationality at Disney World. For example, despite its Herculean efforts, there are long lines and long waits; costs (for food, for countless Disney souvenirs hawked both in and out of the parks) mount up and often make what is supposed to be an inexpensive vacation highly costly. Most important, what is supposed to be a human vacation turns into, at least for some, a nonhuman or even a dehumanizing experience as visitors are forced to deal with employees who relate to them by mindlessly reciting prearranged scripts.

An example of the irrationality of rationality at Wal-Mart is the ill-fated development of hypermarkets. Because bigger and bigger was working so well, Sam Walton concluded that this process was virtually limitless. Why not build hypermarkets that are infinitely larger than the typical supermarket? However, it turned out that there were limits. The stores were just too big. It took too much time to get around them; too much space had to be covered. According to one analyst, "In a hypermarket, by the time you've bought some aspirin, some Kleenex, and a bottle of milk, you could easily walk a mile."[48] Designed to increase efficiency, the hypermarkets actually made shopping less efficient for many consumers. This was especially true for the consumer who needed only a few items.

As we will see in Chapter 8, the failure of the hypermarkets should have been a warning to other cathedrals of consumption (e.g., mega-malls, casino-hotels) that operated on the principle that bigger was better. With the advent of the Great Recession, great size has become an increasing liability.

A good example of dehumanization in another of the new means of consumption is found in the new and increasingly popular "virtual universities." Here is a paradoxical statement from one student in such a program:

> I worried that a professor would be just this faceless entity out there I couldn't relate to. . . . But in the online class I have now, I feel like I know him, even though we haven't met. He could walk right by me on the street.[49]

Most generally, the rationality by which the cathedrals of consumption operate can be seen as playing a role in the irrationality of rationality that was the economic crash that began in late 2007. The highly rational cathedrals of consumption served to greatly expedite the ability of people to consume, to spend all they earned, and ultimately to go into debt. The credit card companies played a key role in rationalizing their operations so that consumers could easily increase their level of debt. Rationalized systems made it easy for consumers to overextend themselves (the same was true of mortgage and home equity loans and the ease with which they could be obtained as banks rationalized their loan procedures). Once the economy began to cycle down, reality began to impinge on these overextended consumers, and as they failed to pay their debts and cut down on their consumption, they contributed mightily to the accelerating recession. This, in turn, led to the decline, and even disappearance, of a number of cathedrals of consumption, and this further contributed to the increasing depth of the recession.

LINKING RATIONALIZATION TO DISENCHANTMENT

As we saw in the preceding chapter, the process of rationalization leads, by definition, to the disenchantment of the settings in which it occurs. The term clearly implies the loss of a quality—enchantment—that was at one time very important to people. Although we undoubtedly have gained much from the rationalization of society in general, and the means of consumption in particular, we also have lost something of great, if hard to define, value.

Efficient systems have no room for anything smacking of enchantment and systematically seek to root it out of all aspects of their operation. Anything that is magical, mysterious, fantastic, dreamy, and so on is apt to be inefficient. Enchanted systems typically involve highly convoluted means to whatever end is involved. Furthermore, enchanted worlds may well exist without any obvious goals at all. Efficient systems, also by definition, do not permit such meanderings, and designers and implementers will do whatever is necessary to eliminate them. The elimination of meanderings and aimlessness is one of the reasons that rationalized systems were, for Weber, disenchanted systems.

As we saw earlier, one major aspect of efficiency is using the customer as an unpaid worker, as a prosumer. It is worth noting that all of the mystery associated with an operation is removed when consumers perform it themselves; after all, they know exactly what they are doing. Mystery is far more likely when others perform such tasks and consumers are unable to see precisely what they do. What transpires in the closed kitchen of a gourmet restaurant is far more mysterious than the "cooking" that takes place in the open kitchen of a fast food restaurant, to say nothing of the tasks consumers perform in such settings.

The same point applies to employees of rationalized systems. Their work is broken down into a series of steps, the best way to perform each step is discovered, and then all workers are taught to perform each step in that way. There is no mystery in any of this for the employee, who more or less unthinkingly follows the dictates of the organization. There is little or no room for any creative problem solving on the job, much less any sense of enchantment.

Compare the efficient and mechanical preparation and consumption of food in the fast-food restaurant to the way food was cooked and eaten in the novel (and later movie) *Like Water for Chocolate*. Food was prepared lovingly over a long period of time:

> On Mama Elena's ranch, sausage making was a real ritual. The day before, they started peeling the garlic, cleaning the chiles, and grinding spices. All the women in the family had to participate. . . . They gathered around the dining-room table in the afternoon, and between the talking and the joking the time flew by until it started to get dark.[50]

And the eating of the food had a magical effect on those who participated in the meal:

> The moment they took their first bite of cake, everyone was flooded with a great wave of longing. Even Pedro, usually so proper, was having trouble holding back his tears. Mama Elena, who hadn't shed a single tear over her husband's death, was sobbing silently. But the weeping was just the first symptom of a strange intoxication—an acute attack of pain and frustration—that seized the guests.[51]

Or,

> tasting these chiles in walnut sauce, they all experienced a sensation. . . . Gertrudis . . . immediately recognized the heat in her limbs, the tickling sensation in the center of her body, the naughty thoughts. . . . Then she left. . . . All the other guests quickly made their excuses, coming up with one pretext or another, throwing heated looks at each other. . . . The newlyweds were secretly delighted since this left them free to grab their suitcases and get away as soon as possible. They needed to get to the hotel.
>
> Everyone else, including the ranch hands, was making mad passionate love, wherever they happened to end up.[52]

With regard to *calculability*, in the main, enchantment has far more to do with quality than quantity.[53] Magic, fantasies, dreams, and the like relate more to the inherent nature of an experience and the qualitative aspects of that experience than, for example, to the number of such experiences one has. An emphasis on producing and participating in a large number of experiences tends to diminish the magical quality of each of them. Put another way, it is difficult to imagine the mass production of magic, fantasy, and dreams. Such mass production may be common in the movies, but magic is more difficult, if not impossible, to produce in settings designed to deliver large numbers of goods and services frequently and over great geographic spaces. The mass production of such things is virtually guaranteed to undermine their enchanted qualities. This is a fundamental dilemma facing the new means of consumption.

Take, for example, the shows that are put on over and over by the various new means of consumption—the Playhouse Disney–Live on Stage! show at Disney's Hollywood Studios, the sea battle in front of the Treasure Island casino-hotel in Las Vegas, or the nightclub shows on cruise ships. The fact that they must be performed over and over tends to turn them into highly mechanical performances in which whatever "magic" they produce stems from the nature and size of the spectacle and the technologies associated with them rather than the quality of the performers and their performances.

In any case, it could be argued that by its very nature, fantasy has more to do with the consumer than with the means of consumption. Ada Huxtable, for example, has defined fantasy as a "freeing of the mind and the spirit to explore unknown places," which she distinguishes from, for example, "a handshake from some unconvincingly costumed actors in a totally predictable and humdrum context."[54] There are inherent limitations on the ability of rationalized settings to create fantasy for people.

No characteristic of rationalization is more inimical to enchantment than *predictability*. Magical, fantastic, or dreamlike experiences are almost by definition unpredictable. Nothing would destroy an enchanted experience more easily than having it become predictable.

The Disney theme parks sought to eliminate the unpredictability of the midway at an old-fashioned amusement park such as Coney Island with its milling crowds, disorder, and debris. Instead, Disney World built a setting defined by cleanliness, orderliness, predictability, and—some would say—sterility. Disney has successfully destroyed the old form of enchantment and in its place created a new, highly predictable form of entertainment. As the many fans of Disney World will attest, there is enchantment there, but it is a very different, mass-produced, assembly-line form, consciously fabricated and routinely produced over and over rather than emerging spontaneously from the interaction among visitors, employees, and the park itself.

A similar point could be made about the "new" Las Vegas. In the "bad old days" when it was run by the "mob," it was a much less predictable place and therefore, arguably, a far more enchanted one than it is today under the control of large corporations and their bureaucratic employees. A good example of this is to be found in the 2003 movie *The Cooler*, which describes the use by an old-style casino of an employee with legendary bad luck to stand close to winning gamblers, making it likely (it was believed) that their winning streaks would end. However, new management wanted to create a more modern casino in which, among other things, the cooler used more predictable techniques (e.g., distracting winners) than simply relying on the aura of "bad luck."

Both *control* and the *nonhuman technologies* that produce it tend to be inimical to enchantment. As a general rule, fantasy, magic, and dreams cannot be subjected to external controls; indeed, autonomy is much of what gives them their enchanted quality. Fantastic experiences can go anywhere; anything can happen. Such unpredictability clearly is not possible in a tightly controlled environment. It is possible that tight and total control can be a fantasy, but for many, it would be more a nightmare than a dream. Much the same can be said of nonhuman technologies. Such cold, mechanical systems are usually the antitheses of the dream worlds associated with enchantment. Again, it is true that there are fantasies associated with nonhuman technologies, but they too tend to be more nightmarish than dreamlike.

An interesting example of the replacement of human with nonhuman technology took place in Las Vegas. Shows in the old casino-hotels used to feature major stars such as Frank Sinatra and Elvis Presley. One could argue that such stars had charisma; they had an enchanted relationship with their fans. Now the emphasis has shifted to huge, tightly choreographed (i.e., predictable) extravaganzas without individual stars. For example, the Rio Hotel and Casino features "ballet dancers who bounce, toes pointed, from bungee cords, hooked to the casino ceiling . . . [and] a mechanical dolphin that dives from aloft with a rider playing Lady Godiva."[55] The focus is on the nonhuman technology (which controls the performers) and not on the individuals performing the acts. The performers in such extravaganzas are easily replaceable; they are interchangeable parts.

The point of this section has been to argue that increasing rationalization is related to, if not inextricably intertwined with, disenchantment. However, as we shall see, there are aspects of rationalization that actually heighten enchantment.

RATIONALIZATION AS ENCHANTMENT

There is no question that although rationalized systems lead in various ways to disenchantment, they paradoxically and simultaneously serve to create their own kinds of enchantment. We should bear in mind that this enchantment varies in terms of time and place. Because these settings are now commonplace to most of the readers of this book, few of them (especially fast-food restaurants) are likely to be thought of as enchanting. However, it should be remembered that they still enchant children, as they did us for some time (and, in many cases, may still); it is certainly the case that they enchanted our parents and grandparents, and they are found enchanting in other societies to which they are newly exported. It is also worth remembering that there are degrees of enchantment; Disney World and Las Vegas are undoubtedly seen by most as more enchanting than Wal-Mart and the Sears catalog.

Reflect for a moment on the highly rationalized, and therefore presumably disenchanted, setting of Sam's Club and other warehouse stores. What could be more disenchanting than stores built to look like warehouses—comparatively cold, spare, and inelegant? Compare them to the "dream worlds" of early arcades and department stores such as Bon Marché. Great effort was made to make the latter warm, well-appointed, and elegant settings that helped inflame the consumer's fantasies—in a word, enchanting. Sam's Club has gone to great lengths in the opposite direction; it seems to have sought to create as rationalized and disenchanted a setting as possible. It comes strikingly close, in the realm of retailing, to Weber's image of the rational cage.

Yet this disenchanted structure produces another kind of fantasy—that of finding oneself let loose in a warehouse piled to the ceiling with goods that, if they are not free, are made out to be great bargains. It is a cold, utilitarian fantasy, but a fantasy nonetheless. As a general rule, disenchanted structures have not eliminated fantasies but rather replaced older fantasies with more contemporary ones. The new, rationalized fantasies involve getting lots of things at low prices rather than the fantasies associated with the older department stores that might involve imagining what it would be like to wear elegant clothing or to surround oneself with luxurious home furnishings.

People often marvel at the *efficiency* of rationalized systems; their ability to manage things so effectively can seem quite magical. For example, the ability of Disney World to process so many of us through the park, or to dispose of all the trash we produce, is a source of amazement to many people.

As we saw in the example of Sam's Club, rationalized systems also often amaze on the basis of the large *quantity* of things they can deliver at what appears to be such a low cost. The cruise is another good example of this, especially the food that is available in great abundance and with great frequency and the bundling of lots of entertainment into one package: casino, spa, nightclub, visits to islands, and so on. Similarly, the continual expansion of Disney World makes it seem increasingly like a world that offers unlimited possibilities for entertainment.

The *predictability* of the new means of consumption can be astounding. This can range anywhere from amazement that the "Big Mac" we ate today in New York is identical to the one we ate last week in London and will eat next week in Tokyo to being struck by the fact that today's water display at the Bellagio casino-hotel is identical to the one we saw on our last trip to Las Vegas.

Perhaps the ultimate in the capacity of the rationalization of the new means of consumption to enchant us comes from their advanced *technologies*. Although at one time enchantment stemmed from human wizards or magicians, it now stems from the wizardry of modern robotic and computerized technology. Ultimately, it is the technology of the modern cruise line, the Las Vegas casino, and Disney World that astounds us, not the humans who happen to work in these settings or the things they do.[56] Our amazement can stem from the technologies themselves or from what they produce. We can, for example, marvel over how McDonald's French fries always look and taste the same. Or we can be impressed by the fact that Wal-Mart's shelves are always so well stocked.

Are the contemporary fantasies associated with rational systems as satisfying as those conjured up in the past? This is a complex and highly controversial issue. Clearly, the huge number of people who flock to the new means of consumption find them quite magical. However, it is fair to wonder whether rationally produced enchantment is truly enchanting or whether it is as enchanting as the less rational, more human, forms of enchantment that it tends to squeeze out. We might ask whether one of the *irrational* consequences of all of this is that these contemporary fantasies come closer to nightmares than did their predecessors. After all, it is far harder to think of a surreal nightmare associated with an elegant department store than with a warehouse. In any case, it is clear that rationally produced enchantment is deemed insufficient as reflected in the many efforts at reenchantment that are the subject of the next two chapters.

CONCLUSION

This chapter has made three related points: First, the cathedrals of consumption can be described as being highly rationalized; second, rationalization leads to disenchantment; third, rational means of consumption can themselves have enchanting qualities inherent in their rationalized natures. Despite the latter, the central problems confronting the cathedrals of consumption remain rationalization and the disenchantment engendered by it.

5

Reenchantment

Creating Spectacle Through Extravaganzas and Simulations

T he cathedrals of consumption must be continually reenchanted if they are to maintain their ability to attract a sufficient number of consumers. Without large numbers of consumers, the mechanisms oriented to control and exploitation will not yield the desired profits. In this chapter and the next, I examine some of the ways in which reenchantment occurs. Spectacle, which I define as a dramatic public display, is key. Spectacles may be created intentionally (these will be called *extravaganzas*), or, as we will see, they may be partially or wholly unintentional.

The basic premise behind this chapter and the next is that it has been not enough (although in the Great Recession it may have become enough) simply to open a shop, a mall, a theme park, or a casino and to wait for the customers to arrive.[1] As a representative of one chain put it, "You've got to romance the product. . . . You can't pile it high and watch it fly. You've got to give something extra."[2]

SPECTACLE

The reenchantment of the cathedrals of consumption depends on their ability to create spectacles.[3] Spectacles themselves are not new and are not restricted to consumption (other examples include the Nazi rallies, American political conventions, Mardi Gras in New Orleans,[4] and Carnaval in Rio de Janeiro). They have appeared throughout history and have often been used to accomplish all sorts of objectives. Fairs, expositions, and the like are early examples of the use of spectacle to sell commodities. In fact, spectacle lay at the base of the success of the most important and immediate precursors of the new means of consumption: department stores. As we have seen, the Parisian arcades were "phantasmagoric," and of the early French department store Bon Marché, Michael Miller said, "Spectacle and entertainment, on the one hand, the world of consumption, on the other, were now truly indistinguishable."[5] The first American department stores used color, glass, light, art, shop windows, elegant interiors, seasonal displays, and even Christmas parades to create a spectacle.[6] Similarly, at the turn of the 20th century, Coney Island relied heavily on the creation of spectacle to attract visitors. Over the years, the bar has been raised progressively, with the result that displays have needed to be bigger and bigger in order to work. Furthermore, spectacles are no longer isolated events but have grown increasingly ubiquitous, both spatially and temporally.

The concept of the spectacle lies at the core of thinking of the French social thinker Guy Debord and his influential work, *The Society of the Spectacle*.[7] To Debord, "The spectacle is the *chief product* of present-day society."[8] He contends that one of the functions of the spectacle is to obscure and conceal "the rationality of the system."[9] I argue here that spectacle has been used to overcome the liabilities, especially the disenchantment, associated with highly rationalized systems. Debord has made the point that the spectacle associated with commodities is a kind of opiate that obscures the true operation of society (including its rationality). It also serves to conceal the fact that the goods and services purchased may ultimately be dissatisfying.

The spectacle is closely linked in Debord's eyes to consumerism and commodities: "THE WORLD THE SPECTACLE holds up to view is . . . the world of commodity ruling over all lived experience."[10] Commodities and the spectacles that surround them have come to dominate not only the economy but also the entire society. As a result, to Marx's alienated production it is necessary to add alienated consumption as a necessity imposed on the masses. That is, consumption is imposed from without, and people are unable to express themselves in the process of consumption or in the goods and services they obtain through it. Ultimately, Debord sees the emergence of a "society of the spectacle, where commodity contemplates itself in a world of its own making."[11] People, as spectators, are not part of these contemporary spectacles; indeed, they are alienated from them. People watch them because they are alluring, but the spectacles are put on *for* them; people are not an integral part *of* them.

David Chaney has done much to clarify the meaning of the spectacle by differentiating between two related but very different cultural orders: the early modern "spectacular society" and today's "society of the spectacle."[12]

In the past, spectacle tended to be an integral part of, and to emerge from, everyday life (e.g., a county fair, a local market day). In contrast, in the contemporary society of the spectacle, such a drama is not an inherent part of everyday life. Rather, we make unusual and lengthy trips to a Disney World where, far from our homes, we participate in various attractions in ways that are largely predetermined by the park's designers and not at all connected to our daily lives. Furthermore, unlike fairs or market days, which are likely to recur regularly, when we leave Disney World, we are likely never, or at best rarely, to return.

In addition, in the spectacular society, there were possibilities of excess and at least limited transgression (the "carnivalesque"[13]). An example might be illicit sexual relations in public. In the society of the spectacle, transgressions are likely to be prevented systematically from occurring by the control over, and close surveillance of, the spectators. Many of the spectacles that will concern us have been sanitized by those who create and control them.

Although these differences are important, we must not take them too far. It is impossible to draw absolute distinctions between past and present spectacles,[14] to say nothing of the cathedrals of consumption in which they occur. Although Mardi Gras (and Carnaval in Rio de Janeiro) has ancient roots, it continues today and retains elements of transgression (e.g., women baring their breasts in response to chants from the crowd at Mardi Gras). And transgression continues to occur in contemporary cathedrals of consumption, ranging from the mundane such as brawls in the stands of modern athletic stadiums to the extraordinary periodic massacres that plague fast-food restaurants.

We should bear in mind that the new means of consumption create spectacles[15] not as ends in themselves but in order to bring in large numbers of people to buy more goods and services.[16] A mall, a casino, or a theme park that is empty, or only half full (increasing realities and problems in recessionary times), not only has a smaller population to sell to but also does not generate the same excitement as a full house. Sparsely populated cathedrals of consumption generate less word-of-mouth appeal and are apt to fail as a result. People seem to be animated by the presence of large numbers of other people, and that animation likely translates into increased sales of goods and services.[17]

While we will discuss it in detail in Chapter 7, it is worth noting that Dubai encompasses a number of spectacles, including many large malls, as well as the tallest building, perhaps the most expensive hotel, and the largest manmade islands in the world. It is that that makes Dubai itself a spectacle and a magnet for global tourists.

EXTRAVAGANZAS

There are obviously many different ways of producing a spectacle, but the most obvious is simply to put on a show intentionally, an extravaganza. This is nowhere clearer than in Las Vegas and in its major casino-hotels, which seek to distinguish themselves by putting on shows that are more spectacular than the ones being presented next door. A variety of devices are used to create a spectacular show—legendary stars (more common, as we have seen, in the past), huge casts, large orchestras, elaborate production numbers, live and potentially dangerous animals (although we may see less of this in the future with the 2003 mauling and near death of Roy—of the famed performers Siegfried and Roy—by one of his white tigers during a show at the MIRAGE that led to the end of the act[18]), blinding light shows, booming sound, ostentatious sets, breathtaking technology, incredible costumes and daring nudity, and so on. Notable in Las Vegas is the various Cirque du Soleil (an avant-garde circus) shows, including "Mystere" at Treasure Island and "O" performed in a permanent 1.5-million-gallon pool at Bellagio.

The exteriors of the casino-hotels are incredible shows in their own right. The Luxor sports the largest pyramid in the world, as well as a monolith and a replica of the sphinx. Excalibur is designed to look like an enormous medieval castle. New York, New York offers an image of the New York skyline with a rollercoaster, complete with screaming riders, weaving around the skyscrapers and even the casino itself. In addition, there is a 150-foot replica of the Statue of Liberty. The Paris casino-hotel includes a 50-story Eiffel Tower built to half the scale of the original and a copy of the Arc de Triomphe at the front of the property. Stratosphere is the highest tower in town—in fact, the highest west of the Mississippi. A volcano erupts periodically at the MIRAGE. A pitched sea battle, complete with the sinking of a British ship by a pirate ship, has occurred several times a day for years outside Treasure Island. Wynn Las Vegas is dominated by a mountain (!) built on the billiard-table flat desert. Of course, the entire Las Vegas Strip, with its enormous neon signs and displays, is a spectacular show.

In the mid-1990s, the downtown Fremont Street casinos were in danger of being overwhelmed by the Strip, its spectacular architecture, and its extravagant shows. To be able to better compete, several blocks of Fremont Street were covered over by a 100-foot-high electric canopy that created an enclosed pedestrian mall and spectacular light and sound shows (the "Fremont Street Experience") that play themselves out on the canopy for 7 minutes on the hour.

The Las Vegas Strip can be seen as the world's largest and most spectacular carnival midway. Owners of each casino-hotel must decide how they are going to seduce visitors into entering their attraction rather than some other. The answer, of course, is that they must build increasingly spectacular exteriors and put on more and more incredible shows out front. As one well-known Las Vegas entrepreneur puts it, "You've got to get people wondering if what's inside is as wacky as the outside."[19] (Virtually all of the external shows, including the light show on the canopy over Fremont Street, last only a few minutes so that those who take the time to watch them will still have plenty of time to gamble before the next show.)

In fact, the entire casino industry in Las Vegas is driven by the need to be spectacular enough collectively to continue to attract visitors to the city. Legal gambling is spreading throughout the United States, and American gamblers therefore need a powerful reason to travel all the way to Las Vegas. The same is true of well-heeled gamblers throughout the world who can now more easily go to other gambling centers (e.g., Chinese gamblers living only a short distance from Macau). Also posing a threat to Las Vegas is the growth of online gambling. To continue to attract large crowds, "the most over-the-top city in America has been forced to become more sensational."[20]

Not to be outdone, the interior structures of the casino-hotels are incredible shows, almost as spectacular as the exteriors. For example, the interior of the Luxor pyramid is a vast open space surrounded on all sides by corridors that lead to guest rooms. Each floor grows smaller with fewer and fewer rooms as one ascends (in glass-enclosed "inclinators") toward the peak of the pyramid. Inside the MIRAGE, one encounters a 50-foot aquarium (with sharks and exotic fish) behind the registration desk, a 1.5-million-gallon dolphin habitat, and the "Secret Garden"—a zoo with rare and exotic animals, including white tigers. "Masquerade Village," which is part of the Rio Hotel and Casino, has a 12-minute show featuring five Mardi Gras floats (with live performers) suspended from the ceiling.

The scenes in the casinos, on the Strip, and on Fremont Street are themselves incredible shows. The large number of people wagering huge sums of money in the casinos is one type of spectacle. The wide range of people in the hotels and in the various shows, bars, and restaurants is another. Yet another is the swarm of people parading up and down the Strip or milling on Fremont Street to view the light shows.

Las Vegas and its casino-hotels represent the ultimate extravaganza, but other means of consumption have sought to learn from Las Vegas (one could speak of the "Las Vegasizing of America," the process by which "American culture is being transformed into one long and uninterrupted show business act"[21]) in developing their own spectacles to attract and keep customers.

As mentioned previously, the most obvious example is Dave and Buster's, one of whose cofounders was a former Las Vegas blackjack dealer. The attractions at Dave and Buster's arcades include "Dactyl Nightmare," a virtual reality game involving the zapping of flying dinosaurs; a virtual driving range for golfers; a Derby horseracing video game; gunfights against laser-activated desperados; and the "Million Dollar Midway" that includes computerized casino games.[22]

Theme restaurant chains are obviously in the business of putting on extravaganzas for their customers. One can imagine oneself in the rock music world in the Hard Rock Cafe and in the Hollywood scene in Planet Hollywood. If you want to imagine yourself in a tropical rainforest, Rainforest Cafe features "cascading waterfalls, tropical rain showers, simulated thunder and lighting, and live tropical birds . . . animated talking trees, butterflies, and crocodiles,"[23] not to mention the retail area selling products with animal themes and sporting the Rainforest Cafe logo.

As for more mundane new means of consumption, we can look to fast-food restaurants. Though hardly spectacular now to jaded American consumers, they are all about extravaganza with vibrant colors, playgrounds, and so forth:

> The competition among fast-food giants has always been as much about appearances as reality—a lot, in fact, like a three-ring circus, with ever new, ever more flashy show stoppers needed to keep the crowds coming into the tent. Toy giveaways, movie tie-ins, glitzy ad campaigns and new food products have all done the job.[24]

In the retail business, there is an increasing need to put on an extrava-ganza in "retailtainment" or "entertainment retailing," involving the "use of ambience, emotion, sound and activity to get customers interested in the merchandise and in a mood to buy."[25] For example, take the "show" at the superstore Niketown (there are now 14 of them) in New York City:

> Niketown's facade is a takeoff on an old New York high-school building. You enter through turnstiles, in the manner of a sports arena, to find yourself in a sleek, futuristic, five-story atrium into which, at 30-minute intervals, a three-story-high screen descends and a video softly plugging Nike products is played along with a crescendo of recorded music. There are displays of sports memo-rabilia and a chance to hit a punching bag . . . the merchandise is secondary to the experience of being in this store, an experience that bears more than a pass-ing resemblance to a visit to a theme park. Niketown is a fantasy environment, one part nostalgia to two parts high tech, and it exists to bedazzle the con-sumer, to give its merchandise sex appeal and establish Nike as the essence not just of athletic wear but also of our culture and way of life.[26]

The Toys 'R Us in the rejuvenated Times Square area in New York City has a number of spectacular elements, including an indoor 60-foot Ferris wheel, a two-story Barbie dollhouse, a huge animatronic T-Rex from Jurassic Park, and R-Zone with loads of electronic games on large plasma screens. Until 2006, the site also featured a life-size version of the board game Candy Land complete with real candy (for sale).[27]

Bass Pro Shops Outdoor World stores include such things as indoor waterfalls, archery ranges, shooting ranges, and outdoor decks where fly fishermen can try out their casts. Then there is the flagship store of Recreational Equipment (REI) in Seattle with its "nearly 100,000-square-foot, warehouselike structure that contains a sixty-five-foot-high freestand-ing artificial rock for climbing, a glass-enclosed wet stall for testing rain gear, a vented area for testing camp stoves and an outdoor trail for mountain-biking."[28] These elaborate new settings seem to work.

What about book superstores? Surely these are places for serious people to do serious browsing and purchasing. Unless, of course, they are one of the modern super bookstores such as Borders. Such a superstore has become much more than simply a place to purchase books:

> It's a place to meet, eat, drink, romance, discuss, *dream* [italics added], read, write or just hang out. A safe, smoke-free gathering place for kids, teenagers, sin-gles, couples, moms, dads, grandparents and rebels with laptops. There are book groups, discussion groups, support groups. There are speakers, writers, story-tellers, musicians and chefs. Breakfast, lunch, dinner. Coffee, juice and milk.[29]

Although obviously sold in large numbers, the books themselves seem little more than the backdrop for this new center of fun. "It's almost like a library. . . . But at a library you can't talk, can't eat, can't drink, you can't laugh and carry on and have fun."[30] For some, it is just another spectacular place to while away the hours, merely an alternative to an adult game center such as Dave and Buster's. Those who tire of the electronic games and the alcohol at the latter can amble on over to Borders for a quieter, more linear variety of fun. It's yet another alternative setting for people to go, hang out, and have a good time. Unlike many of the others, there is no entry charge and very little pressure to actually buy anything. But though many do just go to hang out, many others buy enough to sustain the book superstores. One customer who belongs to several book clubs at Borders spends about $3,000 a year on books. Why? "It's entertainment."[31]

One observer sees putting on a spectacular show as increasingly true for many kinds of stores:

> Retailers are working to make stores provide something that catalogues, the Internet and home shopping cannot—the thrill of an event. Make it spectacular enough and they will come. In a culture that is starved for public experiences and that increasingly consumes entertainment in private, stores are functioning more and more as an escape from the personal space of computers. . . . Stores entice us into their versions of a public realm, offering a Faustian bargain: step into our commercial world and we will give you the kind of communal excitement that it's hard to find this side of Disneyland. . . . What happened? Put simply, retailers came back by figuring out how to compete with other forms of selling. Instead of convenience, they had to give shoppers the one experience that technology could not replace—indeed, the experience that technology almost eliminated in our time. That is, to give the pleasure of physically being somewhere, of going to a place that was bigger, grander and in every way more exhilarating and more energizing than anything the customer could experience at home.[32]

The spectacular new means of consumption are, in turn, forcing other attractions to become more of an extravaganza. There is a move afoot to make skyscrapers more spectacular. The Empire State Building and the panoramic view available on its observation deck are no longer spectacular enough in themselves. The "New York Skyride" (sponsored by JVC) was added, "a theme-park-style simulated space shuttle flight . . . visitors watch from movie-theater seats that jolt and shake as the shuttle zooms over the Brooklyn Bridge, around the Statue of Liberty and along the hair-raising track of Coney Island's roller coaster."[33] By this point in the book, it probably goes without saying that there is a gift shop adjacent to "New York Skyride."

CREATING SPECTACLES WITH SIMULATIONS

Implicit in the preceding section is the use of simulations to create spectacular fantasy worlds. However, the idea of simulations is so pivotal to understanding the enchanting aspects of the cathedrals of consumption that it must be discussed separately. In fact, if I had to choose only one term to catch the essence of the new means of consumption, as well as their capacity to create enchanting spectacles, it would be *simulations*.

The Age of Simulation

Jean Baudrillard has argued that we live in "the age of simulation."[34] This implies that we have left behind a more genuine, more authentic social world. Examples of simulation proffered by Baudrillard include

• *The primitive people the Tasaday, found in the Philippines.* At least as they exist today, the Tasaday are a simulation because the tribe has been "frozen, cryogenized, sterilized, protected *to death*."[35] It may at one time have been a "real" primitive group, but today what exists is nothing more than an approximation of what it once was.

• *The caves of Lascaux in France.* The actual caves have been closed, but an exact replica, a simulation, is now open to the public.

• *Disneyland.* Baudrillard sees it as "a perfect model of all the entangled orders of simulation."[36] One of Disney's classic attractions,[37] the simulated submarine ride to which people flocked to see simulated undersea life, is a good example. Many more go there than to the more "genuine" aquarium just down the road (itself, however, a simulation of the not-too-distant sea).

The widespread existence of such simulations, in the world of consumption and elsewhere, contributes enormously to the erosion of the distinction between the real and the imaginary, between the true and the false. Every contemporary structure and event is at best a combination of the real and the imaginary. In fact, to Baudrillard, the true and the real have disappeared in an avalanche of simulations.

Las Vegas casino-hotels have a field day with the line between reality and unreality. The Bellagio is a simulation of the Italian region of the same name, but it also houses a botanical garden and a gallery of fine art (the entrance fee is $15) with a recent show featuring the modern works of Roy Lichtenstein and Andy Warhol. (In its early years, the museum owned and displayed original works by such masters as Rembrandt, Raphael, and Titian.) At about the same time that the Bellagio opened its doors (1998), the Rio casino-hotel hosted a 6-month exhibit of treasures from Russia's Romanov dynasty. It included Peter the Great's throne and a Fabergé pen used by Czar Nicholas to abdicate in 1917. These authentic artifacts were housed in a replica of the Russian royal galleries, including "a reproduction neogothic ceiling from high density foam." King Tut's tomb in the Luxor hotel is called a "museum" even though everything in it is a reproduction. However, its gift shop sells "genuine ancient coins, 18th century Egyptian engravings, oil lamps and other artifacts." Said an art critic, "The museum had all fakes, and the gift shop had the real thing. It just summed up Las Vegas for me."[38]

Ada Huxtable, following Umberto Eco (and Baudrillard), argues that the "unreal has become the reality. . . . The real now imitates the imitation."[39] For example, the clearly simulated and unreal Disney World has become the model not only for Disney's creation of the town of Celebration but for many other communities throughout the United States. Seaside, Florida, and Kentlands, Maryland, are two examples of popular communities that try to emulate the ersatz small-town America that is championed by Disney World. Specifically, Huxtable has emphasized the growing importance of fake, synthetic, artificial, simulated architecture: "Real architecture has little place in the unreal America."[40]

Our environment has come to be dominated by entertainment and to emulate the theme park. Huxtable's architectural model of this is the casino New York, New York and more generally Las Vegas: "The real fake reaches its apogee in places like Las Vegas. . . . The outrageously fake fake has developed its own indigenous style and life style to become a real place . . . this is the real, real fake at the highest, loudest and most authentically inauthentic level of illusion and invention."[41] Huxtable has argued that visitors seem to find things such as the artificial rainforests, volcanoes, and rock formations in Las Vegas far more impressive than the real thing. In fact, a spokesperson for the industry goes so far as to make the case *against* reality: "You get a very artificial appearance with real rock."[42]

All of our environments are becoming increasingly spurious; Las Vegas is simply the extreme that defines the entire genre of simulated environments, especially those characterized by "unreal" architecture. This is of great relevance because many of the new means of consumption are architectural spaces. In fact, Huxtable has examined several of the new means of consumption from this perspective. Among other settings scrutinized by Huxtable are Colonial Williamsburg (created in the 1920s, a forerunner and another model for Disney World and other settings), Disneyland as faux Americana ("expertly engineered, standardized mediocrity, endlessly, shamelessly consumerized, a giant shill operation with a Mickey Mouse facade"[43]), Edmonton Mall with among other things its replica of Columbus's *Santa Maria* ("fantasy run amok"[44]), and so on.

Simulated People

Not only are some of the new means of consumption simulations, but often so are the people who work in them and the interactions that take place between employees and visitors. The most blatant examples of simulated "people" are the employees who dress up in a variety of costumes. McDonald's Ronald McDonald is obviously a simulated clown. The same is true of the characters—Mickey Mouse, Pluto, Snow White—that one encounters wandering the grounds of Disney World. Then there are the sports mascots such as the San Diego Chicken and the Baltimore Orioles' Bird.

Far more important, however, is the fact that most of the people we encounter in the new means of consumption are simulations, even if they are not wearing costumes. The entertainment director of the cruise ship, the blackjack dealer at a Las Vegas casino, the ticket taker at Disney World, the host on the Home Shopping Network (HSN), the counterperson at McDonald's, the barista at Starbucks, and the cashier at Wal-Mart are all playing well-defined roles. Their employing organizations have developed a series of guidelines about how they are supposed to look, speak, behave, and so forth. The result is that these positions can be filled by a wide range of individuals. There is little or no room for creativity or individuality. It could be argued that the blackjack dealer and the barista are simulations—they *are* fakes.

As a result of the same dynamic, the interaction that takes place between visitor and employee in a new means of consumption often has a simulated character. For example, instead of "real" human interaction with servers in fast-food restaurants, with clerks in shopping malls and superstores, with telemarketers, and so on, we can think of these as simulated interactions. Employees follow scripts,[45] and customers counter with recipied responses (i.e., those routine responses they have developed over time to deal with such scripted behavior),[46] with the result that authentic interaction rarely, if ever, takes place. In fact, so many of our interactions in these settings (and out) are simulated, and we become so accustomed to them, that we lose a sense of "real" interaction. In the end, it may be that all we have are the simulated interactions. In fact, the entire distinction between the simulated and the real may be lost; simulated interaction may be the reality.

Nowhere is this type of simulated interaction more obvious, or more inevitable, than in our dealings with hosts of home-shopping television programs. A typical "interaction" on the part of one of those hosts: "Thank you so, so, so much for calling in today. . . . We took a risk and brought some new items. You responded with an outpouring of support—and we love you for it."[47] Did they really take a risk? Do they really love every member of their audience? All of this taking place in the medium that best exemplifies simulation: television!

Simulations and the New Means of Consumption

Clearly, the new means of consumption contain a variety of simulations. There is little that is "real" about them. Even when real elements remain, there is an almost irresistible compulsion to alter them so that they, too, become simulations. There are undoubtedly many reasons why there is a drive to replace reality with simulations as quickly and completely as possible. It is far easier, for example, to control simulated than real environments. Take Baudrillard's example of the simulated caves at Lascaux. It is much easier to structure the simulated cave (to, for example, reduce the danger to visitors) than it is to restructure the original cave, which one would feel constrained to alter as little as possible. It also is easier to repair the simulation than the original that, in a sense, is not repairable. In fact, once one begins altering the caves, one has begun turning them into simulations. This is a very important point: Most "real" settings have been so altered to accommodate visitors that they already are simulations (see, e.g., the Disneyesque reinvention of Times Square in New York discussed previously and the later discussion of underwater reefs). This buttresses Baudrillard's point that there is no more reality; all is simulation.

Perhaps the most important reason for creating simulations, or transforming "real" phenomena into simulations, is that they can be made more spectacular than their authentic counterparts and, therefore, a greater lure to consumers. Take the example of Las Vegas again: Where else can you find New York City, Monte Carlo, Bellagio, Venice, and Paris within a few minutes' walk of one another? Even if you went to one of those "real" cities, you would be able to experience only it and not the others. In any case, the tourist areas of those cities have themselves become simulations.

Why do so many of us increasingly find simulated settings to be more spectacular than what remains of the real world? For example, although Las Vegas draws throngs of visitors, the natural spectacle of Death Valley a few hundred miles away attracts only a fraction of that number; few who go to Las Vegas bother to take the drive to Death Valley. The stillness, the parched earth, and the great sweep of seeming emptiness simply cannot compete with the noise, the glitter, and the vast expanse of neon that is Las Vegas. For a society raised on the movies, television, video games, and computer imagery, Death Valley can seem dull and uninteresting. The glitter of Las Vegas fits better with the desires and interests of this generation. If some Vegas entre-preneur were to erect a new themed casino named "Death Valley," it might well be a great success. Think of it: faux (of course) desert sand, cactus, sage-brush, and dry heat, leading to excessive drinking, inebriation, and, as a result, great losses at the gaming tables.

Simulations lie at the heart of the fast-food industry. The foods—the ham-burgers, the pizza, the tacos—may be very good simulations of others of their genre, but they are poor copies of their ancestors, bearing only the faintest resemblance to homemade hamburgers, pizzeria pizzas, and road-side-stand tacos. In fact, such "real" food, if it ever existed, has largely dis-appeared under an avalanche of simulations. Today, to most Americans under the age of 40 or 50, the McDonald's burger is the "real" burger. One who wants to unmask these simulations for what they are runs the risk of discovering that there are no "real" hamburgers, and there is no "true" ham-burger (or anything else real or true, for that matter).

There are even completely invented foods. Each of the millions, perhaps billions, of virtually identical (and simulated) Chicken McNuggets, for exam-ple, fits perfectly Baudrillard's idea of a simulation as a copy for which no original ever existed. The original, the "real" chicken, had the temerity to be created with bones, skin, gristle, and so on. But then chickens themselves, given modern factory farming, are nothing more than simulations that bear little resemblance to the dwindling number of their free-ranging brethren.

Then there is the structure and decor of the fast-food restaurant. The Roy Rogers's chain[48] was modeled, I suppose, after the late movie cowboy's ranch house, a ranch house that never existed except perhaps in the movies where it already was a simulation. The whole western atmosphere created by the chain and its commercials had much more to do with the movies (sim-ulations) than it did with the "real" Old West (whatever that was).[49] A sim-ilar point could be made about the fictional Long John Silver (known best to the public, of course, from the movie [i.e., simulated] version of *Treasure Island* rather than the original book, which itself could have been a simula-tion of some real events) chain of seafood restaurants, as well as many other simulated purveyors of simulacra. These examples reflect the importance that the media (movies, television) play in the contemporary world. In these instances, they are affecting us indirectly, but they also have a more direct impact that has been the concern of many postmodern social theorists.[50]

The fact that fast-food restaurants are hard-pressed to distinguish them-selves on the basis of their food, settings, and service leads them to rely on various types of simulations to attract customers within the budgetary lim-its of such outlets. For example, there are the simulated playgrounds that are grafted onto the entrances of many.

The creation of spectacular, simulated interiors has been brought to new heights by the chains of theme restaurants. The very basis of their appeal, given the widely acknowledged inadequacies in their food, has to be these simulated interiors. The presumption is that not enough people would come to restaurants such as Rainforest Cafe and pay the relatively high prices for food were it not for the spectacular simulations. The assumption is that people will find lunch or dinner in a simulated rainforest a spectacular and enchanting experience.

There are also malls that simulate other kinds of settings. One example is the 1.5-million-square-foot Park Meadows Retail Resort in suburban Denver.[51] It is described as a resort to distinguish it from a mall, and that label is reflective of the fact that for many Americans, shopping has, at least until recently, seemed like a vacation. The structure is a simulation of the rustic Timberline Lodge[52] on Mount Hood in Oregon: "On the inside, Park Meadows is full of rustic Colorado overtones with stone fireplaces and wood and copper interiors . . . the experience is less like shopping and more like going for lunch at the ski lodge."[53] Other examples of this trend toward shopping malls as simulations include Newbury Street in Boston, which evokes New England charm, and the small-town feel of Bellevue Square in Seattle.

None of the new means of consumption is more spectacularly simulated than Las Vegas and its casino-hotels. And none has proven better at luring consumers. Las Vegas is built in the most inhospitable of settings—the desert (see Chapter 7 for a discussion of another desert locale—Dubai—that has become a spectacle, in part because of the simulations it encompasses). As a result, virtually nothing natural, or real, is able to survive on its own in the city. The grass, the trees, the shrubs, the flowers—all have been unnaturally imposed on the environment. Furthermore, for all of it to survive, it must be artificially maintained and sustained. Although most true of Las Vegas, these kinds of things take a simulated form in virtually all of the new means of consumption (even inside the MIRAGE). Even in quite hospitable climates, the grass, the trees, and so on are brought in from outside and imposed artificially on the environment. This is true of Disneyland in Southern California and Disney World in Florida, even though the climate is much more appropriate to this vegetation than the Las Vegas desert. Similar things are artificially transplanted in luxury gated communities, most notably in Florida, Arizona, and Southern California—and, needless to say, in simulated towns such as Celebration.

In terms of the hotel-casinos, Las Vegas has drifted more and more in the direction of simulated environments. The earliest post-1947 Las Vegas hotels such as the Flamingo did not try to simulate other environments. Later hotels, such as the Sands, the Dunes, the Sahara, and the Aladdin, had an Arabian fantasy motif, but they did not try very hard to simulate Arabia.[54] They were spectacular, but they did not attempt to copy another reality to the extent that has become common in Las Vegas in recent years. Perhaps the beginning of this change can be traced to the opening of Circus Circus in 1968, which featured a gambling casino surrounded by a simulated circus. It was followed by Caesar's Palace and its effort to simulate ancient Rome. In addition to the spectacularly simulated casino-hotels discussed previously, others include

- *Main Street Station.* Its Victorian design seeks to evoke an earlier era in American history.

- *Monte Carlo.* Built to resemble *Place du Casino* in Monte Carlo, Monaco, its hotel hallways resemble European streets with faux cobblestone and fake building facades.

- *Orleans.* It simulates New Orleans down to the iron balconies and greenery that characterize that city.

The much discussed New York, New York is a beautiful example of a spectacular simulation and, as result, one that has been enormously successful at attracting gamblers (and their families):

Inside this very condensed version of Manhattan, separate banks of elevators— in the Empire State, Century, New Yorker and Chrysler towers (all respectable imitations of those in their 1930s prototypes)—deliver guests near to their rooms. On the outside, the lower-level stage set includes simplified models of the Immigration Hall at Ellis Island, the New York Public Library (minus the lions), the Soldiers' and Sailors' Monument on Riverside Drive and about a dozen other New York (or New Yorkish) facades, jammed eclectically together. At the corner stands a half-size Statue of Liberty, sprayed by jets from two New York fire-boats in a semicircular pool. Downriver on the Strip side rises a superfluous, a miniature Brooklyn Bridge. Through and around all this coils the red track of an awesome roller coaster, intended to honor Coney Island's. Inside the building . . . a stone footbridge meant to evoke Central Park . . . a copy of the pedimented front of the New York Stock Exchange . . . a tribute to Rockefeller Center, with a sleek waterfall and a copy of Lee Lawrie's Atlas statue. . . . The cleverest features of the casino floor are the rambling, asphalt-paved alleyways of the "Villages" (part SoHo, part Little Italy, part Greenwich Village), in which a number of genuine food stalls and shops . . . are surrounded by and enclosed in make-believe shops, townhouses and apartments, their lower floors full size, the upper floors in Disneyland reduction. The fire escapes, mailboxes, trash cans, newsstands, manhole covers, subway entrances and street signs all look reasonably authentic, as do the neatly sprayed-on graffiti, the air conditioners and glowing TV sets that mark upstairs apartments. . . . Of course, this isn't a "real" New York, or anything like it. If you look closely, almost everything dissolves.[55]

A reexamination of this description would yield an extraordinarily lengthy list of simulations. New York, New York can be seen as a simulation, but one that itself encompasses a number of other smaller, but no less meretricious, simulations.

In Tomorrowland at Disney World, there are long lines everywhere, especially at the simulated astro orbiters and rocket rides. The exception is the "real" display sponsored by the Jet Propulsion Laboratory and NASA, which includes a "diorama of that plucky little rover that trundled over the bumpy surface of Mars."[56] Animal Kingdom is rife with examples of the preference for the "fake" over the "real":

> "We have the roseate spoonbill here in Florida, but of course they didn't want to use a Florida bird" . . . "Look, there's fake mist! It's coming out of a spigot. It's fake mist! Unbelievable!"
>
> The triumph of the faux is one aspect of Disney. . . . "They think they can improve on nature." . . . "At some level, that's creepy."
>
> He walks past a fake bamboo fence and some fake boulders and checks out a display that is supposed to include an anteater. But the anteater is hiding in the bushes, so a Disney employee is showing the tourists a photograph of the beast.
>
> "She's passing out pictures of the anteater because the anteater has enough sense to hide." . . . "Oh, that's perfect! It's a great country!"[57]

Virtual reality is by definition a simulation. It may be distinguished from most of the simulations being discussed by its even greater distance from anything resembling "reality." As a result, it possesses possibilities for enchantment that exceed those offered by other simulations. The coming of virtual reality will mean a vast increase in the scope of simulations. There is already, for example, a virtual tour for use at home of the tomb of the Egyptian queen Nefertari.[58] Why bother to leave home, when all one is going to see is simulations? Better to stay at home and view the virtual version, which in some senses is even more spectacular than the simulated version one would have to travel to see.

At least some people are coming to prefer virtual simulations to reality. For example, the Verizon Center, home stadium of professional basketball's Washington Wizards and professional hockey's Washington Capitals, offers a miniature basketball court with a massive video image of a Washington Wizards's star who "interacts" with the player. Said one 11-year-old participant, "I like watching basketball . . . but this is better." A father and his two sons are seen playing virtual hockey 20 minutes after the "real" game starts. Says the wife and mother, "This is not athleticism . . . This is entertainment."[59]

Virtual reality offers the possibility of simulations of simulations. In fact, this is a coming trend in the cathedrals of consumption (see Chapter 8). In the process, we move further and further away from "reality" (whatever that may be) and deeper into a world in which simulation is the reality.

Theming

Theming, or the effort to carry a particular motif throughout a cathedral of consumption (or at least subareas within it), is a natural extension of the idea of simulations discussed in the preceding section. Through theming,[60] many Las Vegas hotels seek to follow through on their simulated image. Many of the employees dress in costumes consistent with the casino-hotel's theme. Internal décor is designed to be in tune with the overall theme. Restaurants often are structured in such a way that they too fit the theme, as does the nature of the food that they serve (e.g., the Orleans Hotel has the French Market Buffet serving Louisiana specialties). The shows put on in the major theaters also are often designed to carry through on the theme. The first show in residence at New York, New York was "Madhattan," in which an array of New York street performers were brought together to represent the New York style of entertainment.

Of course, much the same can be said about the spectacularly simulated and themed nature of the Magic Kingdom at Disney World. Each of the worlds has a theme, and the rides, restaurants, dress, talk, and so forth are designed to support that theme. Theming is so important at Disney World that employees in the costume of one land are not permitted to enter other lands because of a fear that they will compromise the theme and surely destroy the fantasy. There is an elaborate system of tunnel-like corridors beneath Disney World that allow employees to get to the appropriate locale without intruding into others. (The corridors also serve to conceal similarly intrusive deliveries.) One of the spectacular aspects of Disney World derives from the fact that visitors spend time completely enveloped by one land (and one set of simulated themed elements) and then suddenly cross a threshold and find themselves in a completely different land with an entirely different simulated theme.

Perhaps the ultimate illustration of a simulated theme park (as well as of the fact that virtually *anything* can be turned into such a site) is to be found in the plans for "Ossi Park"[61] in what was once communist East Germany (the German Democratic Republic, GDR). Because of inadequate funding, the park was never built, but it is worth describing because it is such a wonderful example of a simulation:

One-day visitors will be *required* to leave by midnight, as they were in the GDR; *guards* will patrol the border; attempts to escape will lead to hour(s)-long *imprisonment*. All visitors will be *required* to exchange a minimum of hard currency for eastern marks . . . [The whole park will be surrounded by *barbed wire* and a *wall* and will] include badly stocked stores, snooping state *secret police* . . . and scratchy toilet paper known as "Stalin's Revenge," whose texture, according to an old GDR joke, ensured that "every last ass is red."[62]

Clearly, being in such a simulated environment would be quite spectacular. Even more fantasy-like would be the knowledge that one could leave anytime one wanted to.

Theming also occurs in much more mundane settings such as the chain of Fry's Electronics stores mainly in the western United States. For example, in California, the store in Palo Alto has a Wild West theme, in Fountain Valley it's ancient Rome, and the Manhattan Beach store has a Tahitian theme complete with a rainforest.[63]

"Authentic Simulations"

Although the creation of entirely new simulations is an extreme case, most "authentic" tourist destinations have been turned into simulations, at least in part. Examples include the colonial town of Williamsburg in Virginia and Windsor Castle in England, among many others. The motivation behind these transformations is that the "real" sites are no longer spectacular enough to attract tourists and their money. Visitor centers, movies introducing the attraction, people in costume, actors putting on shows, and themed restaurants and gift shops are required to draw adequate numbers of people. Of course, adding things such as these to the attraction transforms it into a simulation; it is no longer the original setting. But the increasing demand for a spectacle necessitates greater use of simulations.

Take, for example, the fact that the sea itself, at least in one setting, has been altered (simulated) to accommodate the tourist:

For the snorkeling enthusiast, the place to head is Folkestone National Marine Reserve, Park and Marine Museum at Holetown [Barbados]. . . . The government has built an area where the novice can swim and follow a series of underwater markers that picture what fish are likely to be seen.[64]

Relatedly, a number of tropical islands are now owned and completely controlled by the cruise lines.[65] Only passengers of the cruise line are allowed on shore. The islands are described as "reassuringly Disneyesque."[66] There are already a number of such islands, with more sure to come. In fact, Disney itself acquired Gorda Cay in the Caribbean and renamed it Castaway Cay for its cruise line, which began operations in the late 1990s. Castaway Cay features a "Flying Dutchman Pirate Ship"; separate beaches for children ("Scuttle's Cove"), teens ("Teen Beach"), families ("Castaway Family Beach"), and adults ("Serenity Beach"); and sunken simulated treasures for snorkelers. On such islands, the tourist finds no hawkers, no overbuilding, nothing (except perhaps the uncooperative storm) to mar the "perfect vacation." No cash is needed; everything can be charged to one's ship bill. "Real" Caribbean islands pale in comparison. According to one tourist, "St. Maarten wasn't a very attractive island. . . . It was dirty. The shops were kind of junky." Said another, "Jamaica was pretty run down to us."[67]

On simulated islands, the bathrooms are squeaky clean. On some of these islands, food and drink are brought on shore from the ship, and the onshore service is provided by the ship's crew. There is even an ersatz market; natives (presumably carefully selected and trained so that little or no trace of their real culture remains) of a nearby island sail over to staff it. On one of the islands, "a *replica* of a 16th century ship [was purposely] sunk in the harbor to give snorkelers a thrill."[68] A plane was later submerged (as we will see in Chapter 7, the same sort of thing has been done in Dubai). Some kill-joy academic (an anthropologist) described a visit to such an island as a "virtual experience" and complained that tourists "don't want to see any of the consequences of colonialism—the poverty, the sex trade."[69]

Certainly, there are those tourists, and consumers more generally, who continue to search out authentic settings, and they can, at least to some degree, still find them. However, visits to authentic sites tend to be more expensive than to inauthentic locales. More important, it is likely to grow increasingly difficult to find the authentic. Authentic tourist sites are likely to go the way of the caves at Lascaux. Or they are likely to be so altered by the demands of catering to large numbers of tourists that they are apt to become simulated versions of the originals.

Even museums are being forced to offer simulations in order to compete with the more obvious forms of simulated entertainment:

The art, science and culture museum of the University of California at Berkeley . . . augmented its . . . show of New Guinea artifacts with a "science theatre," where an experience called Nature's Fury produced a rocking earthquake simulation from a minivolcano; going a step further for "lifelike" relevance appropriate to the community, a suggested survivor's kit was displayed in the trunk of a BMW. . . . With nothing to recommend them except their often shabby authenticity, the real objects simply have less appeal than snappy simulations.[70]

Simulated Communities

Moving out of the realm of tourism, luxury gated communities are inherently simulated (artificial community, imported trees and shrubs). Some also seek to give themselves a particular theme or look. Shady Canyon in California, with an ersatz country look, has narrow roads with no sidewalks, limited street lighting, and a layout that conforms to the local topography. Coto de Caza has horse trails, even though few residents have horses. According to the community's vice president for marketing and sales, "Most residents don't own horses, but they like the idea of living in an area with an equestrian-oriented feel."[71] The community was built to accommodate existing trees and, where that was not possible, trees were transplanted. In this "new ruralism," the objective is to create new communities that look like, that simulate old-time communities. The rural look might include houses with front porches, a community square, and shops that are within walking distance of one's home.

Simulation defines the town of Celebration.[72] A whole new level of spectacle is reached when an entire simulated community is created. Journeying to a single simulated setting may be impressive, but it pales in comparison to the spectacle of living one's life in a wholly simulated community. "The town's entrance is straight out of a Disney movie, with white picket fences, wrought-iron street lamps, lush landscaping and an old-timey wood-slat water tower luring visitors with a vision of a simpler time."[73] The simulated character of the town is nowhere more obvious than in the fact that there is a town hall in Celebration, but there is no real town government. The town's sales brochure makes it clear what is being simulated at Celebration:

> There once was a place where neighbors greeted neighbors in the quiet of summer twilight. . . . Where children chased fireflies. And porch swings provided easy refuge from the cares of the day. The movie house showed cartoons on Saturday. The grocery store delivered. And there was one teacher who always knew you had that special something. Remember that place?[74]

Being promised is a resurrection of pre–World War II, small-town America. This is clear, as well, in the town seal (copyrighted by Disney), which is "a cameo of a little girl with a ponytail riding a bicycle past a picket fence under a spreading oak tree as her little dog chases along behind."[75]

Before touring the grounds, prospective homeowners are shown a film with the following script:

> Our memories of childhood. . . . There is a place that takes you back to that time of innocence. . . . A place where the biggest decision is whether to play kick the can or king of the hill. A place of caramel apples and cotton candy,

secret forts and hopscotch on the streets. That place is here again, in a new town called Celebration.

Celebration. . . . A new American town of block parties and Fourth of July parades. Of spaghetti dinners and school bake sales, lollipops and fireflies in a jar. And while we can't return to those times, we can arrive at a place that embraces all of those things. Someday 20,000 people will live in Celebration. And for each and every one of them, it will be home.[76]

Celebration's glorification of tradition does not stop with its architecture, its sales brochure, or its introductory video. There is a Celebration Foundation in charge of the culture of the town. It has created such organizations as Rotary Clubs (Celebration Rotary) and the Boy Scouts, as well as the town's newspaper.

Celebration's houses have many simulated elements. For example, in one model, the panel doors in each room are made of imitation wood. The exterior clapboard is made of a synthetic concrete. With its similarly simulated exterior (e.g., the rustic porches), these houses are described as "outwardly rustic, inwardly corporate."

The town has been described in terms that all but label it a simulation:

The entire awkward struggle to manufacture a tradition for the town revealed . . . a hollowness at its core, the absence of a bona fide purpose such as inspired the creation of most towns. Of course, "bona fide," like "authenticity" and "rigor," is a complicated concept in Celebration. What do such terms mean in a town whose history is retroactive, whose tradition is that of the entertainment company that founded it, whose lake is dammed and whose creek is pumped, whose creators say "lifestyle" for "life" and insert the phrase "a sense of" before every vital principle? Celebration is billed as being in the great American tradition of town building, but it is a town whose mission isn't the pursuit of commercial advantage, or religious or political freedom, or any idea more compelling than a sense of comfortable community. Its ambition is, in the end, no greater than to be like a town.[77]

CONCLUSION

The chapter has documented the fact that the new means of consumption have become ever more spectacular by increasing the number and size of the extravaganzas and simulations (and even simulations of simulations) they offer. Such spectacles serve to reenchant the cathedrals of consumption so that they will be a continuing attraction to increasingly jaded consumers. Extravaganzas and simulations are generally created by those who control the cathedrals of consumption with the intention of reenchanting the settings in which they occur. I turn in the next chapter to other processes that, less intentionally or even unintentionally, also serve to reenchant the cathedrals of consumption.

6

Reenchantment

Creating Spectacle Through Implosion, Time, and Space

(Continued)

In this chapter, I look at the way implosions of various types serve to create spectacles. I will also examine the spectacular use of time and space in the new means of consumption. The implosion of temporal and spatial boundaries is an important source of spectacles. As we will see, there is more to time and especially space as they relate to the new means of consumption than can be discussed under the heading of implosion. For example, there are the seeming abilities to defy the constraints of time and to create a sense of infinite space. Spectacles involving implosions and the extraordinary use of time and space serve to reenchant the cathedrals of consumption. Some of the reenchantment comes about quite unintentionally, but intentional or not, the processes to be discussed do serve to reenchant the means of consumption and thereby to attract consumers.

IMPLOSION

The term *implosion* refers to the disintegration or disappearance of boundaries as formerly differentiated entities collapse in on each other. The explosive growth in the new means of consumption has led to a series of such implosions.[1] Those implosions, in turn, have served to make those means more spectacular and thereby helped them to grow even more.

Implosion involves a kind of chain reaction: The collapse of one set of boundaries leads to the breakdown of a number of other frontiers. Boundaries between the cathedrals of consumption have eroded and, in some cases, all but disappeared. Similarly, borders between the means of consumption and other aspects of the social world (e.g., the family and the home) have also been breached. In this way, we have witnessed the disappearance of many distinctions to which people had long grown accustomed. The result has been a reenchanted world of consumption seemingly without borders or limits.

These imploded worlds represent a kind of spectacle that draws consumers into them and leads them to consume. For example, only a few decades ago, people had to trek from one locale to another for various goods and services; now they can find them all in a single mall. And it was not that many years ago that if one wanted to gamble, one went to Las Vegas, but if one wanted to visit a theme park, one went to Orlando or Anaheim. Now one can go to Las Vegas for the indoor theme park (the "Adventuredome") at Circus Circus; the rollercoaster rides (see below) at the Stratosphere and New York, New York; and the "Lion Habitat," CBS television studio, and water park at MGM Grand. The local Wal-Mart, or corner service station, might well encompass a satellite fast-food restaurant. REI in Seattle not only offers mountain climbing shoes but even a "mountain" to practice on (and a Starbucks so that one can have a warm drink after a tough day on the mountain).

It is often the case that the conscious motivation behind implosion has not been to create a spectacle. Entrepreneurs may be motivated by a variety of reasons such as economies resulting from having two or more means of consumption within one setting, the desire to offer consumers the conveniences and synergies associated with such imploded locales, and so on. Whether or not the motivation behind implosion is the creation of spectacle, the fact is that spectacle often results.

As with many other ideas in the previous chapter and this one, the idea of implosion, at least as it is used in this context, is derived from postmodern social theory, most notably the work of Jean Baudrillard. Baudrillard defines implosion as the contraction of one phenomenon into another; the collapse of traditional poles into one another.[2] To Baudrillard, all things are capable of dissolving not only into each other but also into a single huge undifferentiated mass (a sort of "black hole"). As an example outside of the cathedrals of consumption, contemporary television talk shows are dissolving into life and life is dissolving into talk shows. Consider the well-known case of the now defunct Jenny Jones talk show in which a gay admirer, Scott Amedure, expressed a homosexual interest in, and hugged, a straight male, Jonathan Schmitz, on the air. Schmitz (who expected to encounter a female admirer on the show) later killed Amedure (and was sentenced to 25 to 50 years in prison for it) in a case in which reality and television culture clearly imploded into one another. An even better, and more recent, example is reality TV (e.g., *Survivor, American Idol, Dancing With the Stars*) in which life *is* a TV show. This is also the theme of the (1998) movie *The Truman Show*, in which unbeknownst to him, Truman's life is the orchestrated subject of a television show.

We can get at the phenomenon of implosion in another way by distinguishing between differentiation and dedifferentiation. The modern world can be said to have been characterized by *differentiation*—that is, the creation of more new and different things. Throughout the Industrial Revolution, more and more things were invented, created, produced, and distributed widely. This wide variety of products led to a parallel differentiation in the settings in which they could be consumed. Modernity, then, was characterized by highly differentiated and rigidly separated means of consumption: The butcher shop sold meat, the baker bread, the greengrocer fruits and vegetables, and so on.

Although such differentiation has not completely disappeared, postmodernists argue that today's world is increasingly characterized by dedifferentiation:[3] a growing inability to differentiate among things and among places. They all are coming to interpenetrate, all imploding into one another. This is nowhere clearer than in the contemporary world of consumption in general and in the relationship among and between the new means of consumption in particular. The separate shops of the butcher, baker, and greengrocer have all but disappeared into the supermarket that has imploded into the supercenter into which a discount department store has also imploded. This dedifferentiation produces spectacular settings because so many different entities exist in one place, and this serves to draw consumers to these dedifferentiated entities.

Implosion in the Means of Consumption

The means of consumption are in the process of blending into one another in various ways.

Shopping and Fun

The distinction between shopping malls and amusement parks[4] has always been somewhat illusory, and in recent years, it has grown ever more so. Both have always been means to sell stuff as well as to sell entertainment, but in the past, malls were mostly in the business of selling goods, whereas parks focused on entertainment. That difference is no longer so clear. Malls also offer fun to both adults and children—especially the malls housing themed restaurants, Dave and Buster's, indoor theme parks, and so on. Mega-malls such as the Mall of America and the West Edmonton Mall encompass entire amusement parks, as well. Then there are the increasingly large multi- (or mega-)plex theaters offering 20 or more screens that are of growing importance to many malls.[5] And in the theaters, one might find video game rooms and even food courts. Some of the stores in the malls use devices such as children's play areas to entice people into the stores. The trend in many malls is away from selling goods and toward selling services, especially entertainment.[6] The West Edmonton Mall, which at one time was divided 80% to 20% between retail sales and entertainment, has moved closer to a 60% to 40% split. Anne Friedberg has described a shopping mall as "a consumer theme park."[7]

Ontario Mills (outside Los Angeles) is based on "fun and games."[8] There are no large department stores to anchor the mall; it is a combination of discounted, outlet-like shops, theme restaurants (Rainforest Cafe), and entertainment settings such as a 30-screen movieplex, a comedy improv club, Dave and Buster's, and GameWorks. Ontario Mills has an enormous food court (called "Big Food") that can seat more than 1,000 people. One reason for this shift toward entertainment is that malls need to induce people away from shopping at home. They are becoming destinations in their own right. The chair and chief executive of the company that developed Ontario Mills said, "Shoppers want an experience."[9]

Likewise, amusement parks are marketing more and more goods. An extreme form of this is Santa Claus Village in Rovaniemi, Finland, which offers woefully little entertainment and is almost entirely devoted to the consumption of souvenirs and food.[10] Less extreme is Disney World, which certainly offers entertainment but is also liberally studded with souvenir shops, food stands, and restaurants. Main Street and Downtown Disney Marketplace (basically outdoor shopping malls) areas focus on selling Disney products of one kind or another. Marketplace also has a variety of other consumption sites, including a Rainforest Cafe and, of course, McDonald's. Disney uses its amusement parks to advertise its shops in malls (and vice versa). These shops, of course, are primarily interested in selling Disney merchandise. The vast majority of Disney stores are in the malls. The line between the mall and the amusement park has almost been obliterated.

Also imploding is the distinction between entertainment and the online malls. Even though they are the wave of the future, the Internet in general and online malls in particular need to be entertaining. According to the president of an online advertising and shopping service, "People using on-line shopping want the entertainment experience. They want it to be pleasant. They want access to the cool stuff."[11]

More generally, the distinction between shopping and fun has completely imploded. The fun of shopping for goods and services is no longer enough but must be supplemented by other amusements. Even shopping itself has to be more fun, as reflected in the growth of discount malls and the idea of discovering (supposed) bargains.

For competitive reasons, both fast-food and (to a lesser degree) upscale restaurant (e.g., Morton's) chains are increasingly in the business of fun. The food seems to be secondary, or of little significance at all. Said one diner, "I would rather eat mediocre food in a fabulous room than sit somewhere dull and boring and eat fabulous food. . . . I'm looking for decor, scale, *theatrics*, a lot going on."[12]

Gambling and Shopping

Also eroding is the boundary between gambling and shopping. Time was that people went to Las Vegas to gamble and had little interest in shopping while there. In fact, there were relatively few shopping areas available because the objective was to keep people in the casinos and at the roulette wheels and slot machines. Now, however, shopping is increasingly integral to the Las Vegas experience. One example is the Venetian, which, in addition to a huge casino, 6,000 suites, and a convention center, includes a shopping mall—Canal Shoppes.[13] Planet Hollywood is seemingly surrounded by a themed mall, Desert Passage, with almost 150 shops. Via Bellagio is the Bellagio's upscale mall. There has long been a large mall (Fashion Show) on the Strip. An elegant mall, the Forum, is adjacent to and contiguous with Caesar's Palace. The Showcase Mall, adjacent to the MGM Grand, has a GameWorks, a themed M&M World, and a simulated Grand Canyon Experience (to save visitors the trip to the real thing).

Space in casino-hotels is being increasingly devoted to shops of all types. This has come about as a result of the shift in focus in Las Vegas (now being reversed to some degree) from individual gamblers to families. Malls and shops give some family members ways to spend money while other members gamble. Furthermore, the shops stand ready to take the money of those few who emerge from the casinos as winners. Malls, shops, and gambling operations work in tandem to be sure that visitors leave Las Vegas with little, if any, money.

As the barriers to gambling come down around the country, we can expect to see more gambling in shopping malls. The rapid growth of various new forms of gambling (e.g., lotteries, the proliferation of casinos) combined with the decline in interest in horse racing is making it difficult for racetracks to survive. To keep racetracks afloat, other types of gambling have imploded into them (slot machines, poker rooms, etc.). And lottery tickets are for sale in a wide range of shops in many states.

Touring and Consuming

The changes in Las Vegas are related to a more general implosion of the boundaries between touring and consuming. Of course, touring always involved the consumption of tourist activities and sites. Along the way, tourists generally were interested in purchasing everything from trinkets to trophies. Now, however, there are more and more instances in which the main objective of touring *is* the consumption of goods.[14] For one thing, malls have become tourist destinations. According to a travel consultant, the lure of a mall vacation is that "the malls have everything. . . . They have a water park. They have an amusement park. They have a roller coaster. Mom and dad can get what they want."[15] This combination is spectacular and a powerful lure to the traveler. Airlines offer day trips to the Mall of America; bus lines offer package trips that might involve visits of several days to the mall. Overall, there are 71 package tours to the Mall of America emanating from 32 countries.[16] The Mall of America attracted 12 million tourists in 1995— "more than Walt Disney World, the Grand Canyon and Graceland combined."[17] By 2009, the number of visitors to the Mall of America had quadrupled to about 40 million people a year.[18] In Canada, the largest tourist attraction is not Niagara Falls but rather the Edmonton Mall. Potomac Mills outside Washington, D.C., had 4.5 million visitors in 1995. By comparison, 4 million visited Arlington National Cemetery, 2.5 million journeyed to Colonial Williamsburg, and 1 million visited Mount Vernon. Franklin Mills, outside Philadelphia, drew 6 million visitors in 1995, four times as many as visited the Liberty Bell.[19] Niketown is Chicago's largest tourist attraction.[20] Many tourist destinations are surrounded by outlet or discount malls. People are almost as apt to journey to such locales for the malls as they are for the sea or the air. Indeed, it often seems as if almost as many people are at the malls as are on the beach.

Also worth noting in this context are the cruise ships that have malls on board and that turn the islands on their itinerary into little more than indigenous malls. There are "even shopping cruises, outfitted with shops, catalogues and stops in strategic ports."[21]

Fast-Food Restaurants, Convenience Stores, and Superstores

Fast-food restaurants are imploding into virtually every other new means of consumption. As discussed previously, they are now found within Las Vegas casino-hotels and Disney World. They have found their way onto college campuses and into the nation's hotels and hotel chains.[22] In fact, some hotels have installed mini versions of the food courts we find in shopping malls, airports, and on the nation's highways. As pointed out previously, smaller satellite fast-food restaurants are found in places such as Wal-Mart, gasoline stations, and the like.

Convenience stores such as 7-Eleven have experienced the implosion of many other means of consumption into them: automated teller machines

(ATMs), dry cleaners, theater ticket sales, gasoline stations, coffee shops, and many others.[23]

A good example of implosion in superstores is that taking place in book superstores: "These days, a bookstore is a bookstore, food court, music shop and newsstand rolled into one."[24] And to this list must be added the inevitable coffee shop, especially Starbucks. In fact, so many things have imploded into the superstore that it can now be viewed as a kind of mini-mall:

> The category killer has indeed become a distinct breed of retailer. . . . It's a place to shop, yes, but a place to linger, too, to take a family on a Saturday afternoon, to meet a friend for breakfast, to steal a few minutes for yourself on the way home from work, to daydream, perhaps, over a magazine and a cup of coffee that's infinitely more aromatic than anything at the local coffee shop. . . . Sure, a superstore is a stationery shop or hardware store writ huge. But far more to the point, it's also a mall writ small.[25]

Malls

Malls are turning up in more and more places, accelerating the process of implosion. For example, modern airports, as we have seen, are coming to look more and more like shopping malls. As one observer put it, "What could be a truer gateway to the U.S. than a shopping mall?"[26] (The predecessors to this were the early duty-free shops and shopping plazas at international airports such as Shannon, Ireland, and Schiphol in Amsterdam. London's Heathrow Airport, especially Terminals Three and Four [as well as the new Terminal Five] devoted largely to international flights, offers a wide range of shops under the umbrella of World Duty Free.) The pioneer in the malling of American airports, Pittsburgh International Airport, has 100,000 square feet of shops at its "Airmall." The terminal at Ronald Reagan (formerly National) Airport in Washington, D.C., has been described "as much a mall as it is an airport," or "an airport-cum-mall."[27] It has dozens of retail shops and restaurants occupying 65,000 square feet. Among its shops are national chains that are found at other airports (Brooks Brothers, Joseph A. Bank, Borders), as well as some that are specific to Washington (Smithsonian Museum Store). Among the restaurants are outlets of Legal Sea Foods, Cheesecake Factory, California Pizza Kitchen, Cinnabon, T.G.I. Friday's, and McDonald's. There also are local restaurants such as Tidewater Grill. Minneapolis, home of the Mall of America, has virtually transformed its main terminal into a mall (with about 75 shops and restaurants) and called it Northstar Crossing.[28]

Airport malls exist to lure passengers into making purchases they otherwise might not make. And they seem to work. Retail sales at Pittsburgh's airport more than tripled in the 1990s[29] and does several billion dollars in business each year. The existence of such malls also seems to lure people to use one airport rather than another. In one survey, 11% of passengers said that the mall was one of the reasons they chose to change planes in Pittsburgh rather than at other airports.[30]

Major train stations such as Union Station in Washington, D.C., with 100 shops, have followed the lead of airports, and others have refashioned themselves as malls. Grand Central Station in New York now offers a wide range of shops, restaurants, and food stores.

Athletic Stadiums

New athletic stadiums include far more than simply a playing field, stands, and concessions. Among the things found at newer stadiums are private pools with adjacent hot tubs, virtual reality games, hair salons, cigar bars, and mini-shopping malls. One observer described this as the "amusement-park school of stadium construction."[31] Tropicana Field, the home of major league baseball's Tampa Bay Rays, has a three-level mall that includes places where "fans can get a trim at the barber shop, do their banking and then grab a cold one at the Budweiser brew pub, whose copper kettles rise to three stories. There is even a climbing wall for kids and showroom space for car dealerships."[32] Computers at some upholstered seats allow fans to access video replays and order hot dogs. At the Verizon Center in Washington, D.C., you

> walk through the main entrance to the stadium, a three-story glass atrium. . . . At the other end, a two-level "sports gallery," where fans wind through a maze of "museum" displays . . . and empty into a buzzing, beeping arcade of electronic games. With no clocks, no windows and dim lights, it has all the ambiance of a casino.[33]

The public relations people associated with the Atlanta Braves stadium, Turner Field, describe it as "not just a ball park. It's more like a baseball theme park."[34] In addition to the usual components, Turner Field includes Grand Entry Plaza that has been described as "a virtual Disney World of Baseball."[35] In that plaza is found Scout's Alley (where fans can test their batting skills and learn more about scouting by studying the reports on famous Braves players) as well as the very Disneyesque Cartoon Network's Tooner Field that includes interactive games and souvenir shops. There is also the Braves Museum and Hall of Fame. Over the team store is a bank of television sets that offers live broadcasts of other major league baseball games. A video-board allows fans to interview players. There are electronic kiosks that permit access to scouting reports and the Braves Internet home page. For food, there is the Chop House (overlooking the Braves bullpen) and a beer joint, Taste of the Major Leagues. Then there is the rooftop Coca-Cola Skyfield, a mini-theme park designed to sell the Braves, Coke, and paraphernalia associated with each. It also includes an area where a light mist of water cools off fans overheated by Atlanta's hot and muggy summers (or by excessive use of their credit cards). To further over-heat fans and, coincidently, to help fans pay for all of this, there are several ATMs. A representative of one of the firms involved in planning Turner Field said, "If we are going to hook people on baseball, we don't do it by making them sit through nine innings. If we can make the experience more pleasurable, we should."[36] Said the Braves president, "I like spending. . . . So let's design this (Turner Field) space with something for them to do when they come early. And while we're at it, let's give them a reason for staying late. They will like it more, and we should make more money."[37]

The Braves spring training facility, Walt Disney World's Wide World of Sports Baseball Stadium, is located on the grounds of the Disney complex in Florida. Said the general manager of the park, "I have never seen a (spring) facility like this. . . . This is classic Disney."[38] It is a major cathedral of consumption unto itself and as such involves implosion (and simulation) in various forms. In addition to the baseball stadium that can seat almost 10,000 people, it has other baseball fields, and there is the Diamondplex with six softball fields; a tennis complex with 10 tennis courts and a tennis stadium seating more than 1,000 people; a track and field complex with bleacher seating for 2,000; Hess Sports Fields (sponsored by Amerada Hess) for a wide range of other sports (soccer, football, lacrosse, etc.); the Milk House (sponsored by the milk industry), which is a multipurpose fieldhouse that seats 5,500 spectators; the Jostens Center to accommodate a variety of other sports; and, of course, the All Star Cafe. [39]

Educational Settings

The student unions at some universities are taking on an increasingly mall-like quality:

They stood eye to eye and nose to nose for almost 40 minutes, exchanging heavy talk, soulful looks, and angry glares outside Mrs. Field's Cookies at the food court entrance. . . . It was the kind of minor mall world melodrama that plays out all the time whenever kids gather over their Whoppers, Pizza Hut personal pan pizzas, and Freshen's Premium Yogurt—everywhere from Tyson's Corner Center in suburban Washington to the Galleria in Dallas and Phipps Plaza in Atlanta. The only difference was that this was no shopping center, it was the student union at Boston University.[40]

In addition, educational institutions are growing more and more like theme parks, as well as like other new means of consumption.[41]

Then there is the "shopping mall high school" that offers the student-consumer a variety of choices about which classes to take.[42] There are a number of similarities between such schools and the shopping mall:

• Both are highly oriented to the desires of their consumers; students shop for courses and other services "conveniently assembled in one place with ample parking."[43]

• As in the malls, some students make choices, others browse, others just hang out, and still others never come in. Both need to be fun to attract "consumers."

• "The mall and the school are places to meet friends, pass the time, get out of the rain, or watch the promenade. Shopping malls or their high school equivalents can be *entertaining* places to onlookers with no intention of buying anything."[44]

• "Many contemporary high schools even look like shopping malls. One is a complex of attached single-story buildings whose classrooms open to the outdoors rather than to locker-lined corridors. Between periods students go outside to find their next destination, entering and leaving classrooms as if they were adjacent stores."[45]

• Like shopping malls, high schools must also compete with a variety of other settings for students' time and attention.

• Like shopping malls, "the shopping mall high school is committed to luring and holding the largest possible crowd."[46]

Mausoleums

Perhaps the most astounding example of implosion is the collapse of the distinction between the mausoleum and the theme park. Planned for Vancouver, British Columbia, although long delayed by the controversy it created, is a nine-story mausoleum designed to inter the remains of 90,000 people. Its developer said, "It will be the tallest, biggest, most diversified mausoleum in North America."

Atop the 110-foot-high edifice, mourners will be able to watch loved ones being cremated on a pyre overlooking the city. Below will be theme floors: one for Catholics, with a nativity scene; a floor for Buddhists, with statues and incense burners; one for Canadian military veterans, with medals and weaponry; and a simulated tropical island, with palm trees and piped-in ukulele music, for late members of Vancouver's substantial Fijian community.[47]

Cities and Small Towns

Another kind of implosion is the erosion of the distinction between shopping in rural or small towns and in the big cities. In recent years, New York City has witnessed the entry of the superstores and the threat they pose to small indigenous shops and businesses. While superstores boomed throughout the rest of the nation, New York and other major cities were largely bypassed. Once the center of innovations in retailing—Macy's, Bloomingdales, the discount pioneer Korvette's—New York is in the relatively early stages of having its retail landscape transformed into something shockingly, at least to New Yorkers, similar to small-town and rural America.[48]

Similarly, the reinvention of Times Square, spearheaded by Disney's renovated New Amsterdam Theater, also includes a Disney Store, Madame Tussaud's, Toys 'R Us, a Warner Brothers store, and a Virgin Megastore. Giant multiplexes with as many as 40 screens are on the way as well as, as if to parallel New York, New York in Las Vegas, a "Las Vegas–style theme restaurant called Vegas."[49] As one journalist put it, "The once-greasy, beating heart of New York is being homogenized, sanitized and packaged as a theme park for out-of-town tourists."[50]

Real and Fake

So far I have been discussing the postmodern idea of implosion as it relates to the dwindling distinctions between various means of consumption. However, the postmodernists in general, and Baudrillard in particular, also use the idea of implosion in a more general sense of an implosion of the distinction between the real and the unreal; that is, we find it increasingly difficult to differentiate the real from the fake. Indeed, we come to stop trying and to live with the fake at least as easily, and perhaps more easily, as we live with the real. In this sense, implosion is very close to the idea of the increasingly simulated character of our society discussed in the preceding chapter.

The difficulty involved in differentiating between the real and the fake is well illustrated by the Animal Kingdom at Disney World. As mentioned earlier (Chapter 1), the center of the park is the "Tree of Life," which looks real from a distance but up close is clearly a fake. Africa has "real" live animals; Dinoland has simulations of extinct dinosaurs. Even the real animals live in artificial environments that eventually may change them in various ways, turning them into simulations. An excursion through an artificial savannah takes the visitor to the Conservation Station, which is the "real" headquarters for the care of wildlife in Animal Kingdom. In other words, there are degrees of the fake at Animal Kingdom, and it is not always easy to distinguish the very fake from the not-so-fake.

TIME AND SPACE

The issues of time and space have received a great deal of attention from both modern and postmodern social theorists.[51] Among the modernists, Anthony Giddens is best known for his work on these issues; his entire theory concerns the analysis of institutions across time and space.[52] To Giddens, the primordial human condition involves face-to-face interaction, in which others are present at the same time and in the same place. However, in the contemporary world, social relations and social systems extend in time and space, so we increasingly relate to others who are physically absent and more and more distant. Such distancing in time and space is facilitated by new forms of communication and transportation.

Such distancing has certainly taken place in several of the new means of consumption, especially the dematerialized ones based on the telephone, television, and especially the computer. In such cases, there is no face-to-face interaction, and those who communicate with the consumer can be quite distant physically. In fact, the consumer rarely has any idea, or cares, where such people are. It is increasingly common for those requesting information via telephone in the United States to be connected to an agent someplace in India, to take one major example. In some cases, contacts may be distant in time as well. Information on online malls may have been loaded long before the consumer visits, and infomercials almost always have been taped for later broadcast. Giddens has argued that because of such distancing, place becomes increasingly "phantasmagoric."[53] This is in line with the new means of consumption as being dreamlike, fantastic, and spectacular.

Also relevant is David Harvey's work on time-space compression. Harvey believes that the compression of time and space characteristic of modernity has accelerated in the postmodern era, leading to "an intense phase of time-space compression."[54] While Harvey tends to have a negative view of this process as "disorienting" and "disruptive," the point being made is simply that the new means of consumption have tended to compress time and space. Indeed, it is their ability to do so that has helped make them so phantasmagoric, so spectacular. That ability, that spectacle, has enhanced their capacity to sell goods and services. If consumers stopped to think about it, they would be stunned by the fact that goods once available half a world away (say, French brie or Russian vodka) can be purchased in local shops in the United States (and many other countries). They would be astounded by the fact that products that once took days or weeks to obtain can now be procured overnight, in hours, or in some cases even almost instantaneously (e.g., by downloading music, movies, pornography, and so on over the Internet).

The notion of the compression of time and space has much in common with the idea of implosion, at least as it applies to time and space. To compress time and space, the barriers between various dimensions of time and space must be eroded. Indeed, another way of saying that time and space have been compressed is to say the differences within each have imploded. There is more to implosion than simply time and space compression, but the latter have certainly experienced implosion.

It is worth noting that space is not nearly as amenable to implosion as time. Time creates no barriers to those who seek to use it differently. As we will see, differences between day and night, one season or another, or even the past, present, and future (including past, present, and future incomes) can be overcome in efforts to sell more things to more people. Space, by definition, presents obstinate physical hurdles to those who want to use it in new and different ways. Most of these obstacles are not insurmountable, but they do tend to impede the revolutionary use of space more than they do that of time. Despite the barriers, there have been enormous changes in the spatial characteristics associated with consumption. The spatial boundaries in and around consumption are imploding at an accelerating rate. In so doing, they create spectacles that, although not always intentionally manufactured by those in charge of the means of consumption, serve to heighten consumption.

Space: Implosion Into the Home

Throughout the vast majority of history, people produced and consumed most, and sometimes all, of what they needed inside, or within hunting and gathering distance of, the home. This remained true for most people up to and even through the Industrial Revolution. However, a clear distinction eventually emerged between where one lived and where one worked and, more important, given the focus of this book, where one obtained goods and services. In general, one had to leave one's home and go to some other place (the market, the bazaar, the arcade, the Exposition, the fair, the country store, Main Street, downtown, the supermarket, the mall) to obtain what was needed for consumption. There have long been simultaneous efforts to eliminate the need to leave home, to turn the home into a place to obtain commodities (e.g., the old Yellow Pages campaign, "Let Your Fingers Do the Walking"). The Sears catalog was an early effort. Milk products used to be delivered, and scissor grinders went door to door. Then there were traveling salespeople who might have shown up on one's doorstep in the hopes of using one's house to sell brushes, a vacuum cleaner, or aluminum siding. Another early example were the home "parties"[55] run by organizations such as Tupperware and Avon in which the objective was to turn the home into a site for consumption.[56] Although these kinds of efforts have long existed, the home was, in the main, separate from settings in which one purchased goods and services. That barrier, however, has imploded: The home has become a, perhaps *the*, major site for obtaining goods and services.

There are several longstanding ways to breach the front door. Salespeople can personally visit the home much like the brush-and-vacuum salespeople of a past era. This continues to occur, but it is a rather primitive, labor-intensive, and therefore expensive method. It also requires face-to-face contact and interpersonal skills that people today may be less inclined or able to practice. Furthermore, with many more women in the labor force, there is a greater likelihood that no one will be home when a salesperson calls.

The mail is another traditional invader of the home. The number and variety of mail-order catalogs delivered through the mail escalated dramatically for many years, although that flow is now slowing. Also reaching us by mail are circulars and letters of all types and shapes designed to sell all sorts of goods and services. The credit card companies were, until recently, extremely active in using the mail to interest people in acquiring more and more cards. We were swamped by letters offering us, for example, low interest rates or preapproved credit cards. Mail was considered a relatively inexpensive method of getting inside the home (newspaper, magazine, radio, television, and the Internet are others), but a very large number of things sent through the mail find their way unopened into the trash. Further, with the advent of the Internet, mail came to be seen as increasingly expensive, at least in contrast to e-mail solicitations (almost all of it Spam, or unsolicited "junk" e-mail).

Another traditional way of gaining entrée to the home has been the telephone, and it came to be used more actively and aggressively in the late 20th and early 21st centuries (leading to the 2003 U.S. national "do not call" program [a number of other nations now have such a program] in which the vast majority of Americans are now enrolled[57]). An executive of a firm in the business said that telemarketing had "become the junk mail of the '90s,"[58] and although it has almost certainly declined as a result of the "do not call" program, by the early 21st century, it had grown to a $100 billion a year business.[59] Many could not get through the dinner hour without an overture or two from telemarketers. (Because federal guidelines forbid calls after 9 P.M., most calls are made between 6 P.M. and 9 P.M.) Beyond the sheer volume of calls, telemarketers had revolutionized this process in various ways, and many of them are still in use. For example, they purchase specialized and targeted lists that allow them to focus on the types of people who have some probability of buying their product. They use technologies such as speed dialing and computers that allow them to come on the line when someone picks up the telephone rather than wasting time holding on calls that end up not being answered. As we all know, there are even completely computerized calls that are "dialed" by computer and make the sales pitch with prerecorded voices.

We can think of the personal visit, the mail, and the telephone call as traditional, but limited, efforts to breach the home. The idea is to get a person, a piece of mail, or a voice into the home so that it becomes a site for consumption. These are primitive techniques, but they are obviously effective, especially given the relatively low cost associated with most of them.

The most dramatic changes are associated with newer technologies, particularly the television set and the computer. Television has always used advertising; commercial television programming would be impossible without it. In the main, however, these advertisements have been aimed at motivating us to leave our home at some future point to buy a car or a refrigerator at a retailer. We were not asked to buy those things *in* or from our homes. There were a few exceptions, such as the 1–800 ads for things such as the $9.99 slicer-dicer or the "Greatest Hits of Rock 'n' Roll," but these ordinarily were low-priced or shady operations that did not play a major role in transforming the home into a house of consumption. Such ads continue and, in fact, seem to have accelerated again with the advent of the current recession.

Then came infomercials, shows that fall somewhere between normal television programs and commercials. Without the notice that we are viewing a paid advertisement, we might mistake these for educational or entertainment programs. In fact, those who produce such shows count on the fact that large numbers of people will fail to realize, or forget, that they are watching an infomercial. We are likely to be given a 1–800 telephone number to call to order the product and charge it to our credit card account (or we can pay the bill COD).

Falling into the same category are advertisements and infomercials for spoken services such as the "psychic hotline" and telephone sex. In these cases, the viewer automatically purchases and receives the service by calling the appropriate number. Billed later at a substantial cost per minute, some people have found themselves in deep economic trouble through the purchase of such calls and the "services" they offer.

Of course, advertisements and infomercials pale in comparison to home-shopping television and the television channels and entire networks (Home Shopping Network, HSN) devoted to it. Here our homes are invaded around the clock by slick-talking salespeople, often joined by celebrities (the comedienne Joan Rivers seems especially omnipresent these days) hawking their own products or those from the sale of which they stand to profit. There is no need to leave home to purchase: Just telephone and charge.

Much the same could be said about online malls and other forms of Internet shopping. Increasing numbers of people have computers in their homes, and many of them both work and play on their computers. We may turn on our computers to escape the lure of television's HSN only to find the more seductive (and less annoying) lure of our favorite online malls. Computer-based consumption is even easier than consumption via the home-shopping networks. In the case of HSN, we have to turn our attention away from the television set to make a telephone call. With online malls, we already are online, so that a visit to the mall and a purchase can be accomplished simultaneously. Innumerable other goods and services—including stocks, psychic advice, sex, and gambling—are being sold online, thereby greatly increasing the amount of consumption that can done through our home computers.[60]

Also worth mentioning at this point are those increasingly popular pop-up ads that so plague us (although they can be blocked) when we log on, via computer or smartphone, to a Web site to which they are attached. This is a good example of what is called "in your face" marketing.[61]

Traditional and new means of consumption have been battering so hard and so often at our doors that many of us simply have given up and welcomed them all in. Why not? Spread before our eyes and ears is a cornucopia of goods and services. All that is required is a telephone call, a keystroke, and a credit card number. In this way, our homes have become means of consumption. It is one thing to be trapped at the mall but quite another thing to be trapped at home. No matter how trapped one is at the mall, one must eventually leave. However, most people do not have the option of leaving a home that has become commercialized. In any case, large numbers of people are quite happy with their commercialized homes, and that contentment is likely to increase in the future as the possibility of purchasing more and more goods and services is brought into the home:

> The marriage of technology and commerce will make consuming ever more convenient: Our homes can become retail outlets, we can visit virtual shopping malls from our couches, shop for new homes on CD-ROM. We will, in other words, never have to leave home to fill the needs that marketing creates.[62]

There is spectacle in all of this; for some, nothing could be more spectacular than to be able to acquire the fruits of our commercial world without ever having to leave the comforts of our home.

It is worth noting that the home is increasingly becoming not only a means of consumption but also a means of production. For example, the same computer that is allowing us to shop at home is permitting us to work there. The home, the center of production and consumption before the Industrial Revolution, is once again becoming such a center in our postindustrial society. (And the home is also now becoming, again, an important means of consuming education, through televised and online courses and degrees.) Although production and consumption are once again frequently occurring in the home, they are not the same kinds of production and consumption that occurred during the Industrial Revolution, and they are not occurring in the same way that they did then.

Once again, this illustrates that we are increasingly *prosumers,* that we produce and consume simultaneously.[63] We do this, for example, on Amazon.com (another is ebay.com), where we certainly consume various products, especially books, but we also produce our order by, for example, scanning alternatives, making selections, and providing all the relevant information. We also help produce the Web site by, for example, writing reviews (at no charge) for books available on Amazon.com.

Time: The Implosion of Times Available for Consumption

The ultimate objective in a capitalist economy (and today that is about the only economy that exists in most of the world), at least as far as time is concerned, is to allow people to consume around the clock, every day of the year. In other words, the objective is the implosion of all differences in time as far as consumption (and production) is concerned. Historically, there have been a number of impediments to reaching this objective. Before the advent of electric light, nightfall was a powerful barrier to consumption.[64] Means of consumption were often great distances away, and transportation was slow. As a result, trips to market were infrequent. Large numbers of people lacked the economic resources they needed to do much, if any, consumption beyond that which they collected or produced for themselves. Religion, especially in its promotion of asceticism and a day of rest, also served to impede consumption. The polity was responsible, often as a result of religious pressure, for laws that restricted consumption in a wide variety of ways (e.g., "blue laws" that eliminated alcohol sale on Sundays). Long hours of work on the farm, in the factory, or in the household greatly restricted the amount of time and energy people could devote to consumption. Children and adolescents lacked the resources. People tended to work late into life, leaving few, if any, "golden years" to devote to consumption.

In the past few decades, most, if not all, of these barriers have imploded, or at least eroded, in the United States and in many other parts of the world.

Electricity and other technological innovations have largely eliminated nightfall as a significant obstacle to consumption. Means of consumption seem much closer as automobiles, trains, busses, and even airplanes make it possible for people to get to them more quickly and whenever they want. The increasing wealth of the society, at least until recently, has given more and more people the wherewithal to be active players in the malls of America as well as in all the other cathedrals of consumption. Even those without cash in hand or in the bank can play the consumer game, thanks to the ubiquitous credit card. In our increasingly secular society, religion has come to exert little influence over consumption (except, perhaps, as a spur to the commodification of religion and religious products). Most legal restrictions on consumption have been wiped from the books. Although there is some debate over this, work hours are more limited,[65] and work itself is less arduous, allowing people more time *and* energy to consume. Young people now have lots of resources at their disposal. People are living longer, with the result that large numbers of retirees find themselves with many years to devote primarily to consumption.

As with many things related to the new means of consumption, the United States is the innovator and the world leader in the use of time. Said a student of time as an economic resource, "Compared to Europe, the U.S. is miles ahead in mining the economic value of time."[66] Factors inhibiting the greater use of time in Europe include legal restrictions on the hours businesses can be open and high social welfare costs that work against hiring extra people to handle night shifts. European culture and traditions are another factor. For example, "Much of the small business in Italy is family-owned and operated. Extending hours means going outside the family for labor, which is not the norm. America, on the other hand, is synonymous with new ideas, entrepreneurship and business competition."[67]

Even in the United States, it was not that long ago that there was little or no possibility of purchasing goods and services from dark to early morning. Over the years, hours were stretched, and in some cases, people were able to shop until 10 P.M. In a few cases, such as with the advent of the supermarket and drug store open 24 hours a day and the coming of convenience store chains such as 7-Eleven and Wawa that never close, shopping could be done around the clock. However, there are a limited number of people who are interested in trekking to the market in the middle of the night. Furthermore, with the perception that crime and violence are increasing, a significant number of people are reluctant to venture out of their homes late at night, especially in urban areas.

To truly make all time available for consumption, the means of consumption had to implode into the home. The new means of consumption—especially HSN, online malls, and online catalogs[68]—have served to literally eliminate time as a barrier to consumption. Online gambling casinos are "open" around the clock and every day, as are the Web sites that allow people to buy and sell stocks and bonds. One can watch horse racing for many hours a day thanks to the TVG television network and bet on those and other races on TVGnetwork.com and other online sites.

Time has imploded in other ways. In the past, it might have taken a week or more for a mail order to get to Sears, to pass through its shipping department, and to be delivered to the consumer. Now orders can be placed almost instantaneously by telephone, fax, or computer. Processing has been expedited greatly and the time it takes to move an order out the door reduced enormously. Shipping has been revolutionized with the advent of the express parcel delivery services. The result is that an order delivery cycle (e.g., Netflix) is now often completed in a day or two. Of course, because the new goods are in hand more quickly, one is likely to tire of them more rapidly as well.[69] This means that one may feel the need to plunge more quickly back into the consumer game.

Do any time barriers to consumption remain? Most adults must work many hours a week to earn the income needed for consumption, not to mention to save, and to have the credit base to qualify for credit cards[70] and other forms of credit. Presumably, time on the job is time that cannot be devoted to consumption. But various changes are making it easier for people to work and to consume at the same time. For example, the online malls and other types of online shopping, especially as they will evolve in the future, make it easy for workers to switch from work-related tasks to a quick visit to a "store" within a favored online mall, a favorite online casino, or to trade a stock electronically. Even time on the job will be less and less a barrier to consumption. Among other things, increasing numbers of workers will carry smartphones with them, and they will be able to access the Internet from them at any time and in any place.

Not only is any time of the day, the night, the week, or the year increasingly a "good" time for consumption, but any stage of a lifetime is now a "good" stage to consume. Infants, at least through their parents, grandparents, and so on, have been drawn into the world of consumption by, for example, the growth of baby superstores (e.g., Buy Buy Baby) devoted solely to them. Wal-Mart and the toy superstores are oriented toward children, or at least to those who purchase things for them. Teenagers have become a huge market, and many of the new means of consumption (e.g., music, video, and electronics superstores) could not exist without their business. The retired and the elderly are no longer excused from consumption, either. Among other things, they are expected to consume the homes and lifestyles associated with retirement communities and to become morning mall walkers who might just stay around, or return later, to sample the mall's offerings. Even the dying are expected to purchase the services of nursing homes and hospices, and the dead (or their heirs) are consumers as far as chains of funeral homes and cemeteries are concerned.

Although I am emphasizing the ability of people to consume at all times, we must not forget the spectacular and enchanted (reenchanted) character of all of this, at least from the point of view of the consumer. Suppose the ghost of a 19th-century farmer found itself in the contemporary world of consumption. Many things would be amazing and seem magical (especially the appearance of the ghost), but one of those would certainly be the ability to consume at every minute, of every week of every year, virtually from birth to death. Although entrepreneurs have been instrumental in increasing the time available for consumption, they have not always been conscious of the fact that a spectacle would be created that would help sell goods and services.

Time: Implosion of Past, Present, and Future Earnings

The consumer possesses three basic types of resources of interest to merchants: money currently being earned and in hand; money that has been earned in the past, not spent, and saved or invested; and money that is likely to be earned in the future. Significant differences among the three types of resources have eroded in recent years; there has been an implosion of monies earned in the past, present, or future. As far as the contemporary merchant is concerned, there is no significant difference among them: Money is money whenever it is earned, and in any form it can be transformed into goods and services. A supermarket is more likely to get at cash in hand (although people are increasingly charging their groceries), a new car dealer is more likely to get at longer term savings (past earnings) in the form of a down payment (plus continuing payments), and a home mortgage company will probably get at mostly future earnings via future principal and interest payments. However, the supermarket, the car dealer, and the mortgage company really do not care which "pot" the money comes from as long as they get their share of it. In this sense, the different pots of money implode into one another, leaving merchants with one large cauldron from which profits can be ladled.

Merchants have had, at least until the recent recession, few problems inducing people to spend present income. Past income, in the form of savings and investments, has become harder to tap. Still, the capitalist economy has a wealth of experience with various techniques designed to induce people to spend this kind of money in the present. For example, the advertising industry devotes a lot of attention to creating seductive advertisements for luring people into parting with their savings. In the banking industry, the advent of checks made it easier for people to spend past earnings. The ATM is a more recent innovation allowing people easy access to their money in situations in which cash rather than a check is required.

What is really new and of enormous importance is the incredible expansion of the implosion of future income into the present. It is certainly the case that techniques have long existed to get at future earnings, such as installment buying, but there has been a tremendous expansion in traditional techniques (e.g., home and car loans) and, more important, in the development of new methods and technologies (e.g., the growth in the leasing of automobiles), especially the credit card (as well as credit instruments such as home equity loans). Although merchants care little whether sales are in cash or on credit,[71] credit card companies obviously have a strong preference for customers to spend future income. The reason is that, if money that has not yet been earned is spent, consumers will be unable to pay their credit card bills in full immediately. Such consumers must go into debt to the credit card companies and pay the usurious interest rates associated with their cards.

The use of credit, especially via the credit card, and the spending of future income, have, at least until recently, been an increasingly ubiquitous part of all of the new means of consumption. The most extreme are infomercials, the home television shopping networks, and the online malls and other forms of online shopping that simply could not operate without credit card purchases. Las Vegas and Disney World would not exist, at least at their present scale, without credit cards. Cruise lines would be less affected because they require lump-sum payments that easily could be handled by check. However, even they are moving more into business done on credit. For example, Princess Cruises instituted a program whereby passengers can finance their cruises.[72] More important, cruise lines earn a lot of money from extra expenditures while on board (in the shops, at the spa, in the casino), and much of that is paid for by credit card.

The economy became increasingly dependent on the expenditure of future income, the implosion of future earnings into the present. That is, it was not enough for us to spend all of our cash in hand or in the bank. We also had to spend an increasing portion of money we had not yet earned in order to keep the economy humming at the level it expected and to which it had become accustomed.

Indeed, it is feared that were large numbers of us to reduce or eliminate mortgage, automobile, and credit card debt, to begin living within our means, the effect on the economy would be disastrous. Among the things that would be dramatically altered were there less, or no, debt would be consumer spending. A decline in such spending would reverberate throughout the economy. The banking industry as we had come to know it would be badly shaken and dramatically altered. Many banks had come to rely on consumer loans as one of, if not *the*, most profitable of their businesses. For example, some "monoline" banks relied exclusively on credit card business. Such banks would disappear, and many others would be forced to downsize and reorient their remaining business in order to survive. Some retailers would disappear altogether, and others would shrink dramatically. Particularly affected would be businesses that rely on sales via the telephone and computer. Most of that business would dry up without the credit card. Obviously, a contraction in banking and retailing would lead to a slowdown and scaling back in goods production and service provision.

In fact, of course, that is exactly what happened in the United States, and throughout much of the rest of the world, as the recession that began in late 2007 gained momentum. Credit of all sorts became difficult or impossible to get, and consumption declined dramatically, with disastrous results for the American and the global economy.

Prior to the recent crash, the main spectacle in this context as far as the consumer is concerned was (and still is for many) the seemingly unbelievable ability to buy goods and services without any cash in hand or in the bank. And this spectacle served to draw the consumer into the cathedrals of consumption where it can be played out. While treks to those cathedrals have declined dramatically in the recent downturn, it seems likely that those trips, and the credit needed to undertake them, will return, although it will take a long time for them to return to prerecession levels.

Time as Spectacle

The implosion of time barriers is a spectacle in itself, but there are other types of spectacles associated with time and the new means of consumption.

Speed

In fast-food restaurants, the spectacle is the speed with which one can obtain and devour a meal. Although limited in terms of what it can do with its space,[73] at least within the confines of a small restaurant (and even more so in an even smaller satellite location in, for example, a service station), the fast-food restaurant obviously has been a highly revolutionary force in the realm of time. What once took hours at home, or many minutes in a traditional restaurant, now generally takes a matter of seconds in a fast-food restaurant. We now take this for granted, but when first introduced, it represented a spectacular reduction in the amount of time needed to produce and consume a meal. Furthermore, as the number of these restaurants proliferated, it took less and less time to get to one. It is also worth noting that the nature and spread of these restaurants served to free time that could be used in other ways, especially consuming other goods and services in malls as well as in many other new means of consumption.

All of the chains and franchises serve in one way or another to speed up the process of consumption. For example, if one wants a particular type of jeans, one can pretty much be assured that one or more shops in the mall will have it; this cuts down on the time required to wander from shop to shop, or department store to department store (which are likely to have a much narrower selection of jeans). By the way, the reduction of time spent finding just the right pair of jeans does not necessarily mean that one will spend less time shopping. In fact, the likelihood is that with new jeans in hand, our consumer will wander off to other kinds of shops in the mall. After all, although fast-food restaurants may want to get you in and out quickly, a mall wants to keep you in the mall, moving from shop to shop for as long as possible.

An interesting example of the speeding up of time in a realm in which one would not expect it is in "mass customization." It obviously takes a great deal of time to make and then receive clothing or shoes that are made to order for a specific individual. However, various businesses have dramatically reduced that time through mass customization.[74] Examples include Dell building a computer to customer specifications, fine hotels offering in their restaurants napkins and matchboxes with a customer's name on them, and Planters offering different-size packages of mixed nuts to diverse retailers such as Wal-Mart and 7-Eleven.[75] Logosoftwear.com offers customized caps, shirts, team uniforms, signs, and banners.[76]

Spectacular Use of Time

Fast-food restaurants and other chains reduce the time needed to consume, sometimes spectacularly, but this is not typical of the other new means of consumption. The spectacle in the vast majority of them is generally the feeling of a *loss* of a sense of time, a dreamlike state in which time—very much unlike in the rest of one's life—seems not to matter. In many cases, this works in conjunction with the spectacular size of these new means; getting lost in space also often means getting lost in time. And getting lost in time is often critical to the success of the new means of consumption. It is a key part of the dream they are marketing to customers.

Let us start with the idea that what is being marketed is an experience that offers the spectacle of seeming to be able to defy the constraints and inexorability of time. Las Vegas casinos, as well as the city in general, are famous for this, and they seek to accomplish it in various ways. First, they truly are 24-hour-a-day operations, so that one day rolls seamlessly into another. Second, efforts are made to eliminate any external signs (sunshine, darkness, etc.) of the time of day or night. Third, clocks are forbidden in casinos (and many malls, including the Mall of America). Fourth, the vast, cavernous space operates in conjunction with the absence of indicators of time passing to create a dreamlike world in which time is not a factor, or at least less important than it is elsewhere. Fifth, basically the same kinds of activities are taking place around the clock. Gambling tables are open, drinks are served, the distinctive noise of the casino continues unabated, and people sit in front of slot machines or at the gaming tables, pulling levers, taking cards, throwing dice, and so on. The slot machines themselves make their odd whistles and screeches, and so on.

The casinos are not completely successful in their efforts (fewer people gamble in the early morning than at night, and they are more likely to drink coffee than cocktails), but they come as close as any of the new means of consumption to altering or eliminating a sense of time passing. Representative of what takes place in casinos is the sky effect on the ceiling of the Forum Shops adjacent to Caesar's Palace. The projected sky image changes quickly and dramatically, leaving the viewer with the impression of rapidly passing time. The message? Better hurry and shop and gamble because time is fleeting! Although it works against eliminating the sense of time passing—indeed, it speeds it up—the Forum's "sky" does greatly alter the sense of time, thereby symbolizing the continual effort to disorient the visitor to Las Vegas.

The sports books in the casinos offer betting on horse and dog races around the country, and perhaps the world, from early morning to late at night. Given time zone differences (in fact, in the sports books, time zones implode[77]), one can begin by gambling on East Coast tracks early in the morning and end up betting on races being run at night on the West Coast. Time is magically stretched so that the inveterate gambler can spend 12 hours or even more betting on horse races (compared to the normal 4 or 5 hours a day at a racetrack). Of course, this constitutes not only a spectacular expansion of time but also of space, because a gambler can readily move from betting on races on both coasts as well as on those anywhere in between. One might go from betting on a horse race being run in the snow in Boston to one being run on a sun-drenched 85-degree day in southern Florida or California.

These examples communicate a sense of time passing that is radically different from what is experienced normally. But the spectacular elimination of a sense of time and its passage approaches its ultimate form in shopping on the Internet. For example, 24hourmall.com offers many round-the-clock online stores grouped under more than 30 broad headings (e.g., apparel, toys, and electronics).[78] The "surfer" can see and do exactly the same things at any time of the day or night. There are no indicators of night or day on the Internet; one is adrift there. It is possible, even highly likely, that one is going to lose one's sense of time (and spend one's money!).

An interesting example in this realm is the online casino. Although Las Vegas casinos work hard to eliminate a sense of time, what they can do pales in comparison to the capabilities of online casinos. After all, in an online casino, the gambler is given absolutely *no* sense of the time of day or of time passing (although some help might come from the time indicator at the bottom right of most computer screens). The online player has a similar absence of sense of place; casino operations can take place anywhere in the world. (Other examples of 24-hour consumption include selected Wal-Marts, fitness centers, and bank by phone or by computer operations.)

Another way in which many of the new means of consumption make spectacular use of time is to present attractions that are drawn from many points in humankind's past, present, and future. In that way, the past, present, and future implode into one another, producing what the postmodernists call a pastiche. Las Vegas offers us the ancient past at the Luxor, the Middle Ages at Excalibur, the near past in New York, New York,[79] and the future in the Stratosphere. Malls increasingly juxtapose the ersatz artifacts of museum and nature stores with futuristic gadgets available at brookstone.com. The best example is Disney, which cavalierly juxtaposes the past in the form of such exhibits as "Pirates of the Caribbean" and the future in the form, say, of "Space Mountain" with a number of timeless attractions traceable to Disney characters of one kind or another. The message seems to be not only that Disney can collapse time barriers but also that time itself does not matter (at least as long as one is within the Disney confines and spending a sufficient amount of money to keep the Disney empire operating at the level to which it has grown accustomed).

It is important to remember that the new means of consumption manipulate the customer's sense of time in order to earn greater profits. The assumption is that the spectacular manipulation of time is likely to lead to more customers and more expenditures. And the more time available for consumption, the greater the number of goods and services that will be sold. Furthermore, consumers who are disoriented in terms of time are likely to be disoriented in other ways, including their thinking about money.

Extraordinary Spaces

Beyond the implosion of the distinction between home and the means of consumption, the most general objective in the spatial realm is to offer a sense of an expanse that is somehow different from that ordinarily encountered by the customer. An effort may be made to draw the customers' attention to or away from some spatial aspect of the setting to impress them. This is usually accomplished by creating the sense, often illusory, of a colossal, nearly boundless space.

Manipulating Spatial Constraints

A sense of infinite space is easiest to create in the very newest, dematerialized means of consumption. Online malls, as well as the other modes of selling commodities on the Internet, could be anywhere; they could sell anything; and there appears to be no end to their potential number. Because they are at the outer limit in terms of the spatial dimension, the Internet and its online malls offer the greatest potential for a spectacular sense, and use, of space. Increasing that potential is the fact that one may use the Internet in innumerable ways to sell and to buy. Current examples include ordering airplane or cruise tickets, playing the stock market, purchasing (even reading) books, and enrolling in and taking academic courses.

There are limitations on the Internet's capacity to create a spectacular sense of space. Consumers are likely to be sitting in their studies, offices, or dens and peering at small video screens. Those who control and manage cyberspace must create spectacular images to get viewers to abandon their sense of where they are physically and to lose themselves in the cyberworld. The analogy is a video game in which players are treated to an incomparable spectacle *if* they can suspend their sense of reality and distance themselves from their physical surroundings and immerse themselves completely in the game world. The Internet and online malls offer the same possibility, at least theoretically. If users can, in principle, be led to completely lose themselves, and it remains to be seen whether enough of them can, they become ideal targets to those who control the online malls. Adrift in cyberspace, one has lost touch with reality (at least day-to-day reality) and is in a state that makes one vulnerable to buying things one does not need and cannot afford.

Similarly advantaged is television, especially the television shopping networks, which offer an analogous sense of infinite space. Their signals, like those in cyberspace, are adrift in the ether. The relationship between customer and seller is not restricted by the usual spatial constraints associated with malls or shops. Of course, the den, the television screen, and the telephone necessary to place orders do impose some restrictions. However, space constraints are reduced, if not eliminated, when customers can become as immersed in the goings-on of their home-shopping network as they can in their video games or explorations of the Internet. There are certainly cases of people whose major reality has become their relationship to the hosts of, and the products purveyed on, the home-shopping network. Immersed in this ethereal world, they buy lots of things (often things they have no need for) and, as a consequence, many of them become deeply indebted to their credit card companies. The home-shopping networks have succeeded, at least for some viewers, in creating the kind of boundless space that online malls are trying to create.

Credit cards facilitate this process, as they do much of what transpires in relationship to the new means of consumption. The ability to merely enter card numbers into the computer, or to repeat them to someone who is taking our order over the phone, helps to eliminate spatial barriers to consumption. Of course, although people can defy space while ordering and paying, most goods must still be delivered across physical distances. Exceptions to this are digital products (especially music, videos, and data), stock positions, and so on.

Seeming to Be Everywhere

Some new means of consumption create a spectacle by limiting or eliminating spatial constraints, but most are still limited by material realities that force them to find other ways to make a spectacle of space. One course of action is to be, or at least seem to be, everywhere in the world. The number of outlets of a fast-food chain, combined with the fact that it spans not only the nation but also the world, gives the diner a sense of participating in a massive phenomenon, of being an infinitesimal part of a globe-straddling operation. In eating burgers and fries, Americans may be merely feeding themselves in the most prosaic of ways, but at the same time, they may feel themselves to be players in a colossal national and international operation. The diners at a McDonald's in a remote Russian city are, in contrast, eating what is for them exotic food. At the same time, they may feel that they are participating in an enormous international experience that has its origins in the United States. For many outside the United States, dining in a fast-food restaurant allows them to transcend spatial limitations and dine, in their fantasies anyway, in America—or at least allows them to dine like Americans.

Starbucks has taken this strategy of seeming to be everywhere (there were more than 15,000 Starbucks worldwide in late 2007),[80] although the number is declining with the current recession. Its innovation is to pack a number of Starbucks into limited geographic areas, often in sight of one another.[81] This is true of, among other places, Dupont Circle in Washington, D.C., and the Soho, Picadilly Circus, and Fleet Street areas in London.

For most people, getting to a theme park requires a major trip. To overcome this problem, the parks have, in various ways, moved closer to the consumer.

One example is the Disney stores in many malls. We may not be able to enjoy the rides, but we can still get the souvenirs and have a "Disney experience." Another is the entertainment centers aimed at adults such as Dave and Buster's that are in our malls.

Then there are the GameWorks arcades and "eatertainment" centers.[82] This is an effort to adapt the theme park model (as well as the movies) and bring it into closer proximity to a large proportion of the population. Included at GameWorks are such interactive games, simulations, and attractions as "Rambo," "UFO Catcher," and "House of the Dead 4."

A Sense of Enormous Space

Another course taken by the new means of consumption to create a spectacle is to use enormous physical spaces (or to create the sense of a far larger space than is actually occupied). Most of the cathedrals of consumption are unable to come to us. They therefore must give us a very good reason to leave our homes (with our online malls, home-shopping networks, catalogs, and home-delivery pizza). With their spectacular use of enormous spaces, shopping malls have long sought to draw us out of our homes. Take this description of the Westminster Mall in California provided by William Kowinski, author of *The Malling of America*:

> Westminster Mall was a classic California cathedral . . . it opened into a soaring central court. . . . The court covered an enormous area, both horizontally and vertically. High above was the orange ceiling dome, layered with white. From it hung a huge net sculpture. . . . Altogether this court combined intimate spaces with monumental scale and audacious effects. . . . I was awestruck.[83]

If a student of the malls is awestruck by the physical space and the way it is used in this mall (as well as its amenities), you can imagine the reactions of an ordinary, first-time visitor. Even more extreme are the responses of those from other cultures (although many now have such malls of their own), especially those from developing nations.[84]

Other spatial developments set the stage for such capacious malls and our sense that they are spectacular. Most of us spend most of our lives in confined spaces such as classrooms, small apartments, tract houses, and office cubicles. This helps to make the use of huge spaces by shopping malls (and other new means of consumption) so stunning and attractive to us.[85]

Of course, the spectacle of the mall, as we know, has led, inexorably, to the mega-mall, where the objective is to create much larger settings, to make even more spectacular use of space. For example, as of 2009, the Mall of

America encompassed more than 500 stores and restaurants on 4.2 million square feet (and across the street is a 330,000-square-foot IKEA).[86] Huge numbers of visitors are *not* drawn there by the chains and franchises, because they are nearly indistinguishable from those available in their local mall. What draws them is the sheer size of the place and the fact that it encompasses so many things. People are drawn to what they think will be a colossal cornucopia of goods and services, a phantasmagoria.

The colossal size of the Mall of America permits it to house not only a shopping mall but also a theme park (Nickelodeon Universe) within its confines. The enchantment lies in the fact that one of our fantastic means of consumption—the theme park—is simply a small part of an even more fantastic means—the mega-mall. Nickelodeon Universe covers 7 acres and boasts 30 rides. It also includes entertainment, shopping, and nine places to eat.

In addition to the shopping mall and the theme park, the Mall of America encompasses the Underwater Adventures Aquarium. Visitors to it are transported by a moving walkway through an aquarium that takes them through several areas—Touch of the Wild Woods, The Tunnel, Seacrits of Hollywood Gallery, Circle of Life, and Starfish Gallery. The trip takes an hour; as they progress through it, visitors are surrounded by sharks, stingrays, and many other types of sea life.

Then there is the admission-free Lego Imagination Center that includes more than 30 Lego constructions, play areas for children, and, need we add, a Lego shop. NASCAR Silicon Motor Speedway gives participants the feeling of being in a NASCAR race. Catering to the adults is the fourth-floor entertainment district that includes, among other things, a 14-screen movie theater.

Mega-malls expect the visitor to be impressed not only by their sheer physical size but also by all of the things that space permits under one roof. Impressing visitors in such ways, these malls expect that many other visitors will be drawn to the mall with a similar desire to be astounded. Of course, the ultimate goal is not merely to astonish but to lure the consumer to the mall and into spending.

Although they now may be inside mega-malls, amusement parks or theme parks preceded the malls in the use of great expanses of space to create a spectacle for park visitors. This was clear in Disney's parks, especially in its Orlando site, where it was able to buy up huge tracts of land and create a park with seemingly limitless space. Each of the elements of Disney World is spectacular by itself. But, when taken together, they are designed to overwhelm the visitor with the size of the place and the ever-increasing range of entertainment that is offered. It seems like a self-contained universe that cannot possibly be explored fully on one, or even a few, visits. The addition of more and more attractions and hotels serves to buttress continually that sense, as well as the spectacular image that Disney World works so hard to create.

A similar development has occurred in the cruise business. There has been an ongoing effort to build bigger and bigger liners. The goal is to offer the vacationer a physical space that is mind-boggling in size as well as in what it encompasses:

> Positioning cruise ships as floating resorts is a prime motivation for the many plush spas and high-tech fitness centers, the Broadway-like revues in Broadway-sized theaters, bigger and more attractive casinos, upscale shops and boutiques, miniature golf courses and an ice skating rink aboard a Royal Caribbean ship.[87]

One of the largest cruise ships ever built, a mega-ship (following in the tradition of the mega-malls and reflecting the importance of large spaces to the cathedrals of consumption), is the Carnival Cruise Lines' *Destiny*. It is 102,000 tons (*Disney Magic* is a mere 85,000 tons), but it is worth noting that it is now dwarfed by the *Queen Mary 2* at about 150,000 tons (see below), as well as several other cruise ships (especially Royal Caribbean's *Voyager of the Seas* at over 137,000 tons[88] and with a "super-sized" version of it [see below] on the drawing boards[89]). *Destiny* is almost 900 feet long (*Disney Magic* is 964 feet long), more than 100 feet wide, and has 12 passenger decks with a passenger capacity of almost 3,400 (*Disney Magic's* capacity is 1,000 fewer passengers). There are two 2-level dining rooms, one seating 1,114 people and the other 706. There is also a restaurant seating 1,252, a pizzeria open 24 hours, ethnic restaurants, and a grill. The spa is 15,000 square feet. The central atrium is nine stories high; it has four glass-walled elevators and a glass ceiling, further allowing the passenger to take in the enormous space encompassed by the ship and to give still broader vistas of the sky, day and night. Outdoors there are four swimming pools, a jogging track, a 214-foot-long water slide, and a bandstand. Among the entertainment centers are Millionaire's Club, a 9,000-square-foot casino with more than 300 slot machines and 23 gaming tables; Down Beat, a small jazz club; Point After, a disco with 525 television monitors; Criterion Lounge, featuring comedy and dance; All-Star Bar, a sports bar; and Palladium, a three-story, 1,500-seat show lounge featuring a Las Vegas–type show with fireworks and lasers. According to two analysts of the cruise industry, *Destiny* is "a ship that has truly married the dazzling glitter and entertainment facilities of a large Las Vegas–style resort with a ship's hull."[90]

As mentioned above, Cunard's *Queen Mary 2* (*QM2*), which had its maiden voyage in 2004, now dwarfs *Destiny*, but even more interesting from the point of view of this discussion is what Cunard's Web site chooses to emphasize about this ship:

- *QM2* is five times longer than Cunard's first ship, *Britannia* (230 ft.).

- *QM2* is more than twice as long as the Washington Monument is tall (550 ft.).

- *QM2* is 147 feet longer than the Eiffel Tower is tall (984 ft.).

- *QM2* is more than 3½ times as long as Westminster Tower (Big Ben) is high (310 ft.).

- *QM2* is only 117 feet shorter than the Empire State Building is tall (1,248 ft.).

- *QM2* is more than three times as long as St. Paul's Cathedral is tall (366 ft.).

- *QM2* is as long as 36 double-decker London buses (31½ ft. each).

- *QM2*'s whistle will be audible for 10 miles.[91]

Paraphrasing the mantra of a presidential campaign: "It's the size, stupid."

As mentioned in Chapter 1 and implied above, the *QM2* is about to be dwarfed by the largest cruise ship by far, the $1.4 billion Royal Caribbean *Oasis of the Seas,* which can handle well over 6,000 passengers and a crew in excess of 2,000. It is currently scheduled to be launched by the end of 2009 (a second similar ship is scheduled to be delivered the following year). Among its characteristics:

- It is the longest ship ever built (1,180 feet).

- It is the tallest ship ever built (240 feet; 20 stories).

- It is the widest ship ever built.

- It is the heaviest ship ever built (220,000 tons).[92]

I have emphasized the spectacle of the size of the cruise ship itself, but we should not ignore the fact that cruise ships also attract people by offering them the great vistas open to ships at sea. However, as was pointed out in the last chapter, it may well be that many people on cruises tend to be more impressed by the artificial vistas provided on the ship than by those provided by nature.

The modern hotel offers spectacular use of space as well. Take, for example, the Peachtree Plaza in Atlanta, Georgia, created by world-famous architect John

Portman. Portman's capacious lobbies or atriums have been the paradigm for the use of this kind of space in many other new means of consumption[93] (including cruise ships). In fact, "the Portman name is synonymous with the soaring hotel atrium."[94] Open, glass-enclosed elevators take visitors from the lobby to the hotel floors. The elevators are designed to give guests an unbroken view of the expanse of the atrium. "The elevator is like a seat in a theater, but one in which your vantage point is moving continuously."[95] The elevator can be seen as providing "the same sort of thrill as a ride in an amusement park."[96] The balconies on each floor of the hotel also provide a perspective on the expanse of the atrium. Adding to the impact of the atrium is the inclusion of various types of indoor pools and a park-like setting with lots of vegetation.

It cannot be reiterated too often that all of this attention to things such as the hotel atrium is not an end in itself but designed to further consumption. Portman's work is described as having the "merchandiser's instinct."[97] The lobbies include various places to eat, drink, and shop. These are all important producers of income for hotel owners.

The emphasis on great expanses of space also is certainly the case in the Las Vegas casino-hotels, many of which have been influenced by Portman's concepts. Luxor, the world's second largest hotel by number of rooms, was built at a cost (modest by today's standards) of approximately $650 million. The heart of the hotel is a pyramid with 13 acres of glass. It encloses the world's largest atrium (the Portman influence, again); one could fit nine Boeing 747 airplanes in it (by the way, the Mall of America claims that seven of the old Yankee Stadiums would fit inside it[98]). The pyramid is topped by the most powerful beam of light in the world; at 315,000 watts, it is 40 times stronger than the most powerful commercial spotlights. Almost lost in all of this is the fact that the grounds of the Luxor also contain a 10-story Sphinx, taller than the original in Egypt. The Luxor casino covers 120,000 square feet. Also to be found in the hotel as I write are exhibits including bodies, as well as artifacts, from the *Titanic*. There is a range of themed shops, including the Pyramid and Scarab Shops.

Not to be outdone by mega-malls, several Las Vegas casinos now have, as we have seen, rollercoasters. If you think it is spectacular to ride a rollercoaster in a mega-mall, how about riding one over and through the skyscrapers that make up part of the facade of the New York, New York casino-hotel? Or consider the 1,149-foot-high Stratosphere, the tallest structure in Las Vegas. In addition to the High Roller rollercoaster, the Stratosphere features Big Shot (note the emphasis on size once again), a thrill ride that shoots people 160 feet in the air more than 1,000 feet above the Strip, in the 12-story pod that sits atop this enormous, 100-plus floor, tower. It is touted as the tallest freestanding observation tower in America and the tallest building west of the Mississippi.

Turning to more prosaic means of consumption, superstores offer huge spaces with overwhelming quantities of goods: "To enter a superstore is to know what the scale of Olympus or Eldorado must have looked like in the imaginations of mortals."[99] Here is a description of a Wal-Mart supercenter in those terms:

> The first impressions are obvious but overwhelming. The place, like the country, is big. The Supercenter spreads over 201,000 square feet, the size of four American football fields. Man (or, in this instance, a young woman) resorts to technology to conquer distance: she is employed to whizz around on roller skates, fetching and returning goods.[100]

CONCLUSION

Implosion has served to reenchant the cathedrals of consumption by bringing together two or more means of consumption in one setting. Implosion into the home has created seemingly magical new ways to consume such as television shopping networks and cybermalls. The implosion of times available for shopping has created an enchanted world in which one can shop around the clock for 365 days a year. This has been made infinitely easier recently with the development and widespread use of the smartphone. The implosion of past, present, and future earnings, especially the easier access to future earnings, means that people can buy things they could never have bought in the past. Finally, the spectacular use of both time and space has also served to reenchant the cathedrals of consumption.

Landscapes of Consumption

To this point, we have focused on individual cathedrals of consumption, but it is also important to adopt a larger scale perspective and examine *landscapes of consumption*[1] or geographic areas that encompass two, or more, cathedrals of consumption.[2] In his work on the arcade, which encompasses a number of shops and cafés, Benjamin called it a "primordial landscape of consumption."[3] Just as we have witnessed revolutionary new developments in the cathedrals of consumption, we have seen dramatic changes in the immediate geographic areas that encompass them.

As is often the case in looking at consumption in general and consumption sites in particular, Las Vegas offers us the best example. As we have seen, the lavish casino-hotels that have sprung up over the past several decades in Las Vegas are centrally important new means of consumption that have also served as models for many other such settings throughout the United States and the world. More broadly, all of the most important of these casino-hotels (as well as many other means of consumption) can be found in one geographic area on, or adjacent to, the famous Las Vegas Strip (see Figure 7.1), a delimited geographic area on (or in the vicinity of) Las Vegas Boulevard.[4] Since the casino-hotel can be viewed as the paradigmatic (new) means of consumption,[5] by extension, the Strip can be viewed as the model landscape of consumption. Interestingly, and reflecting the development of a new landscape of consumption in the area, high-end casino-hotels have been built not only off the Strip but also outside the city on manmade (*simulated*) Lake Las Vegas. Interestingly, Lake Las Vegas was created as a *simulation* of Lake Como in Northern Italy, complete with "genuine" Italian gondolas. Lake Las Vegas's landscape of consumption includes MonteLago Village, including MonteLago Village Resort, which comes complete with streets with authentic-sounding Italian names. It encompasses three hotels—The Ritz-Carlton, Lake Las Vegas; Lowes Lake Las Vegas Resort; and the gambling at Casino MonteLago. Shopping and dining facilities are available not only in the hotels but also in MonteLago Village. Lake Las Vegas and, more important, the Las Vegas Strip are examples of landscapes of consumption. Thus, it is not just the development of the individual casino-hotels that is of great interest and significance, but so too is the larger geographic area that encompasses them (and many other cathedrals of consumption—for example, the increasingly ubiquitous shopping malls on the Strip such as the Forum Shops and Desert Passage, as well as great golf courses in both Las Vegas and Lake Las Vegas).

Beyond its own significance, the Las Vegas Strip (and other landscapes of consumption) has served as a model for the development of other social geographies devoted to consumption. This is especially true of the Cotai Strip (see below) under development in Macau. Pigeon Forge, Tennessee (see below), also developed a much smaller scale strip—the Parkway—albeit not one devoted to gambling. There are many other "strips" of consumption that have been influenced directly or indirectly by the one in Las Vegas. Indeed, "strips" devoted to consumption—a road packed on both sides with fast-food restaurants, gas stations, motels, strip malls, and so on—have become the most common landscapes of consumption in the United States. A large, but indeterminate, percentage of all consumption takes place in and around them. Of course, such a strip is only one of many geographic forms taken by

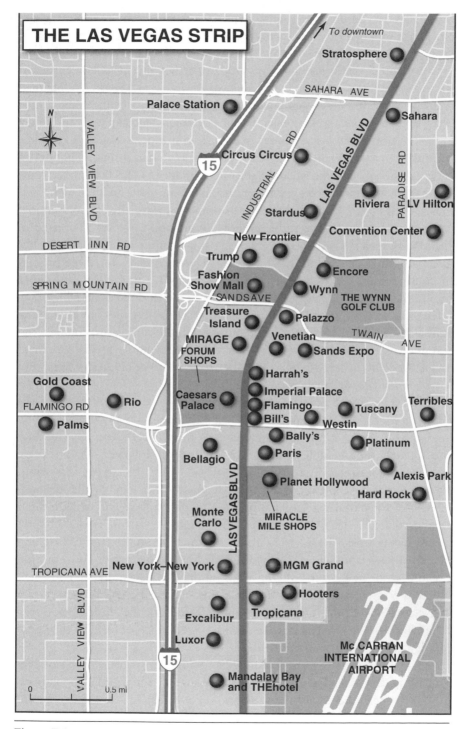

THE LAS VEGAS STRIP

Figure 7.1

landscapes of consumption, with others including a town "square," a city block, less well-defined areas surrounding theme parks and shopping malls, or even, as we will see, entire towns and cities (e.g., Dubai). Yet another is the "power center" that is anchored by a superstore but also includes a cluster of shops. Sometimes power centers locate near one another, creating a "regional retail center."[6] At a much more minute geographic level, even the home can be considered a landscape of consumption because it encompasses such new means of consumption as catalogs, television shopping channels, and online consumption sites. Whatever the scale, the essential point is that an important geographic configuration—a landscape of consumption—has taken new forms and has come to have increased importance in recent years, and it, like the various new means of consumption that it encompasses, is worthy of our attention.

As is the case with the cathedrals of consumption, we are interested in such landscapes not only because they are important new developments but also because of the way in which they have affected and altered the process of consumption. Consumption is different today because of, among other things, the new cathedrals of consumption *and* the landscapes on which they often exist. Like cathedrals of consumption, these landscapes not only allow people to consume, but they also encourage and, in some cases, compel consumption. Thus, landscapes of consumption may be more formally defined as *locales that encompass two or more settings that allow, encourage, and even compel people to consume.*

It could be argued that the globe, the modern world system, Europe, the United States, California, and New York City, among many others, are *all* landscapes of consumption because each of them is a geographic area that encompasses innumerable means of consumption. However, none of these is solely or focally devoted to consumption—many other types of settings exist and events transpire within these large-scale settings. While no landscape is devoted totally to consumption, our concern here will be with those settings that are heavily oriented to consumption. To make this chapter more manageable, the focus will be on much more circumscribed and delimited geographic areas that are defined as landscapes of consumption because of the new means of consumption that they encompass. Thus, neither Las Vegas, Nevada, nor, for example, Pigeon Forge, Tennessee, are considered in their entirety, but the "Strip" in the former and the "Parkway" in the latter are of great interest here and conform to our sense of a landscape of consumption.

While most of these locales will be geographic areas, that need not necessarily be the case. The definition is left vague enough (i.e., the general term *locales* is used rather than *geographic locales*) so that we can examine nongeographic locales as landscapes of consumption. For example, the Internet—or, more specifically, consumption sites on it—can be seen as forming a "locale," albeit one lacking a geographic dimension, at least in a traditional sense. Nevertheless, one can do a spatial analysis on the Internet as a landscape of consumption, focusing on the distribution of such means of consumption as cybermalls, cybershops, online casinos, and sites where one can purchase such things as corporate stocks and pornography.

To make matters a bit more confusing, the means of consumption themselves encompass geographic areas and can be analyzed from a geographic perspective. That is, many means of consumption *also* meet the definition of landscapes of consumption. For example, a mega-mall such as the Mall of America not only spans a fairly large geographic area but also includes several hundred different shops, restaurants, and theaters and an amusement park. Thus, a geographic analysis of a means of consumption is possible and quite useful.

However, in order not to confuse matters, we will not examine here the social geography of such means of consumption as the Mall of America (or the Bellagio in Las Vegas) but rather focus on the social geography of landscapes that, following the definition of this phenomenon, encompass two or more cathedrals of consumption. In this case, each of the cathedrals is separable from one another; often (although not always), the separation is physical, geographic.

ON SOCIAL GEOGRAPHY AND LANDSCAPES

This discussion clearly moves us in a different direction than the rest of this book and into a whole other intellectual tradition—social geography—than that which has come before (or will follow). This is not the place to offer an overview of that field, but a few introductory ideas are in order.[7]

A leading contemporary social geographer, Edward Soja, defines his orientation in ways that are consonant with the approach to be taken in this chapter.[8] He sees himself doing "a new critical human geography"[9] that is "consciously spatialized from the outset."[10] Soja is doing this from the perspective of neo-Marxian critical theory, but in his view, that theory (indeed all theory) has been dominated, even oppressed, by the issue of time, which led to the overwhelming preeminence of a concern for history (e.g., the historical development of capitalism) in that theory. Thus, heavily influenced by the work of the important social theorist Michel Foucault, he seeks to break out of the "carceral historicism of conventional critical theory."[11]

Foucault critiques the emphasis on time (and history) as well as the failure to deal with spatial issues: "Space was treated as the dead, the fixed, the undialectical, the immobile. Time, on the contrary, was richness, fecundity, life, dialectic."[12] However, Foucault believed that the situation was changing, and there was the possibility of reversing the tendency to privilege time over space:

> The present epoch will perhaps be above all the epoch of space. We are in the epoch of simultaneity: we are in the epoch of juxtaposition, the epoch of the near and far, of the side-by-side, of the dispersed. We are at a moment, I believe, when our experience of the world is less that of a long life developing through time than that of a network that connects points and intersects with its own skein.[13]

It is this kind of thinking that helped lead to greater scholarly interest in spatial issues and to the kind of (critical) social geography discussed in this chapter.

However, the key figure in the contemporary outburst of thinking about space is Henri Lefebvre, especially in his *The Production of Space*.[14] Also operating from a largely Marxist position, Lefebvre argues that we have moved from a concern with the "mode of production of things in space" to the "mode of production of space."[15] Politically, this means that the focus shifts from a struggle over the former to that of the latter. Space has come to be not only a means of production but also a means of control, domination, and power. As a Marxist, Lefebvre is interested in practice, both that which occurs in these spaces and that needed to revolutionize these spaces. Spaces, as well as the "pathologies" (hyperconsumption would be an example from the perspective of this book and from the point of view of the Great Recession) associated with them, are socially produced and can therefore be changed by revolutionary social action. Thus, to Lefebvre, "knowledge of space . . . implies the critique of space."[16] The principal stake in contemporary struggles in capitalism has shifted from the realm of production of things (especially commodities) to the production of space.

While we do not need to, indeed cannot, give the reader more than a taste of the vast literature on social geography, there is one specific work in that tradition that requires more detailed treatment here—Sharon Zukin's *Landscapes of Power*.[17] Like the other thinkers discussed above, Zukin is doing a social (or cultural) geography. However, what distinguishes her work from the others is its focus on the kinds of geographic settings—landscapes—of concern here. Furthermore, she has much to say, even more specifically, about landscapes of consumption. While she was not the first to apply the idea of landscapes to the kinds of settings of interest here, Zukin has made the greatest contribution to our understanding of this phenomenon.

The term *landscapes* has a long history in cultural geography. Indeed, there is an ancient geographic tradition known as *chorography*, which involves "the study of how landscapes bring different patterns together in unique ways."[18] Built into this idea is an approach that focuses on "individual and unique outcomes of combinations or circumstances."[19] While chorography is useful in providing historical context for the study of landscapes, it is not at all clear that today's landscapes of consumption are so unique. In fact, in many cases, they are composed of more and more similar elements (e.g., chain stores in shopping malls) and coming to look increasingly alike (e.g., the simulations, to be discussed below, of Las Vegas's Venetian in Macau and of the Bahamas's Atlantis Hotel in Dubai).

Less controversially, to Zukin, the term *landscapes* not only has "the usual geographical meaning of 'physical surroundings,' but it also refers to an ensemble of material and social practices and their symbolic representation." We can see all of these—physical surroundings, material and social practices, symbolic representations—in the landscapes of consumption of concern here.

Power is central to Zukin's notion of landscapes, the power of those in predominant classes, races, and gender over those who are subordinate in these areas. Thus, a landscape involves both those structures we associate with the powerful—"cathedrals, factories, and skyscrapers"—and those linked to the powerless—"village chapels, shantytowns, and tenements." However, the particular combination of these structures is always the result of a struggle between the powerful and the powerless, although "powerful institutions [especially economic] have a preeminent capacity to impose their view on the landscape—weakening, shaping, and displacing the view from the vernacular."[20] Given the nature of landscapes, it is the task of "economic geography to provide a sense of landscape's 'structured coherence.'"[21]

No matter how coherent they may be, landscapes of power are contested. For example, in describing the suburbs as landscapes of power, Zukin sees a contest between the power of large-scale, bureaucratic, economic structures and the power of individuals to define their own way of living. Beyond the suburbs, Zukin discusses other landscapes of power that are in line with the concerns of this book such as amusement parks like Disney World. All are the products of corporate power, but there are always contests with the vernacular, the commonplace, the everyday. Yet Zukin argues that in the long run, "a landscape of power gradually replaces the vernacular."[22] Economic elites may move from one investment landscape (e.g., the center city) to another (e.g., the suburbs), but in all cases, they seek to exercise power and gain control.

While Zukin's views on landscapes of power are useful, they raise several problems for us. First, while one of the main tasks here will be analysis of the "structured coherence" of several landscapes of consumption, we need to be sensitive to the fact that there is also incoherence in these landscapes. Second, it is by no means obvious that the structures of the poor[23] continue to exist in the landscapes of consumption. In fact, in at least some (e.g., the Las Vegas Strip), they have been largely uprooted and relegated to peripheral areas off the Strip. In other cases (e.g., Lake Las Vegas, the Palms in Dubai), new landscapes of consumption have been built that do not allow for any places for the poor (although poor people are allowed in to do menial and low-paid construction and service work). Third, there is the issue of the vernacular and what, if any, place it has in the landscapes of consumption.

It is difficult in Zukin's work to distinguish landscapes of consumption from the related concepts of "landscapes," "landscapes of power," and "landscapes of production." A landscape of consumption is a landscape, and it is also a landscape of power. Clearly, however, the emphasis is on consumption, and this would seem to distinguish it from a landscape of production (e.g., an industrial park). However, in some cases, the settings that Zukin includes under the heading of landscapes of consumption *also* involve production settings. For example, cities (e.g., Miami, Los Angeles) and suburbs (e.g., Westchester) are discussed, at least in part, as landscapes of consumption. What most interests Zukin is the shift within these landscapes from the domination of production to consumption, from places (defined as settings "where people put down roots"[24]; local communities) to the rootless and continually mobile locales that lack a sense of place. This also helps us to understand why Zukin defines "the shopping mall, the department store, and the museum" as landscapes of consumption.[25] These relatively new phenomena are markets that largely lack a sense of place.

Thus, Zukin's work, despite its utility, has a series of important limitations. The first is the kind of conceptual confusion and overlap discussed above. Second, while Zukin is much more aware of the importance of consumption than thinkers like Lefebvre and Soja, it remains secondary in her work. Published in the early 1990s, *Landscapes of Power* is heavily influenced by the changes in American production, especially deindustrialization, in the preceding decades. Thus, her first two case studies are of two steel industries in Weirton, West Virginia, and Detroit, Michigan, which are viewed as existing in two different geographic landscapes, as landscapes of devastation, and as new landscapes of production and power. Even the third case study, of Westchester, New York, is viewed at least in part as a landscape of deindustrialization and devastation (especially Yonkers, New York, which is part of Westchester). All three are also seen as landscapes defined by what Joseph Schumpeter described as "creative destruction."[26] Only Zukin's last two cases—studies of downtown New York, Chicago, and Boston and of the re-creation of an urban form in Miami, Los Angeles, and

Disney World—can be seen as emphasizing landscapes of consumption. Thus, while Zukin sees the shift from production to consumption as a defining structural change, she continues to devote at least as much attention to production as to consumption. Writing almost two decades later, and in a new century, we will be freer to jettison this productivist bias and truly focus on consumption, especially the landscapes of consumption.

LANDSCAPES OF CONSUMPTION

Clearly, innumerable delimited geographic spaces meet the definition of a landscape of consumption. We cannot deal with them all, or with all types, but in the remainder of this chapter, we will focus on three broad types. The first is a landscape that has undergone only *minor change* in recent years; our example is the area around the main cathedral, the Duomo, in Milan, Italy. The second is an *entirely new* landscape of consumption, although one that is threatened by the Great Recession; the examples are Easton Town Center in Columbus, Ohio; Dubai, United Arab Emirates; and the Cotai Strip, Macau, China. The third type is a landscape of consumption *in decline*; Pigeon Forge, Tennessee, is our example.

The discussion of the geographic area around the Duomo in Milan makes it clear that landscapes of consumption are certainly nothing new—indeed, they have ancient roots in marketplaces and squares devoted to consumption. Similarly, the great (and not so great) cities of the world have had central areas devoted to consumption for centuries. Examples include Fifth Avenue, Broadway, and 42nd Street in New York; Bond, Regent, and Oxford Streets in London; the Kurfurstendam in Berlin; the Champs Elysées and Rue du Faubourg Saint Honoré in Paris; and many others.[27] However, almost all of the locales mentioned above have been altered, some dramatically, in recent years. Indeed, many of these older landscapes of consumption have been transformed by the movement into them of many of the new means of consumption.

This leads to the question: What exactly is new here? In fact, the same question arises with reference to the "new" means of consumption and consumption more generally. While we have treated the fully enclosed shopping mall as something new, it has its roots in earlier strip malls, to say nothing of the arcades of Paris (and other major cities of the world, including the galleria to be discussed in Milan) in the early 19th century. The pace of consumption has been accelerated in the new cathedrals and landscapes of consumption, but the nature of what is consumed has also been altered. Earlier cathedrals and landscapes of consumption mainly sold things, but increasingly, the new cathedrals and landscapes also sell experiences, including the experience of the cathedral and/or landscape itself.[28] This is nowhere clearer than the Las Vegas Strip and the casino-hotels that dominate it. The strollers along the Strip are consuming it as well as the casinos that line it. Of course, what is most obviously new about the new landscapes of consumption is the inclusion, if not the increasing preeminence, of the new means of consumption.

The Changing Nature of the Landscapes of Consumption

Before we get to the three types of landscapes of consumption of concern here, it is important to note that these are not static spaces; they are constantly changing. This is always true, but it is especially clear in the current economic downturn. We will discuss the problems in Las Vegas and on the Strip in Chapter 8, but suffice it note that there are major problems there, including the fact that empty lots and unfinished casino-hotels can be seen on the Strip. If the current downturn is severe enough and lasts long enough, we could even see the closing of some of the landmark casino-hotels on the Strip. In terms of the landscapes to be discussed below, even the relatively new and dynamic ones—Easton, Dubai, the Cotai Strip—are being adversely affected by the recession. Pigeon Forge has undergone a major decline with, for example, many of its best-known country music show theaters no longer there. It appears to have grown increasingly threadbare and may be in the process of being replaced by Gatlinburg, which is just down the road. New cathedrals of consumption have appeared there, and it may come to the preferred route into the Great Smoky Mountains National Park. Finally, the landscape to be discussed first in the center of Milan has undergone the least change, undoubtedly because it has existed there for centuries.

Seemingly Minor Changes in a Landscape of Consumption: Milan, Italy

Cheek-to-jowl in a landscape of consumption in the heart of Milan, Italy, are four cathedrals of consumption that represent three very different epochs in the history of such settings (see Figure 7.2). The first is the Duomo, or cathedral, begun in 1386, continued in the 15th and 16th centuries, and completed in the early 1800s on the orders of Napoleon. The second is the Galleria Vittorio Emanuele, an arcade (see the discussion of Benjamin's classic work on arcades in Chapter 3) constructed in the late 1800s. Third, there is a department store, La Rinascente, that is an excellent example of a late-19th-century department store (the department store itself, as was discussed in Chapter 3, has roots in the mid-19th century, and the sources of the arcades date back even earlier). Finally, among other seemingly minor late-20th-century additions, there are two McDonald's (as well as a Burger King).

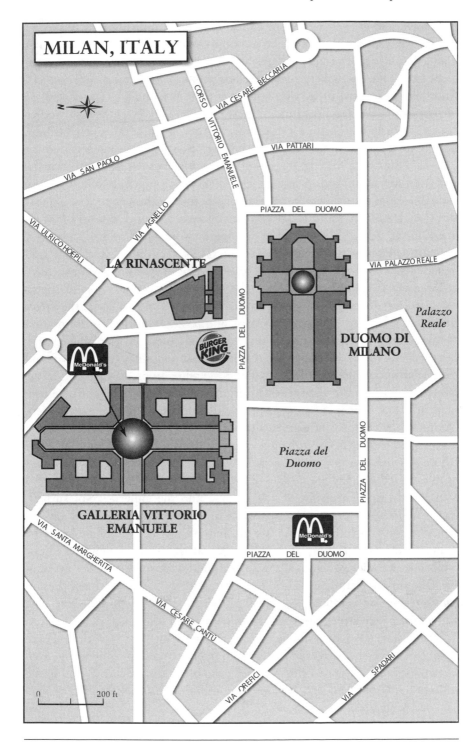

Figure 7.2

The Duomo is a setting for the consumption of a range of religious experiences. The galleria is an arcade that houses a wide array of shops and cafés that sell a far wider range of goods and services. La Rinascente is a department store that, by its very nature, sells a similarly wide range of products. And there is no need to tell you what it is that McDonald's sells. There are obviously huge differences among these four settings as cathedrals and as places of consumption, but in the end, they are all cathedrals of consumption, at least as that notion is conceived in its broadest sense in this book.

To set the scene for this discussion, as well as for the physical location of these four consumption settings and their proximity to one another, let us take a brief tour beginning at one of the four entrances to the Galleria Vittorio Emanuele, the one across a small square from the world-famous opera house Teatro alla Scala.[29] Looming in front of shoppers (or merely strollers—*flaneurs*[30]—or window shoppers) as they enter is a large and magnificent covered arcade with a wide variety of cafés and shops, many quite upscale, lining both sides of the covered passageway. As shoppers reach the middle of the passage and the midpoint in the galleria, they realize that it is shaped like a cross;[31] a second passageway intersects the first at this central point. Standing at this gorgeously tiled center of the arcade, shoppers can look up and see the stunning steel-and-glass roof or turn and see beautiful passageways leading off in four directions. Continuing in the direction to which the shoppers set out, they soon reach the end of the passage and enter onto a great esplanade dominated by the magnificent Duomo, deemed one of the great cathedrals of the world. It is built of white marble and is bedecked with numerous belfries, gables, and statues. The Duomo dwarfs the impressive arcade both in size and in the magnificence of its architecture. Off to the side of the Duomo is La Rinascente. Where is McDonald's in relationship to the Duomo and the galleria? Not surprisingly, it occupies prominent positions in *both* the galleria and on the esplanade on which the Duomo is built. In the galleria, McDonald's is to be found at the very center, at the intersection of the passageways. In the esplanade, another McDonald's is to be found almost directly across from the Duomo (reflecting its secondary status as a fast-food chain, Burger King's restaurant is much less centrally placed but is close to La Rinascente and across a side street from the Duomo).

As an aside, it is worth noting that McDonald's, and its many clones, have routinely placed themselves in the heart of many of the most important, even sacred, locations in the world. Another example is the Starbucks *within* the walls of the Forbidden City, the ancient home of China's emperors in Beijing. Said one Beijing resident on the Web, "Opening a coffee shop in the Forbidden City is like splattering black paint on the portrait of Chairman Mao on

Tiananmen Square."³² At least some observers likely react in a similar way to the McDonald's in the galleria and across the esplanade from the Duomo.

The placement of these cathedrals of consumption is interesting and revealing. It is not surprising that the Duomo would have been positioned at, or become, the heart of a major city in such a largely Catholic country as Italy. More interesting, albeit also not surprising, is the placement of the galleria adjacent to the Duomo and with an entrance onto the esplanade in front of it.

Clearly, and quite sensibly, its designers wanted to take advantage of the crowds that were passing through and around the Duomo. The idea was that many of those who went to the Duomo to "consume" religion could be lured into the galleria to consume many far more prosaic goods and services. Similarly, La Rinascente was positioned to take advantage of the crowds drawn to both the Duomo and the galleria. Much the same logic informed the placement of McDonald's and Burger King. In the case of the former, many of the masses of people in and around the Duomo would see the "golden arches" and be drawn to McDonald's for a quick meal. Similarly, in the case of the galleria, whatever passageway one entered, one would eventually come to its center and there one would find the McDonald's restaurant. It is interesting to note, by the way, that as one approaches the center of the galleria, one must pass by the cafés (examples of what have been called "great good places"³³), many with seating in the passageways themselves, that are the forerunners of McDonald's as means of consuming food and drink and that are fast being driven out of business in many locales by the expansion of McDonaldized chains of restaurants.

What we find, then, are cathedrals of consumption representative of very different epochs that have come to coexist at this central point in Milan (and many other places in the world).

While there are important similarities among and between central Milan's four most important means of consumption, there are also important differences.

While all four are means of consumption, that is not to say that they are structured or function in the same way. While we can think of religion, a wide array of commodities, and fast food as consumables, there are important differences among them as well as the settings in which they are purveyed. Take, for example, the issue of consumption time. The Duomo is built to allow those who so wish to spend almost endless amounts of time sitting in the pews and gaining the consolation they need. The galleria and its shops are constructed to encourage a leisurely stroll, a cup of coffee or a glass of wine at one of the cafés, and relaxed stops in whatever shops (except, perhaps, in McDonald's) catch the consumer's eye. However, while a stay in the galleria might be quite lengthy, it is not likely to be as long as the stays of the true believers in the Duomo. The galleria encourages a leisurely pace, but not nearly as leisurely as that inspired and permitted by the Duomo. La Rinascente also encourages a leisurely exploration of counters and the department store's many floors, but it is not nearly as unhurried as that encouraged by the galleria (or the Duomo). Of course, the situation in McDonald's is very different. Instead of lengthy contemplation, leisurely perusal of shop windows and counters, or enjoyment of a leisurely drink at an outside table of one of the cafés in the galleria, the pace in the fast-food restaurant is frenetic. The restaurant places a premium on getting people in, fed, and out as rapidly as possible—and customers generally happily comply. This reflects the fact that the fast-food restaurant is the most rationalized of these settings, the Duomo the least, with the galleria and the department store somewhere in the middle.

The structure and ambiance of each of these settings also contribute to this difference in the duration of the consumer's stay. The cavernous church, the hushed tones, and the many seats, most of which are unoccupied most of the time, invite a leisurely stay. People are not rushing about, and there are no officials to urge visitors to leave quickly. The passageways and the numerous shop windows and cafés in the galleria are conducive to leisurely strolls, but they are limited by the fact that the passageways are not very long and can be traversed rather quickly, even by the most leisurely of strollers, and there are not that many shop windows in which to gaze (far fewer than in today's shopping malls). While there are other leisurely strollers, there is also a lot of feverish activity in the arcade, including consumers who are rushing through to buy what they need. In the department store, there are innumerable counters on many floors, and this encourages those who want to wander at a leisurely pace through the store. However, there are also many there to purchase a specific item, and their pace is much more rapid. The large number of people who are often found in McDonald's, and the fact that they are generally in a rush, creates the most frantic pace, one that is not conducive to eating a leisurely meal. Other factors militating against such a meal are the cleanup crews that seem ever ready to pounce on the diner's table as soon as the meal seems to be nearing its completion, the press of other diners in search of a table, and the famous chairs designed to make the consumer uncomfortable after only a short period of time.

Most generally, the key point, at least in comparison to the other two case studies covered in this chapter, is that the area of Milan of concern here has experienced comparatively minor changes in recent years. The main change of interest in this context is the addition of a few fast-food restaurants. These humble storefronts are dwarfed by the colossal older means of consumption—the Duomo, the galleria, and the department store. Thus, we are describing in this section comparatively minor changes in a much larger landscape of consumption.

However, it is safe to say that these humble changes have had a disproportionate impact on the landscape. For one thing, they are in highly visible places and make a strong impression on the visitor. For another, they are quite jarring in the sense that they are clearly representative of a very different epoch in the history of consumption than the other cathedrals of consumption and seem out of place in this setting. They are also jarring because their very humbleness stands in stark contrast to the majesty of the classic cathedrals of consumption that surround them. And we cannot ignore the fact that these humble and out-of-place fast-food restaurants seem to attract more than their share of diners. Thus, while the recent changes in the environs of the Duomo in Milan may be minor, their impact is much greater than it appears on the surface.

Nevertheless, the landscape of consumption under consideration in Milan is, and has been, much more stable than those to be discussed next.

New (but Threatened) Landscapes of Consumption: Easton Town Center, Ohio;[34] Dubai, United Arab Emirates; Cotai Strip, Macau, China

Easton Town Center. The "town" of Easton Town Center in Columbus, Ohio, "opened" in June 1999 and within 2 years had doubled in size. It is described here as being threatened because of the Great Recession, which poses a danger to all cathedrals of consumption, especially those devoted to consumption. Many shopping malls have closed, and most others have empty stores. Despite its early success, Easton Town Center is likely to experience similar difficulties (for example, the McDonald's there closed some time ago). It is likely to survive these threats, but it will need to be monitored as the recession unfolds.

All towns and, on a larger scale, cities have had their landscapes of consumption. In some cases, towns and, less likely, larger cities (especially the world's great tourist cities) have come to be dominated by consumption sites and landscapes. However, what is new about Easton Town Center is that it was created *as* a landscape of consumption.[35] That is, it was not, at least originally, a town in which people lived and that developed consumption sites to satisfy the needs of residents and/or those who came to town from the hinterlands to purchase needed goods and services. Indeed, there were no residents, at least at first. Rather, Easton Town Center was, and is, a landscape of consumption designed to be a "destination" for consumers. It is unlike the planned communities mentioned in this book—Celebration,

Kentlands—which were created primarily as places of residence and secondarily to encompass landscapes of consumption aimed primarily at the needs of residents. In Easton, the situation is reversed, and a landscape of consumption has been created as a town without, at least initially, residents and one where residents have been added primarily to suit the needs (e.g., for employees) of the cathedrals of consumption. Despite this reversal, this focus on consumption, the developer is seen as representing the epitomization of the "new urbanism" (reflected, especially, in suburban developments that resemble small towns) that lies at the base of Celebration and Kentlands.[36] In fact, it was the recipient of the 2000 International Council of Shopping Center's Award for Innovative Design and Construction of a New Project.

Of course, Easton is not "really" a city, or is it? In most ways, it is a large shopping center within the confines of a larger city, Columbus, Ohio. However, it is huge (with 1.7 million square feet of retail space, hotel, and residential properties), it sits on approximately 1,200 acres, and it has streets (or "streetscapes"), metered parking spaces, open-air town squares, fountains, parks for children, and outdoor shops. More important, it has more than 3 million square feet of office space, about the same amount of office space available in downtown Columbus. There are also three hotels to house out-of-town visitors as well as attendees of the many conventions held there. However, what makes Easton most interesting is that hundreds of apartments have been constructed. Thus, it not only looks like a town, but with the addition of these apartments, it has become a town, or at least a town within a city (of Columbus). In fact, the developer now regrets not putting apartments among the shops rather than making them a separate development. A later project—Kansas City's Zona Rosa—has done just that with 60 apartments placed in the center of the retail area.[37] To make Easton feel more like a town, there are six city blocks, and the streets are often lined with two-story red-brick buildings with a number of street-front restaurants and cafés; parking is on the street (the two parking garages are found at the edges of the development); the scale of the development has been kept small so that visitors are not overwhelmed by the size of the structures and can easily walk from one site to another; the library is, in fact, a Barnes & Noble; and the art deco movie theater actually houses Pottery Barn. "At the center of it all is a small park, where parents can relax on benches while children play in the fountains; in the summer there are concerts, and it is the scene of holiday activities in the winter."[38] Said the president of the design and development company that took the lead in creating Easton, "I look at it as this Norman Rockwell middle America hometown vernacular."[39]

A number of other measures have been undertaken to make Easton feel and appear more like a small town. There are bright red phone booths on many street corners, some of the roadways are brick, and the town police car looks like a 1950s-style cruiser. During the Christmas season, there is a parade and a ceremony to light the town tree, horse-drawn carriages are available to take one around town (for a small fee, of course), and carolers in period clothing roam the "town," which is lit by more than a half-million white lights. Easton also offers a community room free of charge to local groups, has a booth available to groups interested in public exposure, donates all proceeds from its parking meters to local charities, and recently established a scholarship program for two local high schools. It is such efforts that won Easton a 2003 Business First Corporate Caring Award.

The historic emphasis in towns and cities of creating living space has been reversed here with consumption sites—especially new means of consumption—coming first. Furthermore, Easton will always be more of a consumption site than a living space. This reversal of historic emphasis helps us to associate Easton with hyperconsumption. The result is a site designed to foster such a heightened level of consumption; it is a site of hyperconsumption. Reflective of this are the data that show that Easton does more business per square foot than traditional malls. And it is designed to be the kind of destination that will lure consumers over great distances to engage in such an exaggerated level of consumption. Hotels offer "experience Easton" vacation packages (including various incentives) for those who come from more than 50 miles away.

Thus, while Easton in particular and the new landscapes of consumption in general are continuous with earlier forms, there is something qualitatively different about them. John Urry uses the term *cities of consumption* (as opposed to traditional *industrial cities*), and although Urry is thinking of more traditional shopping malls, this idea fits Easton (as well as the other landscapes of consumption to be discussed below—Dubai and the Cotai Strip) even better.[40] First, whereas in the past, living was prioritized over consumption, in the new landscapes, consumption is granted priority. Second, they tend to be dominated by new means of consumption. Third, they are settings that are structured to be conducive to high levels of consumption. Finally, in fact they succeeded, at least in the past, in leading people in the direction of this heightened level of consumption.

That there is something new here is reflected in the fact that observers are struggling to come up with a new term for Easton and what it represents. Some terms that one runs across to describe Easton (and locales like it such as CocoWalk in Miami) are *streetscape, lifestyle center, town-center-style center, new urban retail,* or *neo-village.*[41] In fact, with strip malls and even some traditional fully enclosed malls now showing signs of weakness, the trend is toward outdoor landscapes like that found in Easton. However, while most of these are shopping centers designed to look like towns,[42] Easton (belatedly) has become a town.

One the ironies associated with Easton is that it is designed to be a simulated small town center, but the new means of consumption that were built on the outskirts of "real" small towns—like the shopping mall, as well as discounters such as Wal-Mart and superstores such as Bed Bath & Beyond— bore a heavy responsibility for their demise. The historic pattern was for Wal-Mart, for example, to open on the outskirts of a relatively small town and quickly devastate downtown businesses, turning the area into a ghost town. Interestingly, in recent years, some of the big box stores (or superstores) have been failing (nearly 250 Wal-Mart stores in the United States are wholly or partially empty), and huge empty stores and lots now also litter the American landscape.[43]

Ironically, Easton is having a similar impact on neighboring malls. The one in downtown Columbus—City Center—is nearly empty (its last anchor, Macy's, closed in 2007). In addition, Northland, a nearby traditional shopping mall, was forced to close its doors in 2002 because of competition from Easton; it was demolished in 2004.

To what degree does Easton, as a landscape of consumption, use the techniques discussed throughout this book to create the spectacle needed to attract large numbers of consumers (and some permanent residents)? As is clear above, most obvious is the use of simulation—a simulated small-town center—to create a spectacle.[44]

Easton certainly uses implosion since many of today's best-known means of consumption have collapsed into it. Thus, in addition to the Barnes & Noble and the Pottery Barn, there is a huge movie theater complex (*not* in Pottery Barn's ersatz art deco theater) with 30 screens, an indoor shopping mall with nearly 200 tenants, and much more.

We have previously mentioned the use of enormous spaces to create spectacle. In one way, Easton employs this device since it encompasses such a large geographic area and so many cathedrals of consumption. However, what is interesting about Easton is that it *also* seeks to underwhelm (Disney's "Main Street" does much the same thing; see Chapter 8) rather than overwhelm the visitor with the size. The idea is to make the space seem manageable, so the streets are narrow, they are lined with buildings restricted in height, store ceiling heights inside the buildings are limited to about 13 feet, distances between settings are small (thus it, like other lifestyle centers, has "walkability"[45]), big box stores (e.g., Gaylan's) and the three large hotels are on the periphery of the town and are carefully placed so that they do not loom over the central area (and they do not block or overwhelm the vistas available to visitors), and so on.

Because it is outdoors, Easton is able to do less with the manipulation of time than indoor spaces, which can manipulate lighting and cover over windows to prevent the visitor from having a sense of time of day and of time passing. However, the vibrant small-town environment and active street life are designed to get people to linger longer and stay later. Several nighttime hot spots have turned Easton into an 18-hour-a-day operation. Yet there is manipulation of time here, especially in the form of giving Easton the feel of a small town from an earlier period of American history. This is reflected in efforts to associate it with things like Norman Rockwell's early to mid-20th-century artwork and the *Ozzie and Harriet* television show of the 1950s. Thus, in addition to other touches already mentioned, "there is an old-time ice cream shop."[46] Overall, while Easton may use some of the techniques somewhat differently, the fact remains that simulation, implosion, and manipulations of space and time are at the heart of creating spectacle there as they are in the cathedrals of consumption discussed throughout this book.

While Easton was founded to be a new landscape of consumption, other areas and even whole towns are moving dramatically in a similar direction. For example, the cathedral town of Canterbury, England, has undergone a major transformation. Once a city subordinated to the famous cathedral and primarily a place in which people lived and, as a result, shopped, Canterbury has been transformed into a town that is increasingly almost solely about consumption. Of course, it has long been about the consumption of religion and of the architecture of the cathedral as well as of the religious experience that it housed, but more recently, the major new means of consumption (e.g., chain stores of many types) from around England and the world have been drawn to it in order to create outlets within its confines. As a result of the demand for space created by the chains, fewer residents can afford the increasing rents and housing costs. In any case, living space is giving way to commercial space. In fact, it could be argued that Canterbury is moving in the direction of Easton, and in the end, there will be little (except for the age of the buildings) to differentiate the two. That is, there will be little difference between a town created as a landscape of consumption and an older town that has been transformed into one. While some residents will remain in Canterbury, the town will increasingly be a shopping destination for tourists headed to see the cathedral as well as for locals from the surrounding communities. Coming from opposite directions, the creation of Easton and the transformation of Canterbury make it abundantly clear that a sea change is taking place in the landscapes of consumption, as well as in what we think of as towns and at least small cities.

Of course, it could be argued that Canterbury has been a landscape of consumption for centuries (the beginnings of the cathedral are traceable to 597 A.D.). While some of the means of consumption that grew up in the town existed for residents, many others catered to those who were visiting to see and attend services at the cathedral. However, what is different today is the increasing ubiquity of the new means of consumption in Canterbury. For example, Starbucks now occupies a building that is adjacent to the entrance to the cathedral (at least it's not *in* the cathedral—at least not *yet*). In addition, with fewer and fewer residents, these new means of consumption are increasingly there to serve visitors and tourists. In a way, even the residents and locals can be thought of as tourists—*tourists in their own community*. As such developments accelerate in more and more communities, we can increasingly be thought of as tourists (and consumers) in our own living spaces.

Dubai, United Arab Emirates. No global locale demonstrates the spectacular landscapes and cathedrals of consumption (and their stunning reverses in the Great Recession[47]), as well as their globalization, better than Dubai, especially the Palm Islands (Palm Jumeirah, Palm Jebel Ali, and Palm Deira) being built with sand trucked in from the desert and reclaimed from the sea around Dubai. Also created in the Persian Gulf is the World—300 manmade islands literally simulating the shape of the world, some of which sold for between $15 and $45 million.[48] However, Dubai itself can be seen, at least to a large degree, as a landscape of consumption that encompasses not only the above but also numerous malls and mega-malls, condominiums, hotels, and, in the planning stages, an amusement area that will dwarf all of Disney's worlds together.

The Palm Islands (Figure 7.3) are of special interest as landscapes of consumption within (or, really, just off the shore of) Dubai. Under construction as I write, these are to be the three largest artificial (simulated) islands in the world—the product of the largest land reclamation project ever undertaken. All three are to be islands shaped, albeit somewhat differently, as palm trees and surrounded with crescents (that also serve as breakwaters). All three are spectacular because of their enormity (the largest, Palm Deira, is planned to be bigger than Paris). All together, the Palm Islands will add over 500 kilometers of beaches to Dubai. Also spectacular is the way in which they were, and are being, created through massive movements of sand and rock. Over 100 million cubic meters of sand and rock each were required to form Palm Jumeirah and Palm Jebel Ali. They are minuscule in comparison to Palm Deira, which will require 1 billion cubic meters of sand and rock. It will dwarf Palm Jumeirah, already the largest manmade island in the world.

Of course, the developers were not content with the spectacle of the islands themselves. The islands are to be populated by luxury hotels, theme parks, shopping malls, condominiums, and the like; in other words, each will be a distinct landscape of consumption (and all three islands, taken together, will be an even more spectacular landscape of consumption).

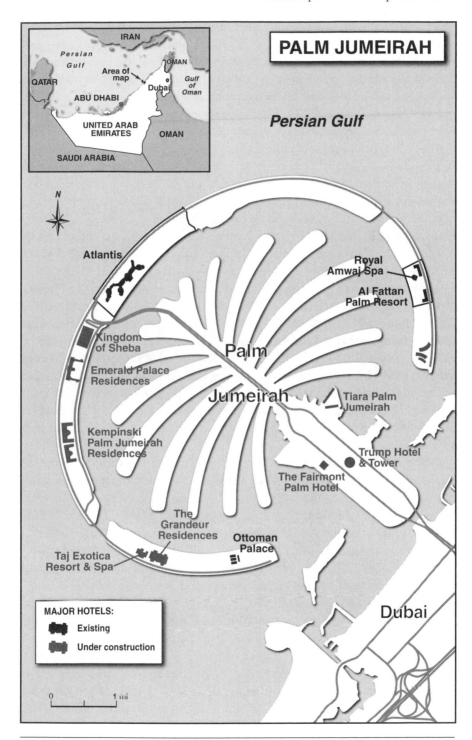

Figure 7.3

This massive project was undertaken despite many dangers and risks. For example, no one knows how well the islands will stand up over time and whether they can survive the hoped-for but now likely illusory, at least for the foreseeable future, massive influx of visitors and condo residents. In addition, it is not clear how the development, and the huge amount of dredging that was needed, will affect the ecology of the area. It is also not clear how much the project will cost, but given the magnitude of the work involved in creating the islands, the costs will be astronomical.

Palm Jumeirah is the furthest along, but the others are under construction as well. There are elaborate plans for each, but given the current economic downturn, it remains to be seen how quickly they will be completed and what proportion of the plans will be fulfilled in the near future. The Atlantis Hotel opened in late 2008 on Palm Jumeirah, and a number of other hotels, residences, and so on are completed, under construction, or planned. Among them are the following with scheduled opening dates (original and in some cases already delayed[49]) in parentheses: the Fairmont Palm Hotel (2009; now projected for 2010), Tiara Palm Jumeirah (late 2007; now projected for 2009), Jumeirah Al Fattan Palm Resort (2009), Grandeur Residences (2009), Kempinski Hotel Emerald Palace (2009), Kingdom of Sheba (2009), Royal Amwaj (2009), Taj Exotica Resort & Spa (2009), and Trump International Hotel and Tower (now on hold). To allow people to get from the mainland to Palm Jumeirah, a monorail (Las Vegas has such a monorail) is being built between Gateway Station on the island and the Atlantis Station on its crescent. There will also be a 300-meter bridge to the island, as well as a tunnel under the sea to the crescent.

Beyond the shopping available at the hotels on Palm Jumeirah, there will be an outdoor shopping street—The Golden Mile—and a giant indoor mall aptly named Luxury Mall. And there will be a simulated version of an early cathedral of consumption, a souk, a "traditional" Middle Eastern bazaar where "meandering paths lead visitors through a bazaar-like atmosphere in which open-fronted shops and intimate galleries spill into paved walkways."[50] It includes 75 boutique shops and 23 cafés, bars, and restaurants all on the waterfront. It has a 442-seat theater and even air-conditioned walkways to help visitors continue to shop despite the often extreme desert heat.

To add to the spectacle, two F-100 Super Sabre jets were sunk off the coast of Palm Jumeirah. They are to create an artificial reef so that divers can enjoy the marine life that will congregate in and around the planes. The one-time flagship of the Cunard line, HMS *Queen Elizabeth 2,* was purchased in mid-2007 so that it can be refurbished and serve as a floating hotel off Palm Jumeirah. The QE2 is, of course, itself an older cathedral of consumption, but it will now just be one of many on and off the coast of Dubai.

However, the cathedrals of consumption on Palm Jumeirah, as well as those to be constructed there and on the other Palms, only scratch the surfaced of the cathedrals of consumption already built, under construction, or planned for Dubai. Even in the current downturn, building cranes are everywhere as are construction workers (although the numbers of both are down significantly from the peak before the beginning of the recession). Many huge skyscrapers are already in existence, and many others are under construction. The skyline is quite a spectacle. It (like Las Vegas) was clearly planned that way in order to draw tourists to what is otherwise a torrid and in many other ways an unappealing, even forbidding, desert locale. In fact, Dubai exemplifies the idea of spectacle perfectly because few people would go there to live and to consume were it not for the man-made spectacles.

Dubai's shopping malls are both numerous and spectacular. Take the following examples:

• The Dubai Mall opened in late 2008, and when it is complete, it will house 1,200 stores. Imploded into it are a gold *souk*, an aquarium, and an ice rink.

• The Mall of the Emirates has 350 shops, a 400-room Kempinski hotel, and most notably a 400-meter indoor ski slope (copied by Xanadu).

• The Ibn Battuta mall is themed à la Disney World. It encompasses six worlds—India, Persia, Egypt, China, Tunisia, and Andalucia. It also encompasses a 21-screen cinema and the only IMAX in the United Arab Emirates.

• Wafi is a mall shaped like a pyramid (à la the Luxor in Las Vegas), and imploded into it are both Planet Hollywood and Khan Murjan—a simulation of a 14th-century souk.

• Mercato is a mall with Italian, Spanish, and French Renaissance architecture and themes.

In the planning stages, and undoubtedly delayed by the Great Recession, is Dubailand, which will encompass 107 square miles, have six themed worlds, and be twice as large as *all* of the Disneyland/Disney World theme parks combined.[51] It is planned to eventually be a city that encompasses, among many other things, a number of theme parks (including Six Flags), an equestrian and polo club, an autodrome, golf city, Mall of Arabia (planned to be the largest in the world), and the Great Dubai Wheel (planned to be second only to the observation wheel in Shanghai).

It seems clear, assuming the likely event that oil prices and oil wealth rise dramatically once again, that most of the cathedrals of consumption planned for and under construction in Dubai will eventually be completed. It is even possible that the number of cathedrals of consumption, and the spectacle offered by them, will expand dramatically in the coming years. While other parts of the world may well see a slowdown in, or even the devolution of, some of the cathedrals of consumption, the revolution in this realm is likely continue apace, if not accelerate, in Dubai. The same is true, although to a lesser degree, in the next landscape of consumption to be discussed—Macau. However, in Macau's case, the motor force will not be oil prices but the booming economy of China (for more on this, see Chapter 8).

Cotai Strip, Macau, China. Macau is an island off the tip of China that has had gambling since the 1850s. In more recent years, the giant firms from Las Vegas have built copies of (simulations[52]) of Las Vegas casino-hotels in the older hotel-casino area of Macau. That area can be seen as a landscape of consumption within the larger such landscape that is Macau.

Even more recently, these corporations have been moving in the direction of the further "Las Vegasification" of Macau by developing the Cotai Strip (a separable landscape of consumption) designed not only to resemble but to rival the Las Vegas Strip (Figure 7.4). The U.S.-based Sands Corporation (the name comes from one of Las Vegas's early and legendary cathedrals of consumption, imploded to make way for the Venetian) owns, and is building, casino-hotels, on the Cotai Strip. The casino-hotels in Macau, especially on the Strip, are themselves simulations of the "originals" in Las Vegas, and none is a better example of this than the Venetian (owned by the Sands Corporation), which opened in August 2008.[53] It is a simulation of a simulation (the "original" Venetian in Las Vegas), which, itself, is a simulation of Venice, Italy (which as a tourist city may now be a simulation of itself). Like its predecessor in Las Vegas, the Macau Venetian has a Cirque de Soleil arena and show—ZAIA (Cirque de Soleil has simulated its shows in many locations). Venetian Macau also reflects the importance of time and space in creating spectacular simulations. Like its counterpart in Las Vegas, it seeks to resemble and embed itself in old Venice. Like all Vegas-style casino-hotels, it emphasizes its size. The fact that it is the largest building (10.5 million square feet) in Asia says it all. Beyond that, it has 3,000 guest rooms (all suites), more than 30 restaurants, and 1.2 million square feet for conventions and meetings. It also claims to have the world's largest casino with 3,000 slot machines and 750 gambling tables. And it illustrates implosion in that it encompasses both a large (1 million square feet) shopping mall (Grand Canal Shoppes) with over 350 shops *and* the 15,000-seat Cotai Arena.[54]

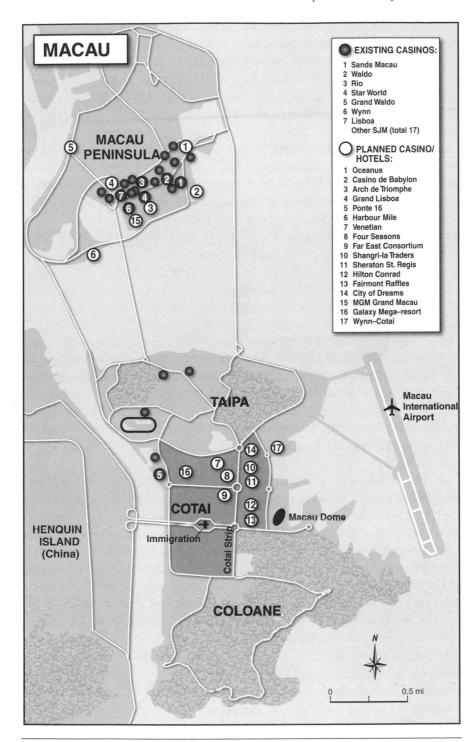

MACAU

EXISTING CASINOS:
1 Sands Macau
2 Waldo
3 Rio
4 Star World
5 Grand Waldo
6 Wynn
7 Lisboa
Other SJM (total 17)

PLANNED CASINO/
HOTELS:
1 Oceanus
2 Casino de Babylon
3 Arch de Triomphe
4 Grand Lisboa
5 Ponte 16
6 Harbour Mile
7 Venetian
8 Four Seasons
9 Far East Consortium
10 Shangri-la Traders
11 Sheraton St. Regis
12 Hilton Conrad
13 Fairmont Raffles
14 City of Dreams
15 MGM Grand Macau
16 Galaxy Mega–resort
17 Wynn–Cotai

MACAU
PENINSULA

TAIPA

Macau
International
Airport

COTAI

HENQUIN
ISLAND
(China)

Immigration

Cotai Strip

Macau Dome

COLOANE

N

0   0.5 mi

Figure 7.4

A number of other major casino-hotels are being built or are planned for the Cotai Strip, including projects from Las Vegas–based MGM MIRAGE and Wynn. Given the future economic growth of China, the source of a large proportion of Macau's gamblers, they are likely to be built as are other casino-hotels on the Cotai Strip. In the end, it seems likely that Macau in general, and the Cotai Strip in particular, will be a world-class landscape of consumption like Dubai.

Nevertheless, there are currently signs of trouble in these two locales. In Dubai, the Atlantis on Palm Jumeirah had a $20 million star-studded opening in late 2008 that was highlighted by an over-the-top fireworks display that literally could have been seen from space. Shortly afterward, the state-controlled Dubai company (Nakheel) involved in the development of Palm Jumeirah laid off 500 people—15% of its global employees. Said a Lebanese businessman, "The people with Nakheel spend $20 million on fireworks and don't have money to pay their own people . . . It's a disaster."[55]

A more important indicator of deep problems is the decision by Nakheel to halt work on its huge $38 billion project, the Nakheel Harbor and Tower in Dubai. It was to have been twice as high as the Empire State Building and higher than the tallest skyscraper in the world, the 162-story, 818-meter (2,700 foot) high Burj Dubai[56] currently under construction nearby and scheduled for completion in December 2009.[57] The Nakheel Tower was planned to be almost 2,000 feet *taller* than Burj Dubai. Spectacle is being created on a monumental scale in Dubai. However, the Burj Dubai, too, is in trouble, with sales on its condominiums (its high-end condos are known as the Armani Residences) dropping sharply and asking prices being cut by as much as 50%.[58]

In Macau, a number of construction projects have been halted or put on hold. This is closely related to the global economic crisis, but other factors are in play such as the fact that China, apparently concerned about the gambling problems of some of its citizens, has restricted travel to Macau through visas that limit visitors to one trip of no longer than 7 days in a 3-month period.[59] What is especially troubling is the decline, and potential bankruptcy, of the Las Vegas Sands Corporation. In late 2008, the company reported a huge shortfall in its ability to handle fixed charges, and there was fear that it would lead to defaults on almost $9 billion in long-term loans.[60] The corporation is having problems elsewhere in the world, including the construction of a casino-hotel at Marina Bay in Singapore. Work continues there, buoyed by the fact that the Singapore government considers it "too big to fail," and there is talk of the Singapore Tourism Board taking over much of the Sands's debt in order to complete the project.[61] It may turn out that the developments in Dubai and Macau will also be deemed too big to fail by the local governments.

A Landscape of Consumption in Decline: Pigeon Forge, Tennessee

While virtually everyone knows a great deal about Las Vegas, few who read this chapter are likely to know very much about Pigeon Forge, unless they happen to live in the general region.[62] The town is in southern Tennessee, 33 miles southeast of Knoxville and 5 miles from one of the main entrances to the Great Smoky Mountains National Park. The development of the Parkway (the consumption "strip" mentioned above) in Pigeon Forge is undoubtedly attributable to its proximity to the national park and the fact that it lies on the main approach to the park from the nearest large city, Knoxville.[63]

While Las Vegas is dominated by the Strip, Pigeon Forge is even more dominated by the Parkway, and the means of consumption that exist on it or are a short distance from it. (There is little else in Pigeon Forge, while Las Vegas has become a large and diverse city. Furthermore, casino-hotels and other attractions not only exist on the Strip and in the downtown Fremont Street area but also have arisen just off the Strip as well as in various places throughout the city and even outside the city limits [e.g., Lake Las Vegas]. For example, there has been a significant proliferation of casinos throughout the city that cater to locals rather than tourists.)

The Parkway offers a number of attractions such as The Miracle Theatre (in 2009 offering a musical devoted to the life of Jesus Christ), Wonderworks, The Black Bear Jamboree, a *Titanic* exhibit (scheduled to open in 2010), Magic Beyond Belief, Memories Theatre (with a salute to Elvis), Dinosaur Walk Museum, The Smith Family Theatre, Tennessee Shindig, and signs pointing the visitor to Dollywood, a theme park found just off the Parkway. Named after, and created by, the country music star Dolly Parton, Dollywood is an amusement park with an Appalachian theme. The park has a number of attractions such the Southern Gospel Music Hall of Fame and rides such as Tennessee Tornado, River Battle, Smoky Mountain River Rampage, Timber Tower and Daredevil Falls, Dolly's Home-on-Wheels, and The Polar Express 4-D Experience. A one-day pass in 2009 ($53.50 for adults, $42.35 for children) covers all rides and attractions in the park, although there are many opportunities to spend a great deal more money on food, souvenirs, and gifts at places such as the Dollywood Emporium, Dolly's Closet, and The Ole Woodcutter. On or just off the Parkway is a series of "attractions" such as the Elvis Museum, miniature golf courses, a number of "raceways" designed for go-carts, museums, water parks, indoor skydiving, Ultrazone and Lazerport for laser games, and a variety of others. Also of note in Pigeon Forge, and another of the new means of consumption, is a series of outlet malls.

While all of the above, or signs pointing to them, are the most visible landmarks on the Parkway, the most common sights there are the gasoline stations, motels, and restaurants. Among the latter are "themed" restaurants such as Smoky Mountain Pancake House and Smokies Restaurant. There are many other local restaurants and, of course, McDonald's as well as many of the McDonaldized chains that have come to dominate increasingly not only America's restaurant business but also strips of road such as the Parkway throughout the United States. Beyond the mandatory McDonald's, there is the usual list of suspects, including Arby's, Burger King, Cracker Barrel, Hardee's, International House of Pancakes, Kentucky Fried Chicken, Pizza Hut, Shoney's, Sonic, Subway, Taco Bell, and Wendy's. It is also worth noting that the outlet malls are dominated by shops that are also part of large chains that are found in almost all of the outlet malls that have sprung up throughout the United States, especially in or near resorts like Pigeon Forge and tourist attractions like Dollywood and the national park.

While there is much on and around the Parkway, what is notable is the disappearance of a number of cathedrals of consumption that existed there not too many years ago and were described in previous editions of this book. In fact, at that time, the Parkway was built on a country music theme (Dollywood was a large part of that). It was dominated by large show theaters such as the Anita Bryant Music Mansion Theatre, Louise Mandrell Theatre, Country Tonite Theatre, Smoky Mountain Jubilee, and Elwood Smooch's Hillbilly Hoedown. These are all gone, as is much of the country music theme, and they have either not been replaced or replaced by far less attractive means of consumption. The Parkway has clearly experienced a significant decline (now likely being exacerbated by the recession). It seems to be losing out to another entry point to the Great Smoky Mountains National Park and a landscape of consumption on the ascent, just down the road in Gatlinburg. We will have a bit more to say about the latter at the close of this section.

Nevertheless, the Parkway in Pigeon Forge is still devoted to consumption. Particularly notable is the significant presence of entertainment settings of one kind or another, including not only the obvious ones discussed above but also "eatertainment" and "retailtainment" venues. The result is the striking presence in this small town and area of many of the new means of consumption, including a theme park, outlet malls, chain stores, McDonaldized restaurants, and entertainment venues of one kind or another.

One of the things that is different about the Parkway in Pigeon Forge, like the Strip in Las Vegas, is that it is *not* mainly about the consumption of everyday needs at the supermarket or department store, but it is about the *consumption of fun* and the *fun of consumption*.

First, there is still clearly lots of fun to be consumed in Pigeon Forge at Dollywood, in the various entertainment venues, and at the range of attractions and rides. In all of these places, people are paying money to buy fun. Second, other venues offer fun while one is consuming more material commodities. The outlet mall falls into this category where the fun of finding a bargain, of outsmarting the shop owner, creates an atmosphere where people will be more willing to part with their money for products for which they may have little or no need. In fact, as in Las Vegas and other similar locales, people find the atmosphere of a fun resort to be conducive to spending money on all sorts of things they might not otherwise purchase. In Las Vegas, it has been found that even substantial gambling losses do not deter people from also buying expensive products at prices they might never dream of spending at home.

Of course, it could well be argued, and quite legitimately, that people "need" fun, and places like Pigeon Forge's Parkway provide settings in which that need can be filled. Indeed, it could be argued that people have long had such needs, and in the past they have been satisfied in settings such as fairs, circuses, and expositions. However, the latter were almost always impermanent settings that were set up for a day, a week, or maybe several months. One of the things that is new about Pigeon Forge, as well as Las Vegas and other locales (e.g., the Palm Islands, the Cotai Strip, as well as places like Branson, Missouri), is that they are designed to be *permanent consumption settings*. Furthermore, instead of coming to the consumer as did (and still do) fairs and circuses, the consumer is expected to travel, often great distances, to the consumption setting.

The Parkway in Pigeon Forge and the Strip in Las Vegas have become geographic *destinations* in their own right (although Pigeon Forge appears to be less a destination and to have less to offer these days as a destination than it did not too long ago)—places to which people are willing to travel great distances, and to spend large sums of money, in order to get there. Of course, there have been areas that have long been destinations for tourists—especially notable are resort cities such as Miami Beach, Acapulco, Maui, Aspen, and Innsbruck. But these became destinations, and continue to be destinations, because of climatic conditions and/or because they exist in some of the most beautiful locations in the world. People came, and continue to come, mainly for weather and the natural attractions; that is, they came largely to consume fun. It was only later, as magnificent hotels, shopping areas, and in many cases casinos were built, that they became centers for *both* the consumption of fun and the fun of consumption.

There is no physical beauty in Las Vegas (although there is nearby) or Dubai.[64] Few would be drawn to the desert (unless it is developed as it is in Las Vegas, Palm Springs, or Dubai) for vacation. The only reason that Las

Vegas has become a destination is the existence of the casino-hotels. This is less clear in the case of Pigeon Forge because it undoubtedly became the consumption center that it is because of its proximity to the Great Smoky Mountains National Park (Gatlinburg offers similar proximity). However, the city is several miles from the park; it is on the road to and not in the park. Furthermore, one wonders how many of those who consume in Pigeon Forge also go on to spend time in the park. How much time do visitors to Pigeon Forge spend there, and how much time do they spend in the park? It may well be that the park and Pigeon Forge cater, at least in part, to entirely different clientele. On one hand, there are those who want to spend time and money consuming fun and commodities. On the other, there are those who want to avoid Pigeon Forge at all costs and spend time and little or no money "consuming" nature in the national park. Of course, some enjoy both and devote much time, energy, and money (camping gear can be costly) to both settings and the activities they offer. However, the joys of Pigeon Forge and the national park are so different that it seems entirely possible that they attract very different populations.

This leads to the more general issue of the relationship between the two and the construction of Pigeon Forge and its new means of consumption on the road to, and in sight of, the Smoky Mountains and the national park. At one level, the two exist in a symbiotic relationship to one another (whereas Pigeon Forge is in competition with Gatlinburg). Pigeon Forge would not have developed as it did were it not for the proximity of the park, and the park would not attract nearly so many visitors were it not for Pigeon Forge. It could be argued that they need each other, although that may become less true in the future if they become, at least to some degree, different destinations for different populations of people (or if Pigeon Forge becomes an increasingly less attractive destination).

However, what is most interesting are the stark contrasts between these two settings and the conflicts that exist between them. The Great Smoky Mountains National Park is a vast geographic area of natural beauty that straddles the border between Tennessee and North Carolina. It is, in a sense, a means of consuming the Smoky Mountains. More specifically, the roads in the park make it possible for large numbers of people to consume easily at least a small part of the park. Of course, much more of the park is open to those willing to leave their cars behind and trudge up and down mountains with little more than their backpacks.

Pigeon Forge, especially the parkway, is a much smaller geographic area that is astride one of the main routes to the park. While there is natural beauty (the Smokies) in the background, it is impossible to describe Pigeon Forge as naturally beautiful. It is defined by the structures and signs that, to a large degree, line both sides of the Parkway. The structures were not built with architectural beauty in mind, and few would find the signs to be beautiful. Indeed, these kinds of strips, repeated in miniature in an increasing number of places throughout the world, are most often viewed as unattractive necessities and even public eyesores. If the park is a means of consuming the mountains, the town, especially its Parkway, is a means of consuming, well, the new means of consumption that are its most important and defining reality.

We need a term to define these geographies that allow people to consume things. They are, in a sense, means of consumption, but we cannot use that concept if for no other reason than the fact that these areas allow people access to the means of consuming things; these areas are not the same as those means of consumption. In the case of Pigeon Forge, it is the theme park, amusement venues, and McDonaldized restaurants and motels that are accessed in and through the town. In the case of the Great Smoky Mountains National Park, it is the orientation center and the like that are accessed in and through the park. The roads and walking paths in the Great Smoky Mountain National Park, as well as the Parkway in the town, then, are means to access the means of consumption encompassed by them. We can think of such settings as offering *geographic access* to various means of consumption. We can therefore think of a kind of hierarchy with geographic accesses offering people approaches to means of consumption, which, in turn, allow them access to and the ability to consume various kinds of goods and services.

We need to look not only at the issue of geographic access in these settings but also at the overall topography of these settings. One crucial geographic fact associated with Pigeon Forge is, as pointed out above, its existence on one of the main roads to the Smokies and the fact that that mountain range looms as a backdrop to the town. A second is the geography of the means of consumption that have been developed on, and adjacent to, the Parkway. Virtually all, if not all, of them, and/or signs pointing to them, exist along the road leading to the national park. If one takes that road (and there are other ways of getting to the park), one cannot avoid all of the means of consumption that define Pigeon Forge. Clearly, these are irresistible to many who visit the area. Indeed, it is undoubtedly the case that many have visited the area specifically to drive down the Parkway, stay at one of its many motels, and partake of its at least regionally famous attractions (Dollywood is probably known to many people throughout the United States). Such people may have little or no interest in the Smokies and may avoid the park entirely.

The geography of the Great Smoky Mountains National Park, at least for the tourist, is defined to a large extent by its roads, paths, campgrounds, visitor centers, and the like. The roads and paths offer geographic access to the means of consumption within the park such as campgrounds and visitor centers. The vast majority of those who visit the park are not going to venture far from these access points and means of consumption and go off on their own into the mountains. Thus, for most, the mountains are defined by the geography of these roads, paths, campgrounds, and so on; visitors only see and visit that which is visible and accessible from these venues. Just as the visitors to Pigeon Forge rarely venture very far from the Parkway and its environs, the vast majority of those who visit the park stick mainly to the well-known routes and places. On one hand, it seems likely that those who visit the park in this way are also likely to spend time in Pigeon Forge. On the other, it seems somewhat unlikely that those who venture off on their own into the bowels of the park are going to be attracted to Pigeon Forge and its means of consumption.

Thus, both the park and the town offer geographic access to the means of consuming what they have to offer. But this similarity should not conceal important differences between the two. For one thing, Pigeon Forge allows access to means of consumption that, in turn, allow people to consume human products and services. The Great Smoky Mountains National Park allows access to means of consumption that, in the main, allow people to consume nature rather than any human product or service. For another, the costs associated with a stay in Pigeon Forge are vastly higher than a visit to, or even a stay in, the park. The means of consumption that define Pigeon Forge are profit-making enterprises, whereas much smaller amounts of money are needed to gain entrée to the park, and the charges associated with its means of consumption are used in the main to pay the costs of running the park and maintaining the means of consuming nature; the park is not a profit-making enterprise. Thus, the town clearly supports and fuels high levels of consumption, while the park plays little or no role in such heightened level of consumption.

Thus, there is a temptation, at least from the point of view of critics of consumption, to value the park over the town. After all, in the park, one is consuming natural beauty at relatively low cost, while in the town, one is consuming far less impressive human products at much greater cost. While this is a tempting perspective, one needs to be cautious here. After all, both the town and the park offer geographic access to the means of consumption that exist within them; conceptually, they are the same and function in much the same way. Thus, they may not be as different as first appears.

The similarity between them is clearest when we examine one of the key factors associated with the study of the means of consumption—simulation. It comes as no surprise that Pigeon Forge offers a wide range of simulations, most generally of the Appalachian way of life. More specifically, there is a long list of simulations associated with, or found within, the means of consumption within the town (e.g., many of the rides in Dollywood, including Tennessee Tornado).

There are no such obvious simulations in the national park. However, the imposition of roads, paths, campgrounds, and visitor centers has altered the area; it has, at least to some degree and in some places, become a simulation. A notable example of this is a short, looping road that has been constructed to allow visitors with limited time and opportunity to get a glimpse of the park. Most visitors to the park experience it in this way and from this road rather than by hiking through remote areas of the park. The amount of traffic and the number of people on this road have served to alter what one sees, and what takes place, in this limited area. For example, the wildlife has become accustomed to cars and people, and therefore animals have altered their behavior to accommodate the presence of civilization. On a visit a few years ago, I saw deer that normally would shy away from people and their technologies allow cars to come right up to them; the deer exhibited a total absence of fear. More strikingly, I saw a bear eating high in a tree adjacent to a road that had become jammed with traffic that had slowed or stopped to watch it. Furthermore, many people had parked, climbed a fence, and surrounded the tree to gawk, shout, take photographs, and the like. Uncharacteristically, the bear was unmoved by all of this human activity and simply went on munching away at the leaves of the tree. In acting in these unnatural ways, the deer and the bear (and undoubtedly other types of wildlife) were no longer acting in an "authentic" manner; they had become simulations. (Such changes occur even more extremely in zoos; one sees simulated animals in the zoo.) While the changes in the behavior of the deer and bears are less obvious simulations than those in Pigeon Forge and at Dollywood, both can be seen as simulations.

What of the point that there is a symbiosis between the town and the park and that they both benefit from their proximity to one another? There is clearly much truth to this. The town certainly would not have developed as it has were it not for its proximity to the Smoky Mountains, and the park gains visitors it might not otherwise get because of those drawn to Pigeon Forge. But this symbiosis has a different effect on the two settings. The town is likely to draw visitors to the park who are predisposed to appreciating simulations and are therefore likely to be appreciative of the town as it is. Few park visitors in search of authenticity are likely to venture into the town and, if they do, it is likely to be only for brief periods in order to obtain things that they need. Thus, in the main, the park and the majority of its visitors in search of simulation are likely to support Pigeon Forge and reinforce its simulated character.

However, it is a different matter with the park. Virtually all those who are drawn to the area by Pigeon Forge are likely to prefer their experiences to be simulated, perhaps as highly simulated as possible. Thus, when they venture into the park, they are likely to stick to the most simulated areas and, more important, to push park authorities to simulate more and more of the park and its attractions. More indirectly, the greater number of people who venture into

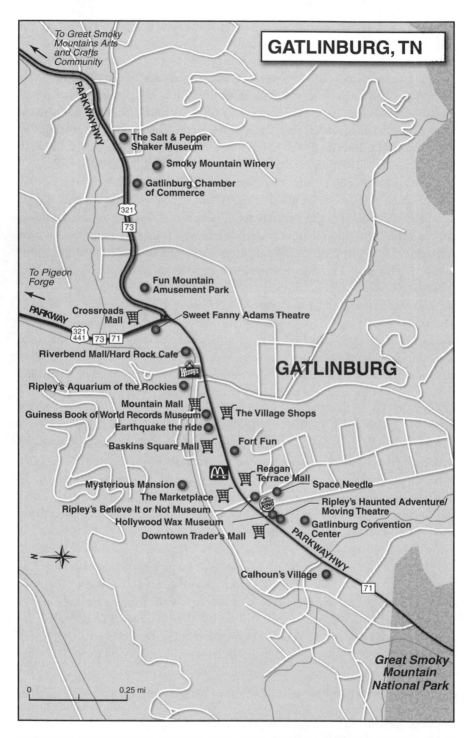

Figure 7.5

the park because they have been attracted to it by Pigeon Forge's attractions are likely to force park authorities to build more roads, paths, campgrounds, visitor centers, and so on. The result will be more simulations and simulated experiences—the animals will grow even more accustomed to people, and their behavior will be increasingly different from that of "authentic" animals. Thus, the symbiotic relationship between Pigeon Forge and the national park is most likely to push *both* in the direction of increasing simulation.

Interestingly, the once more traditional arts and crafts city of Gatlinburg, about 5 miles from Pigeon Forge, has developed a mini-Parkway of its own (see Figure 7.5) with attractions both on and near it. They include Sweet Fanny Adams Theatre presenting original musical comedies, Fun Mountain Amusement Park, Earthquake the ride and several Ripley's attractions—the Aquarium of the Smokies, Moving Theatre, Haunted Adventure, Mirror Maze, and of course a Believe It or Not!—on or near it.[65] Interestingly, the more traditional arts and crafts are now part of a landscape of consumption of their own on an 8-mile loop about 3 miles from Gatlinburg. On the loop are over 120 studios, galleries, shops, and restaurants of various types. In developing new means of consumption and maintaining more traditional ones, Gatlinburg has, at least for the moment, come to outstrip Pigeon Forge both as a landscape of consumption and as a gateway to the Great Smoky Mountains National Park.

CONCLUSION

This chapter has shifted the focus from the cathedrals of consumption to the limited geographic areas that encompass them. The key point is that we have witnessed not only the creation of new means of consumption but also the development of, and changes in, the geographic areas that encompass two or more of them. We focused on three broad types—one that has experienced only seemingly minor change (the area around the Duomo in Milan, Italy); new, but still threatened, landscapes of consumption (Easton Town Center, Dubai, Cotai Strip); and a landscape of consumption in decline (Pigeon Forge).

The Cathedrals (and Landscapes) of Consumption

Continuity and Change

The preceding chapters have been revised to bring them, and the information provided in them, up-to-date. The main concerns in those chapters—the cathedrals (and landscapes) of consumption and the hyperconsumption that supported and was heightened by them—were largely revolutionary products of post–World War II America. They expanded rapidly throughout that period and at a fever pitch in the late 20th century and in the first several years of the 21st century. This book has its roots in, and in many ways takes as its subject matter, the heyday, even the excesses, of a consumer society and more generally an economy that had continued to boom until late 2007 and the onset of the Great Recession. Indeed, these extremes, especially in consumption, were major causes of that recession. Many of the economic excesses[1] that lay at the root of the current economic crisis have now been wrung out of the system, often with quite wrenching consequences. Of specific interest here is the fate of the cathedrals of consumption, some of which have become "monuments to excess," at least in the current economic environment.[2]

Some might argue that the revolution in consumption in general, and in the cathedrals of consumption in particular, has ended (as President Barak Obama put it in his first press conference: "The party is now over"[3]). Both consumption and the cathedrals of consumption have experienced recent declines and setbacks, and it is possible that those declines will be transformed into a long-term devolution where consumption retreats to levels not seen in decades and the cathedrals of consumption experience a period of decline, even regression. Some of those cathedrals will disappear not only because of the recession but also because of the irrational exuberance that preceded it and led to overbuilding and to a great deal of excess capacity (a problem currently being confronted by, among others, the global automobile industry). Others may be replaced by newer settings of consumption that overcome some of the weaknesses (e.g., the high cost to build and to maintain them) of their predecessors. We are also seeing efforts to find new uses for some of the cathedrals of consumption (e.g., for empty, or soon-to-be-empty, big box stores[4]). In some cases, we may even see true devolution as contemporary means of consumption are replaced by early modern consumption settings such as small, independently owned shops. In some malls (enclosed and especially strip malls), we already see shops that have been vacated by the chains being occupied by small independent entrepreneurs.[5] With the decline or disappearance of some chains, they have a better chance of succeeding, and mall owners are eager to have them occupy what would otherwise be dead space (a disaster from the point of view of mall owners). In some cases, the costs of renting or leasing have been reduced to meet the needs of small entrepreneurs.

The coexistence of the modern with the early or premodern (those small entrepreneurs, "mom-and-pop" shops) is often seen as one of the hallmarks of the postmodern. The revolution-devolution pairing is comparable to, and has some similarities with, the pairing of the modern idea of explosion with the postmodern idea of implosion by Jean Baudrillard. The implication is that we may be on the cusp of a postmodern era in which hyperconsumption (especially for the wealthy) coexists with less frantic forms of consumption and modern cathedrals of consumption coexist with, and may even be replaced by, early or premodern consumption settings.

It is in the United States that devolution is likely to be greatest because it is there that revolution in this domain started and reached its peak. Having risen far, the fall may well be great and with devastating consequences. Globally, however, we *may* witness *devolution while the revolution is still in its infancy.* This best describes the situation facing the casinos on the Cotai Strip in Macau and the hotels on Palm Jumeirah in Dubai, currently under construction or planned for the near future (see Chapter 7 for a discussion of both). Here we may well see a decline *before* a rise; devolution *before* revolution. This all sounds eerily postmodern.

The American, as well as the global, economy is at the moment highly fluid, and its future is, at best, murky. This is all particularly true of consumption and its excesses, especially hyperconsumption and the cathedrals of consumption that both helped to create, and fed off of, such excessive consumption.

In the past few years, we have certainly witnessed the decline of hyperconsumption and many of the cathedrals of consumption. Some of that decline, especially as it relates to the cathedrals of consumption, has been discussed at appropriate places throughout the preceding chapters. In this concluding chapter, however, we need to examine whether this is but another passing phase in the "boom and bust" history of (consumer) capitalism or whether this change is of a more permanent nature. Is this only a temporary decline, or are we witnessing the end of the era of continually escalating consumption and ever more spectacular cathedrals of consumption?

While it is difficult to answer those questions and, more generally, to predict the state of the economy in general, and consumption in particular, after the current economic crisis plays itself out, this book operates with several premises about the nature of that future, premises that lead us to see *both* change *and* continuity in the future of consumption and the cathedrals of consumption. First, people will, indeed must, always consume. Second, when the economic environment improves significantly, at least some people will once again begin consuming beyond their basic needs. Third, people have long needed, and will continue to need, settings (e.g., agoras, bazaars, arcades, grocery stores, supermarkets, shopping malls, online malls) in which to consume. Fourth, along with an eventual improvement in the economy and increased consumption will come a revival of many of the consumption settings of specific concern here—the cathedrals of consumption—as well as the revival of older and the development of newer and more innovative consumption settings. In the long run, in order to compete with one another, many of the cathedrals of consumption will be forced to engage in essentially the same processes described in detail in this book; that is, they will continue to seek to be more spectacular than their competitors.

That being said, it seems highly unlikely that any aspect of the world of consumption will return any time soon to the heights of its recent "glory days." The effects and the lessons of the ongoing economic crisis will continue to reverberate for years to come (as they did in Japan after a similar economic meltdown in the 1990s led to its infamous "lost decade"[6]). Thus, I think the possibility of the revival in consumption described above will be tempered by a number of factors. First, consumers have lost trillions of dollars, and much of it will not be recovered; this is money that will never be spent on consumption. Second, credit of all types will be much harder to come by for some time to come, and this will serve to tamp down consumption. Third, consumers are now reversing a long-term pattern and saving more, and the money being saved will not be spent, at least immediately, on consumption. Fourth, in addition to having less to spend on consumption, many consumers will also find their "need"[7] to consume diminished (again, as in the Japanese case) by recent and continuing economic conditions. Fifth, cathedrals of consumption will continue to exist, but many will be forced by economic exigencies to abandon the kind of reckless spending we have seen epitomized in Las Vegas and Dubai and to find more economical ways of creating spectacles.

There are precedents for this. For example, as discussed earlier in this book, Wal-Mart and others followed the dictum of "bigger is better" and created massive hypermarkets. However, they found that what they created was simply too big; consumers could not and/or would not navigate these vast spaces. They were forced to backtrack to smaller, and less expensive, supercenters. The latter are still spectacular (especially spatially), but they are more manageable and are more economical to build and to run.

In light of the Great Recession, many superstores have opened smaller and more specialized shops. For example, OfficeMax (others doing this are Best Buy and Radio Shack) has opened three new Ink Paper Scissors stores in Seattle. They are about one ninth the size of a typical OfficeMax (2,000 vs. 18,000 square feet) and offer a small number of basic and more profitable products. There are many advantages to such stores—less space, lower rental costs, less inventory, fewer workers, easier to enter new (often smaller) markets, more rapid entry into a market (and exit if things don't work out), and most generally less risk because of lower investment. Such stores can also attract new customers attracted by the speed associated with shopping in small stores (shorter and easier to navigate aisles; shorter checkout lines) and who have been put off by the time needed to negotiate a superstore. Thus, in

at least some ways, "retailers are going back to their roots, evoking the corner store. At many new stores, personalized service is being emphasized, like
explaining the features of a product."[8] Said one corporate official,
"Consumers want stores that are more convenient, less time-consuming and
more personal. . . . There is such a thing as too much variety."[9] To some consumers, stores that return to some degree to their roots can be seen as offering a spectacle, albeit a very different one that is also far less costly to create.

A similar trend is the emergence of "pop-up shops."[10] These are temporary storefronts that open for as little as a few weeks. Of particular interest
here are those pop-up shops that offer low-priced and discounted products
during these recessionary times. There is a kind of spectacle here as these
shops come and go, as well as in the fact that some offer luxury and designer
products.

The "dollar" stores are succeeding these days not only because of low
prices but also because they are smaller than the superstores, the staff is
more accessible, and the aisles are less crowded. One customer pointed out
another advantage of the dollar store: "You don't have to navigate the big-
box parking lot."[11]

The idea of a more *economical spectacle* is central to this discussion. Such
a spectacle seems like an oxymoron; producing a spectacle seems all about
excess, including economic excess. However, while spectacles, especially as
they apply to cathedrals of consumption like Las Vegas casino-hotels and
modern cruise ships, are usually expensive (see Chapter 7 for a discussion of
the opening of the Atlantis hotel in Dubai), it *is* possible to produce spectacles
that are more cost-effective, that require fewer "bucks for the bangs," and that
offer "more bangs for the bucks." For example, while implosion is employed
to create a spectacle, it also can be used to create economies of scale. It is less
expensive to manage a mega-mall than physically and geographically separate
shopping malls and theme parks. Much greater use can be made of implosion
as a way of limiting costs, while still producing a spectacle.

A real reflection of the tenor of the times, as well as an interesting example of an effort to create an economical spectacle, or at least one that
appeared to be economical, was the opening production number of the 2009
Academy Awards show. Such numbers are always quite lavish, but cog-
nizant of the Great Recession, the producers of the opening production number made it seem homemade, appear to be created on a shoestring budget.
The backdrop for the number was "crude, supposedly garage-made card-
board sets."[12] This was undoubtedly more appearance than reality, and the
seemingly low-budget number actually was quite costly. Nonetheless, it
reflected the new economic realities and the need to create at least the illusion of an economical spectacle. Many of the cathedrals of consumption to

be built in the near future will be forced to do far more than create the illusion of being economical.

This concluding chapter, then, needs to reflect, and reflect upon, the above developments and prognostications. However, even though much has changed in the wake of the Great Recession, we must not lose sight of great continuity as well as of the fact that the basic sociological realities described in these pages remain operant. The processes (implosion, simulation, and manipulations of time and space) discussed in Chapters 5 and 6 will continue to be employed to create spectacles in the cathedrals of consumption, although they are likely to be modified, at least in the short run, to better fit the new economic realities and to be joined by other means of creating spectacle.

It is now clear that the massive expansion of the cathedrals and landscapes of consumption, as well as the hyperconsumption that lay at their base and characterized the West in general, especially the United States, and quickly spread to other parts of the world such as Dubai and Macau (see Chapter 7), was unsustainable in the light of the Great Recession. In Dubai, the fuel for the development of the Palm Islands and of massive resort hotels to be built on them was the explosion in oil prices (reaching nearly $150 a barrel in 2008, declining to almost $40 a barrel, but as I write in mid-2009 having recovered to over $70 a barrel).[13] In Macau, long a gambling center, the expansion in casino-hotels was based on the boom in Las Vegas gaming and the ambitions of Vegas-based companies (e.g., the Sands, MGM MIRAGE) to become more important global players. An even more important factor in the case of Macau was the skyrocketing economy of China (of which Macau is, like Hong Kong, a special administrative region). In the United States, the growth in cathedrals and landscapes of consumption was fueled by a rapidly rising stock market, abundant credit flowing from banks and government agencies, and seemingly endlessly increasing home values. As a result, many American consumers were awash with money, and they also found credit easy to obtain to buy not only homes but almost anything else. Escalating home prices led banks to extend credit to consumers in the form of home equity loans (auto loans were also easy to obtain). The credit card companies were similarly eager to find new cardholders and to increase the credit limits of those who already had cards and had reached their upper credit limits. As a result, in 2008, Americans were in debt to the tune of about $13 trillion in the form of mortgage ($11 trillion), automobile ($1 trillion), and credit card ($1 trillion) loans.[14] It is little wonder that the American consumer was labeled "the most over-extended consumer in world history."[15]

All of that excess (and much more) came to a screeching halt in 2008 with the near collapse of the American, and global, stock markets and of the world's banking, financial, and credit systems. Credit all but disappeared, and banks (e.g., IndyMac, WAMU) either went belly up or refused to lend money, even to other banks. The banking crisis, like all of the other economic problems discussed here, had its origins in the United States but quickly became a global crisis, revealing the tight linkages among the world's economies and more specifically their leading banks and financial institutions.

More specific to our interests here is what happened to the leaders in the global casino-hotel business. MGM MIRAGE owns many of the premier casino-hotels on the Las Vegas Strip, including the MGM Grand; Bellagio; Luxor; New York, New York; and Mandalay Bay. It has other properties in the United States (including the Gold Strike in Tunica, Mississippi—see Chapter 1) and the MGM Grand Macau. It is also heavily involved (in partnership with Dubai World) in the new City Center project in Las Vegas (see below), which is in danger of bankruptcy. The stock price for MGM MIRAGE dropped from over $60 a share at the end of March 2008 to just over $2 a share in March 2009. The Las Vegas Sands Corporation (it owns, among others, the Venetian in Las Vegas, Marina Bay Sands in Singapore [opening in late 2009], as well as the Sands and Venetian, Macau) has experienced a similar dizzying fall from a share price of over $74 to $3.01 during the same time period. Since they were the most excessive, the Las Vegas casino-hotels (and their offspring) have experienced some of the most precipitous declines, but almost all the other major cathedrals of consumption have also declined (and, as we saw above, some have disappeared).

OPTIONS FOR THE AMERICAN ECONOMY

While it is clear that we are not returning in the near future to the frenetic pace of consumption (or banking, etc.) that existed in the first decade of the 21st century, are there viable alternatives for the American economy (and at least some other economies) to a return to at least a modified form of consumer society? The American economy has been dominated, sequentially over its history, by agriculture, durable goods-producing industries, service industries, and consumption. All not only had their day, but they all continue to coexist today and will continue to coexist in the future. However, over time, agriculture and goods production declined, while service industries became ascendant, as did the realm of consumption that was often facilitated by the service industries and service work. If those are America's four major economic alternatives, it seems clear that the United States is *not* returning to an economy dominated by agriculture or even to one in which goods-producing industry is preeminent (although alternative energy technology or the rebuilding of America's crumbling infrastructure may become growth industries). Agriculture is now just too efficient and high tech to employ all but a small portion of the American population (most of whom, in any case, would have a hard time returning to an earlier point of the nation's history and to working the land).

While it has declined, production of durable goods in the United States is not moribund. Bright spots include "civilian aircraft, drilling tools, telecommunications equipment, agricultural machinery and excavators."[16] However, various nations have captured other industries that America once dominated (textiles, tires, steel, automobiles). Those industries will be nearly impossible to recapture either because they are so advanced technologically and/or because they have employees who are willing to work for far less than Americans have been willing to accept, at least until now. However, while it is remote, it is not beyond the realm of possibility that America will enjoy an industrial renaissance and build even more technologically advanced factories where its citizens are willing, even eager, to accept wages that are closer to those earned by workers in Bangladesh or Vietnam.

It seems far more likely that we will see an array of efforts to restore America's service industries, consumer culture, and its cathedrals of consumption (in which many service workers are found), at least in some limited and greatly modified form. Much hope lies in the service sector, especially in the higher end, creative,[17] postindustrial[18] service jobs that require high levels of training and skill and rely on great creativity. However, the United States is facing stiff competition even in the area of service provision. Examples include the loss of call center jobs to India and other places in the world (the Philippines) and the outsourcing of many other jobs—some very high paying (e.g., radiology)—to many global locales.[19] While some higher level service jobs exist in the realm of consumption, the latter is dominated by lower end service work ("McJobs" such as counterperson at McDonald's and card dealer at a casino-hotel).

From the 1950s on, the United States became the great innovator in the realm of consumer culture and exported interest in it, as well as many of its physical trappings (McDonald's, shopping malls, Disney Worlds, credit cards, exotic loans and investment vehicles, iPods, iPhones), to much of the rest of world. While service industries will continue to expand, a return to agriculture or heavy industry is highly unlikely. Thus, beyond the service sector (much of which is tied to consumption), there are few, if any, alternatives on the horizon in the United States but a return to a focus on consumer culture.

Of course, there are other, much more radical, alternatives such as completely reimagining our lives, our values, and the nature and structure of our society so that the economy shrinks and consumption occupies a far less prominent place in all of them.[20] We may yet see such a radical change, but it is going to require that the wall our economy has hit remain in place, or even become more of a barrier, for years, perhaps a decade or more (as was the case in the Great Depression and in Japan's lost decade). Failing that, what we are likely to see, as the title of this chapter suggests, is *both* continuity and change in the economy, consumption in general and in the cathedrals of consumption in particular.

FROM CATHEDRALS TO DINOSAURS (IN NO TIME AT ALL)

While the low-cost cathedrals of consumption (Wal-Mart, McDonald's, "dollar" stores[21]), those that offer economical spectacles, seem to be weathering the current perfect economic storm well, the higher end, especially the costliest to build and to maintain, cathedrals of consumption are experiencing the greatest difficulties. This is certainly clear in the United States in general, and Las Vegas in particular, as the epicenters of the development of the paradigmatic cathedrals/landscapes of consumption. By late 2008, visitor volume to Las Vegas was down 3%, and gaming revenue declined by over 8%[22]; in October 2008, revenue was lower by over 25% compared to October 2007; daily room rates were down over 14% for that same period. When one of the great cathedrals on the Strip—Wynn Las Vegas—opened in 2005, a bargain rate for a room was $250 a night. The month after Encore (an adjacent casino-hotel also built by Steve Wynn) opened, rooms in January 2009 could be had for $159 a night.[23] True to the need to be ever more spectacular, Encore, which cost $2.3 billion to build, is three stories higher than the neighboring Wynn Las Vegas and features the original art of Fernando Botero, a 231-carat pear-cut Wynn diamond, and a nightclub that seats 3,000 people. Such a casino-hotel requires lots of visitors spending and losing enormous sums of money. That is going to be much more difficult to achieve in the midst of a deep recession. This has resulted in great economic pain, including a massive budget deficit for the state of Nevada, a drop in new construction of 92% from October 2007 to October 2008, a huge decline in housing prices, and a rise in statewide unemployment from a minuscule 0.4% to 10% by February 2009.

However, bigger problems confront new Las Vegas cathedrals of consumption that were planned, and on which construction had begun, or was even well along, before the plunge in the economy. Construction on the planned $4.8 billion Echelon resort was halted in August 2008, with three of its towers having already reached 12 stories (one was to have been 55 stories). Other projects (e.g., the Fountainbleau) are on hold. However, some huge projects were too far along and could not be held up or stopped. The nearly $4 billion Cosmopolitan Resort and Casino, a complex of hotels, casinos, and condominiums scheduled to open in early 2010, was forced to file for bankruptcy. However, the bank that financed it (Deutsche Bank) decided that the project needed to be completed.

At the same time, an even larger and more spectacular $11-plus billion project, City Center, a joint endeavor of MGM MIRAGE and Dubai World, is being built adjacent to the Cosmopolitan in Las Vegas (the two projects may eventually be combined). In keeping with the emphasis on size, it is reputed to be the most expensive privately funded construction project in the history of the United States. The first phase of City Center is to open in 2009, and the project as a whole is planned to eventually include, among other things, the following:

• The 4,004-room 61-story ARIA Resort & Casino designed by Cesar Pelli

• A 165,000-square-foot casino also designed by Pelli

• The Mandarin Oriental Hotel/Residences with 400 hotel rooms and 227 condominiums

• The Harmon Hotel/Residences with 400 hotel rooms and 207 condominiums

• The Vdara Condo/Hotel tower with over 1,500 units

• Veer, which will be twin, 337-unit luxury condominium towers

• The Crystals Mall will encompass a 500,000-square-foot retail and entertainment area under a "crystalline canopy"

• There will be $40 million worth of modern sculptures and installations by world-famous artists[24]

While much else is planned for City Center (for example, a 2,000-seat stadium, its own fire station, and power plant), it remains to be seen how much of it will actually be built. Even if it is not fully completed as planned, it may encompass the last of the spectacular cathedrals of consumption and landscapes such as City Center that encompass several of them, in Las Vegas and the United States more generally, for some time to come. Unless the U.S. economy recovers far more dramatically in the next few years than is anticipated, it is likely that City Center will, at the minimum, face a rocky start.

Thus, with existing Las Vegas casino-hotels confronting a major downturn in business and others to be completed in the teeth of the continuing economic crisis, it may be that at least some of these cathedrals of consumption should be better seen as *dinosaurs* of consumption. As was the case with the real dinosaurs of yore, they are in imminent danger of extinction. They are huge and enormously expensive to build and to maintain. Hotel occupancy needs to be high, if not near capacity, and the casino floors must be flooded with gamblers, especially high rollers. However, occupancy rates are down, and bettors, even well-heeled ones, are not coming in as great numbers and tend to be wagering less. The casino-hotels relied on competing with one another in terms of the magnitude of the spectacles offered. They could afford to do this and continually up the ante by offering ever greater spectacles because they simply passed the cost of the spectacles on to consumers in higher room rates, higher prices for food, more money spent on goods in pricey shops and malls, and, most important, ever greater sums lost in the casinos. However, in tough economic times, the casino-hotels have had to resort to something that they have long resisted—competing on the basis of price rather than spectacle.

What has happened, and is happening, in Las Vegas can be understood from the perspective of Paul Baran and Paul Sweezy's theory of "monopoly capital."[25] As Marxists, and writing in the 1960s, Baran and Sweezy focused on production, but their thinking can easily be applied to consumption. In an earlier era of "competitive capitalism," entrepreneurs competed with one another on the basis of price; the ones that offered the lowest prices were able to win out over their competitors. The problem with this is that it served to reduce profits or, in the case of "cutthroat" competition, all but eliminate them. Furthermore, many capitalists were driven to the wall, and some were forced out of business as a result of this kind of intense price competition. As capitalism rationalized, an increasing number of capitalists came to the realization that such price competition was self-destructive. The focus increasingly shifted to "sales" competition where the emphasis was on outdoing the competition on the basis of things like advertising and packaging rather than on the basis of a lower price. It was sales techniques such as these that came to draw in consumers, *not* low prices. Prices could be kept high while the cost of these sales efforts and mechanisms could be passed on to the consumer. The result was not only a less vicious economic environment but also higher profits to the capitalist producer than under a regime of price competition.

The modern, highly spectacular cathedrals of consumption came of age in the era of the dominance of sales competition in the production arena. As a result, and taking their lead from the dominant players in the realm of production, cathedrals of consumption tended to focus on sales rather than price competition. Thus, Las Vegas casinos, cruise ships, fully enclosed shopping malls, and so on concentrated on building bigger, better, and more expensive consumption sites. The latter was their distinctive contribution to sales competition in the consumption arena, whereas in the production realm, such competition focused on design, advertising, and the like (these were not ignored by the cathedrals of consumption). These massive expenditures were made possible by the belief and longtime reality that those costs, no matter how massive, could be passed on to consumers who would willingly pay higher prices for the privilege of being "allowed" to consume in such palatial settings. Now, however, these consumption settings, like many of their predecessors, are being forced to rely less on sales competition and to focus more on cutting prices and being more competitive in terms of price.[26]

In fact, Las Vegas recently launched a new promotion, "Vegas Right Now," which seeks to increase the number of visitors by offering discounted hotel rooms, tickets to shows, and spa packages. Room prices are down all along the Strip, and promotions are rife (a free buffet meal with a room rental; discounted and even free show tickets at the major hotels). This may succeed in bringing more visitors to Las Vegas, but those who come as a result of lower prices are not likely to be the big spenders and high rollers who are required to support the massively expensive cathedrals of consumption. These cathedrals, built during the heyday of Las Vegas, may become dinosaurs ill suited to survive in this new economic climate. They may simply be too big and too expensive, employ too many people, and be too costly to operate. If the current downturn is brief, most or all will survive and perhaps thrive once again. However, if the downturn is severe, at least some of these cathedrals may, indeed, become dinosaurs and follow the "real" dinosaurs into extinction. Especially vulnerable are the ones currently under construction and nearing completion. Where will a sufficient number of the needed tourists, gamblers, and condo purchasers come from? The newer, very expensive casino-hotels (e.g., Encore) will also have great difficulty in this environment, although it may be that the very wealthy are best positioned to weather the economic storm and still afford such luxuries. The wealthy and near wealthy will allow the high-end casino-hotels (e.g., Bellagio) to survive and maybe even prosper. It may also be that the older casino-hotels on the Strip (e.g., Caesar's Palace) that have long since earned back their capital investments are in a good position to survive. They are better able to compete on a price basis and still earn a profit. Also likely to survive are the least expensive casino-hotels (e.g., Circus Circus, where, at this writing, rooms can be had for $29 a night). However, the older the casino-hotel (and both Caesar's Palace and Circus Circus are in this category), the more modest the spectacle being offered, at least in comparison to the newest casino-hotels. While this is a source of their price advantage, will it attract enough consumers to them and to Las Vegas as a whole?

It also could be argued that continuity is traceable to the fact that many of these casino-hotels are, like banks and financial institutions such as Citibank, AIG, Fannie Mae, and Freddie Mac, "too big to fail." While the failure of some of these casino-hotels would be catastrophic, especially for Las Vegas and Nevada, it seems unlikely that either the city or the state would have the funds needed to rescue them. It seems even more unlikely that the U.S. government would rescue them; the public uproar over saving such centers of gambling and other "sins"[27] would be enormous. However, as in the case of City Place, large investors may well find it in their interest to continue to pump money into the casino-hotels with the hope and expectation that their fates will improve in the future.

While the problems are most extreme in Las Vegas, probably because the cathedrals there were, at least until very recently, the most spectacular (and spectacularly expensive), they are also afflicting the other spectacular cathedrals of consumption. Cruise lines are responding by offering low-price promotions; the Disney cruise line is allowing children to travel free. Cruise ships have an advantage because of the perception, or the reality in some cases (if those who cruise do not purchase expensive add-ons such as side trips at various ports of call), that their package rates are a bargain, or at least allow the travelers to have a clearer sense of just what their total costs will be.[28] Nevertheless, many of the most popular cruise ships are huge and must attract thousands of customers every week, at least in season. The ships themselves are expensive and costly to operate, requiring large crews to handle the thousands of passengers.

Shopping malls throughout the United States (there are about 1,500 of them) and elsewhere have seen declines in the number of customers visiting malls, the amount spent per customer, and the total amount of business. They have responded by offering sales, promotions, contests, and so on. However, malls are plagued by an increasing number of empty shops (a devastating sight in malls that adversely affects the spectacle they are endeavoring to create), and many of these shops are outlets of chains that are retrenching or themselves going out of business.[29] Closed shops mean less revenue to the mall owners and make it more difficult for them to survive. Many malls are themselves in danger of closing, are in the process of closing, or have already closed (see www.deadmalls.com) as a result of the recession.[30] Also contributing to mall closures is the credit crisis associated with the recession and the inability of malls to get needed financing or refinancing. The result is the proliferation of "dead malls" such as the Randall Park Mall outside Cleveland, Ohio, which closed in late 2008.[31] However, strip malls and even fully enclosed, "big box" malls have been experiencing problems for some time. Part of the reason is that too many of them were built (retail space per capita in the United States

doubled between 1990 and 2005, but consumer spending, adjusted for inflation, rose only 14% during the same period[32]), and many were just too big; they
are also losing business to other spectacular shopping sites such as "lifestyle"
open-air malls (e.g., Easton Town Center in Columbus, Ohio [see Chapter 7],
which is, as we've seen, having its own problems).

One of the major developers of malls, the Mills corporation, experienced
severe economic difficulties and was taken over in 2007 by Simon Property
Group (and Farallon Capital Management)—the company is now called The
Mills: A Simon Company (General Growth Properties, the largest mall
owner in the United States, is deeply in debt and announced in April 2009
that it was filing for bankruptcy). Mills had built a number of the United
States' biggest and best-known malls (e.g., Sawgrass Mills, Potomac Mills,
Ontario Mills), and it had constructed malls elsewhere in world, including
Spain, Scotland, and Canada. At the time of its sale, Mills was building a
spectacular new mall—Meadowlands Xanadu—just outside New York
City. The project was taken over by a private investment firm. It was originally scheduled for completion in 2007, but that has been pushed back until
2010 (certainly not likely to be an opportune time to open such a mall).

Xanadu is an interesting example of a *dinosaur of consumption in the making* (another is the *Oasis of the Seas* [see Chapter 6], which has been described
as "a dinosaur—a floating emblem of a bankrupt era"[33])—a shopping mall that
may be extinct before it opens it doors. Even if it survives, it may be the "last
shopping mall" of its kind,[34] at least for some time to come. The fact that this
mall seeks to be a spectacle is clear in its name, which comes from a poem by
Samuel Taylor Coleridge, who describes Xanadu as a "stately pleasure-dome"
built for Kubla Khan (based on Chinese emperor Kublai Khan). The mall will
cost over $2 billion to build, and it will encompass 2.4 million square feet of
space.[35] Among the attractions imploded into that space are the following:

- A ski jump whose structure will also encompass a facility for indoor
skiing and snowboarding

- An 18-screen movie theater

- A concert hall and live theater

- An extreme-sports store with an indoor wave pool

- A skydiving simulator

- A 286-foot Ferris wheel (the largest in North America) offering a view
of the New York skyline

- A huge video screen in the sports area

- Five themed areas

- Children's Science Center

- Legoland Discovery Center

- Wannado City where children can play at being firefighters, police officers, and so on

At one time, all of this would have seemed quite normal for a new mall, but it seems very different in this new economic era. It seems more like a huge mistake akin to giving birth to a dinosaur when a gecko would be better adapted to the times. To top off Xanadu's problems is the fact that it is built in a monumentally ugly environment—the polluted wetlands of New Jersey and alongside the Jersey Turnpike—and it is itself described as horrendous: "a mishmash of big-box structures covered in aqua, blue and white tiles, with a little mustard yellow and brown thrown in to finish off the 1970s-nightmare look . . . 'Looks like bathroom tile from the 1970s.'"[36]

While some restaurant chains (e.g., low-priced ones such as McDonald's, Taco Bell, and Subway) are thriving, others are not. Some of the chains in trouble are at the low end (e.g., Arby's, Krispy Kreme), but most are mid-range, casual dining chains such as Applebee's and Outback Steakhouse (themed as an old-time Australian restaurant). Even high-end chains such as Morton's are struggling, in part because they have lost many of their expense account customers. As in the case of many cathedrals of consumption, the restaurant chains overbuilt, with the result that there are far more of them than are needed. A painful restructuring of the chain restaurant business is in process.[37]

Amusement parks, especially Disney's theme parks, may fare better in the current recession than many of the other cathedrals of consumption discussed here. In part, this is due to the fact that Disney World is such a cultural icon (but Las Vegas is, as well, and it is hurting). However, Disney theme parks, like cruise ships, seem to offer low prices (although this often turns out not to be the case when all other costs are added up—food, souvenirs, hotels in or near the park, etc.) through their one-price passes for one-day or several-day visits. In addition, many Americans can drive to one of the U.S. parks, thereby saving on expensive airfares for several family members. More regional amusement parks in the United States, such as Cedar Point outside Sandusky, Ohio, are, or are perceived to be, even more economical vacation sites (e.g., the drive for many is shorter), with the result that they are even more likely to be resistant to recession. This is true, as well, of other parks around the globe such as Tivoli Gardens in Copenhagen, which can be reached by public transportation.

THE NOT SO CREATIVE DESTRUCTION OF STILL-BORN CATHEDRALS OF CONSUMPTION

Whatever the future, as I write what we are witnessing in the realm of consumption, as well as in the larger economy, is another of the economic "gales" that were the focus of the work of Joseph Schumpeter. What defines capitalism to Schumpeter is a process of "creative destruction" where new economic structures are created and old ones are destroyed in order to make room for them. Schumpeter, of course, was focusing on production (e.g., manufacturing plants), but much the same argument can be made about consumption (and, say, casino-hotels and shopping malls). Thus, from a Schumpeterian perspective, new—but still spectacular—cathedrals of consumption (albeit perhaps built more economically, more reliant on advanced technology) will arise and, in many cases, replace at least of some of the "dinosaurs" (e.g., superstores like Linens 'n Things) that dominated an era that now appears to be in rapid retreat.

It is one thing for extant cathedrals of consumption, especially those that have been in existence for some time, to be destroyed (in the name of creative destruction), but it is quite another for those that are in the advanced planning stages or, worse, well along in their construction. The image conveyed by the theory of creative destruction is of a business that has succeeded for a time but has fallen on hard times and/or has been made increasingly marginal by a variety of changes (e.g., economic, technological, social). While we might fret about the destruction of such a business and the loss of jobs facing its employees, there is at least the consolation that it/they had their successes.

While we are witnessing many examples of such classic creative destruction in the current recession, there are many other cathedrals of consumption that are not being built even though much time, money, and planning have already gone into them. Furthermore, there are many others that will experience dramatic and costly delays. However, a much greater problem is created for the structures that have been destroyed during the process of being created (e.g., the Echelon in Las Vegas; see above) or are being completed even though they face a bleak future (at least immediately) and may face the possibility of destruction soon after completion (e.g., the Cosmopolitan and City Place in Las Vegas; the same might be the case for some of the hotels under construction on Palm Jumeirah in Dubai).

In these cases, we have no past history of success, as was the case for, say, Circuit City, to soften the blow of failure, no history of past profits, and no sense that they had their time in the sun but that that time has now past. All we have in these instances is failure (or the great likelihood of failure). This is not a situation that is considered by the theory of creative destruction and its generally optimistic outlook. If we would like to salvage creative destruction as a theory (although there is no imperative that we must), we need to do so by taking into consideration situations such as these. Creative destruction *may* be a theory that has relevance to the contemporary economic situation, but it is not salvageable without a major overhaul. Among other things, it needs to be able to deal with such still-born organizations.

Creative destruction also needs to be reexamined in the context of globalization. Schumpeter wrote long before the current "global age," with the result that his theory of creative destruction focused only on what transpired within a given country. Thus, his image was, for example, of a factory closing in the Midwest but being replaced by a newer and more efficient one in the South. From the perspective of the United States, this could be seen as a rather benign process since the country as a whole lost nothing and likely gained by such creative destruction. However, in the global era, it is likely the case that that which is new and more efficient might well be created in some other, very distant part of the world. Thus, in the era of globalization, creative destruction is not such a welcome process, at least for some of the companies and nations involved.

We might see this repeated in the case of the cathedrals of consumption. For example, one could conceive of a circumstance in which much of the Las Vegas Strip is decimated by a prolonged depression and/or a dramatic shift in the global economy away from the United States. In that case, it might be that the Cotai Strip in Macau becomes the world's main landscape of consumption as far as gambling is concerned and comes to be populated by the most spectacular casino-hotels. Furthermore, if the global economic center of gravity is indeed shifting to China, India, and Southeast Asia, then it makes sense for Macau to replace Las Vegas as the paradigmatic landscape of consumption, at least as far as gambling is concerned. However, this is not a benign process of creative destruction, at least from the perspective of the United States. The decline of the Las Vegas Strip would be an economic disaster for the city of Las Vegas, the state of Nevada, and perhaps even the United States as a whole.

A WORST-CASE SCENARIO: THE DEATH OF AT LEAST SOME OF THE CATHEDRALS OF CONSUMPTION

There is another scenario to discuss in this concluding chapter, and that involves the ultimate step in the devolution of at least America's cathedrals of consumption—the demise of many of them! In Schumpeter's terms, this is destruction *without* creation.

The warning signs are everywhere. Of particular interest are not only the cathedrals of consumption that have already disappeared but also those that may soon join them. Among those that have the potential to disappear as I write are the Rite Aid chain of pharmacies (with almost 5,000 stores and 100,000 employees), Blockbuster (a video rental chain with about 60,000 employees), Sbarro (a pizza chain with over one thousand stores and 5,500 employees), Six Flags (an operator of a chain of 20 theme parks), and Station Casinos (which operates 15 casinos off the Strip in Las Vegas and employs 14,000 people).

More generally, at some point in the future, all of the cathedrals of consumption, like all structures throughout history, will die. What sociologists and historians of the future will be left with are the remnants of today's cathedrals of consumption, much as we have today in the case of Stonehenge or the ruins in various locales that are all that remain of the Roman Empire. Returning to the dinosaur metaphor, specifically the bones that remain of them, we will be left with many of the relics of today's leading cathedrals of consumption. Like the dinosaur, these cathedrals of consumption were well suited to one type of reality (economic abundance) but totally ill suited to what may come later (economic decline or other large-scale changes).

Let's assume we are at a relatively early point in the process that will lead in the end to the death of at least some of today's cathedrals of consumption. In thinking about these cathedrals from this point of view, we have much to learn from Walter Benjamin's *The Arcades Project* (see Chapter 3 for a discussion of this work). Benjamin wrote this book over a number of years in the 1920s and 1930s, but he was writing about a largely 19th-century phenomenon that was at the time in its death throes ("the arcades are dying") or at least in decline. Thus, he treated the arcades as "monuments" that had been left behind by, and had left "traces" of, an earlier age or, more negatively, as the "detritus" of that era. For example, the Eiffel Tower in Paris is a monument (it's hard to think of it as detritus) left behind by the Paris Exhibition (or World's Fair) of 1889 (the same is true of the Unisphere that remains from the New York World's Fair of 1964–1965). He was interested in studying such structures as detritus that offer insights into a prior epoch. He saw the arcades as "dreamworlds"[38] that cast light on the collective dreams of the era in which they were constructed.

Today, arcades continue to exist in various places in the world, especially in Europe, where they can be studied from Benjamin's perspective. Furthermore, many other cathedrals (or, as Benjamin called them, "temples" [the arcades were such temples in his view]) of consumption, created both before and after the arcades, continue to exist (although they are in decline) and can be studied in much the same way. In fact, the discussion in Chapter 7 of the landscape of consumption in the heart of Milan, Italy, dealt with not only an arcade but also the Duomo that preceded it by several centuries, as well as a department store (La Rinascente) that succeeded it by a few years. All three can be seen as examples of monuments that can be studied for what they tell us about the eras in which they were built and reached their peak.

It could be argued that all of the cathedrals of consumption discussed in this book will experience the same fate sooner or later. However, what the Great Recession has indicated is that some of them are farther along in this process of decline than others. For example, the strip mall, which was already in decline before the recession, has devolved still further in recent years. Those that remain, either as functioning or dead malls, can be seen as detritus of an earlier era when comparatively little spectacle was needed in order to construct a cathedral of consumption. These were, and are, very functional sites that have, in many cases, been abandoned for the more spectacular fully enclosed malls and mega-malls.

Even if we assume that all of the above is true or comes to pass, the point is that a study of all of these monuments is worthwhile for what it tells us about the age, just past or now passing, that gave us the ultimate, at least until now, cathedrals of consumption. Furthermore, it would be useful to think of all cathedrals of consumption as having a life cycle with some in their early stages of life (e.g., online malls, shopping via a smartphone) while others (e.g., strip malls) are in their twilight years. This gives us a more processual view of all cathedrals of consumption and allows us to compare and contrast them from this perspective. If nothing else, this will allow us to see that what now seem to be permanent structures are really in the midst of a process that will end some day, as did the Roman Empire, in their "decline and fall."

GLIMPSING THE FUTURE OF SPECTACLES

It seems likely that once the price competition discussed above is set in motion, it will continue for some time, even if the economy recovers more rapidly than is expected. Consumers come to expect price cuts, sales, and bargains, and the cathedrals of consumption will have no choice but to continue to satisfy those expectations, at least for a time. This could become part of a process of deflation that many observers fear could develop in the wake of the Great Recession and is already occurring in Spain, Iceland, and elsewhere.[39]

However, as soon as it is feasible, the cathedrals of consumption will seek to shift back to sales competition. On one hand, this means a focus on the same kinds of things that one finds throughout the economy such as advertising and marketing. However, as we have seen, what is unique about the cathedrals of consumption is their reliance on spectacle as a means of competing on the basis of sales. Thus, it is argued here that we will see a return to spectacle and to the specific methods discussed in this book to create spectacle. However, the lessons of the Great Recession will not be lost on those who own and control the cathedrals of consumption. They will come to see that some mistakes were made in the creation of spectacles, and we are likely to see less use of at least some of those techniques in the future. Conversely, it will become clear that other methods made sense and will continue to make sense down the road. Furthermore, it is likely that efforts will be made to rediscover older, or to create new, methods for generating a spectacle.

Here we need to differentiate between extant cathedrals of consumption and those likely to be built in the near future. In terms of the former, the cathedrals exist, and they need to attract large numbers of people in order to survive. They will rely on not only price competition but also traditional methods of generating spectacle in order to save themselves, if not to prosper once again. They will also be attuned to searching for new ways of generating spectacle, but they will be hampered in that search by the nature of their structures. That is, massive structures are likely to continue to require equally massive spectacles. Furthermore, such spectacles are inherent parts of most of those structures. However, this means a continuation of the cycle that got these cathedrals of consumption into great difficulty in recent years—massive expenditures to build and operate great cathedrals of consumption with enormous and very costly spectacles in order to attract huge crowds.

In light of this discussion, one of the most interesting and telling responses of indoor malls in trouble is to turn to traditional spectacles in order to save themselves by luring potential customers. In early 2009, a number of U.S. malls began planning to install a huge and costly (approaching $2 million to install) contraption called a Flowrider in spaces in the mall vacated by, for example, department stores. The Flowrider is a glass-enclosed wave pool with a machine that propels 35,000 gallons of water over a slope at 30 miles per hour.[40] Some potential customers are drawn to play in the pool; many others just come to watch the spectacle. Of course, as with all spectacles, the hope is that people will stay in the mall and consume in various shops. However, the Flowrider represents a continuation of the belief that cathedrals of consumption need large and expensive spectacles in order to survive.

The cathedrals of consumption to be built in the future will not labor under the constraints on extant cathedrals. Furthermore, they will, or should, have a clear-eyed view about what has happened to the economy, consumption, and the cathedrals of consumption. This will enable them to learn better from past mistakes. They are in a better position to build on those lessons because they are not as constrained as extant cathedrals of consumption. Thus, they will examine critically the traditional methods of creating spectacle, and they will be more determined to find and to experiment with new methods of creating spectacle.

As mentioned above, it is the cathedrals of consumption under construction that are in the most difficult situation, although their fate will vary by their position in the global economy. In the United States, there is the new condominium complex, Icon Brickell, at the confluence of the Miami River and Key Biscayne in downtown Miami, Florida. It cost $1.25 billion to build and has the following spectacular characteristics:

> It has 1,646 condos, a 28,000-square-foot fitness area and a two-acre pool deck with a 12-foot-high limestone fireplace. The 22-foot-tall sculptured columns, 100 of them, marking the entry way were inspired by the monumental moai statues on Easter Island and cost $15 million.[41]

It has three towers, the smallest is 50 stories high (said one real estate executive who, seems belatedly, to have come to his senses, "Bigger is not better"[42]), and the complex includes a boutique hotel. The problem is that this building complex was completed and its condos came on the market as the Great Recession emerged and also in the face of massive overbuilding in Florida in general (yet another example of excess and irrational exuberance). Between 2003 and 2009, 83 towers were built in Miami, putting 23,000 new condo units on the market. As of December 31, 2008, 45% of them had not been sold. In the case of Icon Brickell, only 30 of the 500 condos (priced between $400,000 and $800,000) that were ready for closing at the end of 2008 actually closed. Like many cathedrals of consumption of this bygone era, Icon Brickell is spectacular and spectacularly expensive. For the moment, it sits largely empty and looks very much like one of many dinosaurs still standing in Miami Beach, as well as elsewhere in the United States and the world.

The key point is that Icon Brickell is in existence, and the expensive spectacle associated with it is going to do it little good in the current economic environment. It is going to need to compete, very reluctantly, on a price basis, and that means cutting prices, probably drastically, until its inventory of condos, and that of others, is eventually sold. It, like all other extant cathedrals of consumption, has little choice, but those currently being contemplated can rethink the nature, extent, and type of spectacle they wish to create.

However, it should be pointed out that the actions taken and the fate of cathedrals of consumption will vary by geographic location. Within the United States in general and the Miami, Florida, area in particular, the cathedrals of consumption are going to have a difficult time, and it will not be easy for them to avoid becoming dinosaurs. Other areas of the world—Dubai and Macau, in particular—are likely to continue to experience some difficulties, but in the long term, their cathedrals of consumption are more likely to escape the perils of "dinosaurization."

The one type of spectacle that we are certain to see less of in the future is that which relies on spatial manipulations, especially the creation of huge, and hugely expensive,[43] spaces (although the Flowrider discussed above indicates this will not disappear). Instead of "more is more," the dominant ideology is going to be "less is more." As has been discussed previously, huge physical spaces have become liabilities. No matter how spectacular a cathedral of consumption is physically, it is quite unspectacular if it is more or less empty. In boom times, luring large crowds is not a problem, but it is in depressed times and even in a more normal economy. While overall, there will be less reliance on large spaces to create spectacle, there will, once again, be global variation in this. Given its likely economic decline, there will be fewer such spaces in the United States, but in other places that are likely to expand economically—China and the Arab States, for example—we are apt to see a resumption of the building of such spaces once the recession ebbs.

The other type of spatial spectacle—being in many different geographic locales—is also likely to be used less, although it will not decline as much as the use of great spaces. Lower end global chains like McDonald's, IKEA, and Wal-Mart are likely to expand their reach into ever more locales, while those on the higher end will slow down in terms of expansion or even retreat, at least until the economy picks up dramatically. Building yet another locale in still another part of the world is, in the end, a comparatively low-cost undertaking, especially for low-end chains, and if it doesn't work, it can be closed with relatively little effect on the massive corporations that created it. In fact, the companies mentioned above have not been shy about either building or closing locales as demanded by market considerations.

Creating spectacle via implosion has a mixed future. On one hand, this has often involved huge spaces and great costs (e.g., Xanadu). Given what has been said above about size, we are likely to see fewer implosions of this magnitude in the future. On the other hand, implosion does not necessarily require great spaces and huge expenditures. Implosion can occur in very modest settings with a multitude of offerings, making them attractive to consumers. 7–11 is a chain that, over the years, has changed from its roots as a convenience (grocery) store; a number of other means of consumption have imploded into it—newsstand, restaurant, coffee shop, bank (ATM machines, etc.), phone store (purveyor of prepaid phone cards), and so on. There is a spectacle to all of this, but it is a highly economical form of implosion. It is likely that cathedrals of consumption will make more use of such economical forms of implosion. They create a spectacle and a synergy that leads to greater sales and profits (and lower costs). It is certainly not eye-popping; it is more a spectacle of convenience, but given the global proliferation of 7–11s and their clones, it seems to work and to be highly profitable.

Given the fact that many of the cathedrals of consumption are likely to continue to exist, we are apt to see new forms of implosion into at least some of them. While some fully enclosed malls will be closed or used for other purposes, many of them will look to new forms of implosion for their salvation. Among the likely new inhabitants of malls are not only more small independent businesses but also libraries, medical facilities, classrooms for community and technical colleges, dance studios, nonprofit arts groups, and even religious centers.[44]

Manipulations of time will continue to be attractive sources of spectacle, again largely because time can be manipulated in an economical manner. Being spectacularly fast does not necessarily mean high costs, as is well demonstrated by the fast-food restaurants, 7–11, the express package delivery services, and the like. Seeming to be everywhere is also not extraordinarily costly, as reflected, again, in the same examples. Combining a variety of different time periods in one setting is also not inherently a costly operation, although it has at times been done at high cost (e.g., Disney World, the Las Vegas Strip). Similarly, concealing the time of day or obscuring the fact that time is passing is also amenable to being accomplished at low cost. Finally, while we will discuss technology at more length below, the manipulation of time is particularly amenable to the use of various advanced technologies, and as will be argued, technology represents an important tool in the production of future spectacles, especially those that are done economically.

While many well-known simulations have been extraordinarily costly, there is no reason inherent in them that requires that they be expensive. At the extreme high end have been the simulations that define Las Vegas and the casino-hotels on the Strip. However, at the lower end of the continuum in terms of cost, there have been, and are, fast-food restaurants (e.g., Long John Silver, the now-defunct Roy Rogers), as well as more upscale chains (e.g., Rainforest Cafe) that simulate some other world. There is nothing to prevent the creation of highly appealing, even spectacular, simulations that cost relatively little to produce.

Beyond the possibilities associated with the methods of creating spectacle discussed above and earlier in the book, there are other possibilities for creating economical spectacles. One example is moving away from the idea of overwhelming consumers and to the opposite direction of underwhelming them. Clearly, as a general rule, it is going to be far more costly to overwhelm than underwhelm consumers. The idea here would involve such things as packing a great deal into a small space, producing a cathedral of consumption that is highly manageable rather than being unmanageable, and relatedly focusing on producing a space that is defined by its walkability rather than requiring all sorts of conveyances (e.g., monorails) to traverse the property. There are, in fact, spectacles such as this, including, as mentioned earlier, Main Street in Disneyland/Disney World and Easton Town Center. Another is Madurodam near The Hague in the Netherlands. It is a "typical" Dutch city, with characteristically Dutch buildings, built on 1/25th the actual scale of the buildings. Not a lot of attention has been devoted to producing spectacles that are underwhelming, but they have been done, and more important, there is a lot more that can be done with them.

However, the most important factor in producing less costly spectacles in the future will involve the use of new and advanced technology. Most of the major cathedrals of consumption discussed in this book are based on brick-and-mortar structures that employ large numbers of people. Such structures, as we have seen, are very expensive to build and maintain. Furthermore, they all tend to be highly labor intensive, and the employment of large numbers of human workers is very costly. The future would seem to depend on the invention of new and in many cases unimagined technologies that will be, or will produce, spectacles that do not require large and expensive structures or large numbers of people to operate. Here we are still in the realm of science fiction, but a technology that is capable of creating virtual reality or holograms in which consumers can immerse themselves and that requires few employees to staff and maintain comes to mind.

However, the use of advanced technology to create spectacle is already with us in various realms such as video and online games and on much of the Internet, especially Web 2.0 (e.g., Second Life). While this technology is initially expensive, once it is up and running, the costs are minimal. Better yet, because they exist in an immaterial world, the spectacles are free of material limits. This means that one is much freer to create and to experience a spectacle than in the material world. The possibilities for using the techniques discussed in this book to create spectacles—simulation, space, time, and implosion—are infinitely greater on the Internet than they are in the material world. Furthermore, relating to the point made above, it all occurs in a far more manageable world on one's computer and computer screen.

By the way, a cost saving associated with the Internet, especially Web 2.0, is using the consumer to do labor at no charge that in other instances would require payment (e.g., doing the "paperwork" involved in ordering books on Amazon.com). Another way of saying this is that the consumer has been transformed, at least in part, into also being a producer. The fusion of the producer and the consumer, as discussed earlier, has come to be called the *prosumer*.[45] Making greater use of prosumers should aid in the creation of more economical spectacles. That is, prosumers will create at least part of the spectacle on their own and at no cost to the businesses involved.

In the end, if the cathedrals of consumption must choose between price and sales competition, they will always choose the latter, specifically in terms of the creation of spectacle. The new economic realities brought on by the Great Recession will lead to rethinking spectacles, to focusing on some and deemphasizing others, and, most important, with experimenting with new, different, and often more economical spectacles. However, while the nature, form, and cost of producing spectacles may change, the fact remains that spectacle will remain the preferred mechanism by which cathedrals of consumption compete with one another, allowing them to attract, they hope, larger numbers of consumers.

Notes

Chapter 1

1. Yiannis Gabriel and Tim Lang, *The Unmanageable Consumer: Contemporary Consumption and Its Fragmentation,* 2nd ed., London: Sage, 2006.
2. Jean Baudrillard, *The System of Objects,* London: Verso, 1968/1996.
3. The focus is on the macrostructures in which consumption takes place and *not* microlevel consumers and their actions. To put it another way, the focus is on structures and *not* on consumers as agents.
4. For a discussion of some older means of consumption, see Ray Oldenburg, *The Great Good Place,* New York: Paragon House, 1989; David Nasaw, *Going Out: The Rise and Fall of Public Amusements,* New York: Basic Books, 1993.
5. An important issue is whether there is really anything "new" about the new means of consumption.
6. Alan Bryman, "The Disneyization of Society," *Sociological Review* 47 (1996): 25–47; *The Disneyization of Society,* London: Sage, 2004.
7. It is interesting to note how many of the new means of consumption have their roots in the 1950s. This is undoubtedly traceable to the increasing affluence of American society as well as the growth of facilitating means of consumption relating to transportation—automobiles, highways, jet planes, and so on.
8. DisneySea, at a cost of $2.5 billion, was constructed in Tokyo Bay.
9. Stephen M. Fjellman, *Vinyl Leaves: Walt Disney World and America,* Boulder, CO: Westview, 1992; Alan Bryman, *Disney and His Worlds,* London: Routledge, 1995.
10. Judith A. Adams, *The American Amusement Park Industry: A History of Technology and Thrills,* Boston: Twayne, 1991, p. 111.
11. John F. Kasson, *Amusing the Million: Coney Island at the Turn of the Century,* New York: Hill and Wang, 1978, p. 44.
12. Coney Island *did* have some structure and Disney World *does* offer some respite from the structures people encounter in their daily lives.
13. Kasson, *Amusing the Million,* p. 50.
14. Michael Sorkin, "See You in Disneyland," in Michael Sorkin (ed.), *Variations on a Theme Park,* New York: Hill and Wang, 1992, p. 231.

15. Bruce Handy, "It's Only a Day Away: Tomorrowland Gets an Update. Too Bad Tomorrow Has Gone Out of Style," *Time*, June 1, 1998, p. 66; for an even more acid critique, see William Booth, "Planet Mouse: At Disney's Tomorrowland, the Future Is a Timid Creature," *Washington Post*, June 24, 1998, pp. D1, D8.

16. Douglas Frantz and Catherine Collins, *Celebration, U.S.A.: Living in Disney's Brave New Town*, New York: Henry Holt, 1999; Andrew Ross, *The Celebration Chronicles: Life, Liberty and the Pursuit of Property Values in Disney's New Town*, New York: Ballantine, 1999.

17. Sharon Zukin, *Landscapes of Power: From Detroit to Disney World*, Berkeley: University of California Press, 1991.

18. From Michael D. Eisner, "Letter to Shareholders," *Business Wire*, January 3, 2002.

19. It is worth noting that despite its enormous success and expansion, not everything Disney has undertaken has succeeded. For example, the company sold its money-losing sports teams (Anaheim Angels in baseball; Anaheim Mighty Ducks in hockey) and closed many of its Disney stores. Its Club Disney sites were closed down some time ago.

20. Eisner, "Letter to Shareholders."

21. Charles V. Bagli and Randy Kennedy, "Disney Wished Upon Times Sq. and Rescued a Stalled Dream," *New York Times*, April 5, 1998, pp. 1, 32.

22. Everett Evans, "'Sleaziest Block in America' Transformed Into Family-Friendly Heart of New York," *Houston Chronicle*, March 8, 1998, p. 1, Travel.

23. Although I am calling them *structures*, these settings are increasingly taking a dematerialized form as, for example, the case of cybermalls or home-shopping television. For a general discussion of dematerialization in the realm of consumption, see Don Slater, *Consumer Culture and Modernity*, Cambridge, UK: Polity, 1997.

24. Stuart Ewen, *Captains of Consciousness*, New York: McGraw-Hill, 1976; Roland Marchand, *Advertising the American Dream*, Berkeley: University of California Press, 1985; Jib Fowles, *Advertising and Popular Culture*, Thousand Oaks, CA: Sage, 1996; Adam Lury, "Advertising: Moving beyond Stereotypes," in Russell Keat, Nigel Whiteley, and Nicholas Abercrombie (eds.), *The Authority of the Consumer*, London: Routledge, 1994, pp. 102–115.

25. Adam Arvidsson. *Brands: Meaning and Value in Media Culture*, London: Routledge, 2006.

26. Richard S. Tedlow, *New and Approved: The Story of Mass Marketing in America*, New York: Basic Books, 1990.

27. A study of changing tastes in food in Great Britain concluded that little could be said about the issue because data are sparse and inconclusive (and this is even more true of tastes in consumer goods in general). The author was able to say much more that is definitive about the production of food as well as the means of consumption that make that food available to consumers. See Alan Warde, *Consumption, Food and Taste*, London: Sage, 1997.

28. Stuart Ewen, *All Consuming Images: The Politics of Style in Contemporary Culture*, New York: Basic Books, 1988.

29. Gilles Lipovetsky, *The Empire of Fashion: Dressing Modern Democracy*, Princeton, NJ: Princeton University Press, 1994.

30. Campbell offers an even broader sense of this process "involving the selection, purchase, use, maintenance, repair and disposal of any product or service." Campbell's use of the term *shopping* (selection and purchase of goods and services) is closer to our sense of this process, but it does not apply well to our interest in theme parks, cruise lines, and casinos; we usually do not think of people as "shopping" in these settings. See Colin Campbell, "The Sociology of Consumption," in Daniel Miller (ed.), *Acknowledging Consumption: A Review of New Studies*, London: Routledge, 1995, pp. 102, 104.

31. See, for example, Sharon Zukin, *Point of Purchase: How Shopping Changed American Culture*, New York: Routledge, 2004; Pasi Falk and Colin Campbell (eds.), *The Shopping Experience*, London: Sage, 1997; Hoh-Cheung Mui and Lorna H. Mui, *Shops and Shopkeeping in Eighteenth-Century England*, London: Routledge, 1989; Alison Adburgham, *Shops and Shopping: 1800–1914*, London: Allen and Unwin, 1964.

32. George Ritzer and Todd Stillman, "The Postmodern Ballpark as a Leisure Setting: Enchantment and Simulated DeMcDonaldization," *Leisure Sciences* 23 (2001): 99–113.

33. This extension to museums makes it clear that it is increasingly difficult to distinguish between "high" and "low" culture.

34. This means, among other things, that the exchange need not necessarily be completed. That is, something like "window shopping" would be part of our concern, even if no purchase takes place. See Anne Friedberg, *Window Shopping: Cinema and the Postmodern*, Berkeley: University of California Press, 1993.

35. Corrigan has recently described an earlier means of consumption, the department store, in a similar way: "It is not an exaggeration to see department stores as similar to cathedrals: they attracted people to worship at the temple of consumption." See Peter Corrigan, *The Sociology of Consumption*, London: Sage, 1997, p. 56.

36. Bill Keller, "Of Famous Arches, Bœeg Meks and Rubles," *New York Times*, January 28, 1990, section 1, p. 12.

37. Bob Garfield, "How I Spent (and Spent and Spent) My Disney Vacation," *Washington Post*, July 7, 1991, p. B5.

38. Alexander Moore, "Walt Disney World: Bounded Ritual Space and the Playful Pilgrimage Center," *Anthropological Quarterly* 53 (1980): 207–218.

39. William Severini Kowinski, *The Malling of America: An Inside Look at the Great Consumer Paradise*, New York: William Morrow, 1985, p. 218.

40. Ira G. Zepp Jr., *The New Religious Image of Urban America: The Shopping Mall as Ceremonial Center*, 2nd ed., Niwot: University Press of Colorado, 1997; see also Moore, "Walt Disney World," pp. 207–218.

41. I will have a lot more to say about atriums, and the contribution of the architect John Portman, in Chapter 6.

42. Zepp also discusses Disneyland, baseball stadiums, and airports in these terms. All of these means of consumption will be discussed in this book.

43. John Drane, *The McDonaldization of the Church: Spirituality, Creativity, and the Future of the Church,* London: Darton, Longman and Todd, 2000.

44. This is not impossible because it could be argued that this is exactly what takes place in thousands of churches and synagogues on the Sabbath.

45. Thomas S. Dicke, *Franchising in America: The Development of a Business Method, 1840–1980,* Chapel Hill: University of North Carolina Press, 1992, pp. 2–3.

46. Ibid.

47. There are two basic types of franchising arrangements. The first, *product franchising,* is a system in which "a manufacturer markets its output almost entirely through highly specialized retailers who, in turn, rely on the manufacturer for most of the products they sell." McCormick harvesting machines and Singer sewing machines involved product franchising, and most important, to this day so does the sale of new automobiles. The second, *business-format franchising,* "is where the outlet itself—together with a comprehensive package of services to support it—is the product." The fast-food franchises are the best example today of business-format franchising, but this type has expanded into many other types of retail businesses since the 1950s. See Dicke, *Franchising in America,* p. 3.

48. http://www.entrepreneur.com/mag/article/0,1539,275271,00.html

49. David Seagal, "In Hopes of a Chain Reaction," *Washington Post,* April 30, 1997, pp. C11, C19.

50. http://www.mcdonalds.com/corp/invest/pub/2007_annual_report.html

51. Richard Gibson, "Fast-Food Spinoff Enters Pepsi-Free Era," *Wall Street Journal,* October 7, 1997, pp. B1, B2; http://www.yum.com/company/ourbrands.asp

52. http://www.nationmaster.com/encyclopedia/Walmart

53. David Handelman, "The Billboards of Madison Avenue," *New York Times,* April 6, 1997, section 6, p. 50ff.

54. There were precursors (e.g., arcades) to the modern shopping mall in Europe in the late 1700s and 1800s.

55. Margaret Crawford, "The World in a Shopping Mall," in Michael Sorkin (ed.), *Variations on a Theme Park,* New York: Hill and Wang, 1992, p. 20.

56. Laura Bird, "Huge Mall Bets on Formula of Family Fun and Games," *Wall Street Journal,* June 11, 1997, pp. B1, B12.

57. Paco Underhill, *Call of the Mall,* New York: Simon & Schuster, 2004. p. 201.

58. Suzette Barta, Jason Martin, Jack Frye, and Mike D. Woods, "Trends in Retail Trade," *OSU Extension Facts,* WF 565, n.d., p. 2.

59. John Holusha, "The Key to the Mall? That's Entertainment," *New York Times,* February 9, 1997, section 9, p. 1.

60. Peter A. McKay and Maryann Haggerty, "Entertaining New Mall Ideas," *Washington Post,* June 19, 1998, pp. F1, F10.

61. Barta et al., "Trends in Retail Trade," p. 2.

62. www.forbes.com/business/2007/01/09/malls-world-largest-biz-cx_tvr_0109malls.ht

63. theseoultimes.com/ST/db/read.php?idx=1962

64. "The Outlet as Destination for Those Who Love a Sale," *New York Times Travel,* April 5, 1998, pp. 12, 24; http://realtytimes.com/rtcpages/20010628_malls.htm; http://www.cardelhotels.com/News_herald_online_0211_2002.asp

65. Frank DeCaro, "Looking for an Outlet," *New York Times,* April 6, 1997, section 6, p. 70ff.

66. Ibid.; http://www.charleston.net/stories/090103/bus_01outlets.shtml; http://travel.mainetoday.com/todo/shopping/0307140utlet.shtml

67. Danielle Reed, "A Tale of Two Leaves: Outlet Shopping . . . ," *Wall Street Journal,* October 17, 1997, p. B12.

68. Michael Barbaro, "Retailers Embrace the Great Outdoors," *Washington Post–Business,* December 1, 2003, pp. E1, E12.

69. Gregory Richards, "Shopping Malls Without Halls," *Florida Times-Union* (Jacksonville), September 22, 2003, p. FB12.

70. http://www.icsc.org/srch/rsrch/scope/current/ (International Council of Shopping Centers public statistics page)

71. Marc Fisher, "Naming Your Price," *Washington Post,* June 30, 1997, p. C2.

72. Gary Gumpert and Susan J. Drucker, "From the Agora to the Electronic Shopping Mall," *Critical Studies in Mass Communications* 9 (1992): 186–200.

73. Linda Castrone, "The 'Couch Potato' Medium: College Class Analyzes Infomercials' Huge Appeal," *Rocky Mountain News,* December 17, 1996, p. 3D; http://www.marketwatch.com/news/story/infomercials-move-mainstream-tv-stay/story.aspx?guid={B287AF76-C8FB-44BE-AC61-7F929796DB83}

74. Some traditional advertisements do this as well.

75. Mike Mills, "A Pentagon Plan Became the Internet: The Network Was Born From a Divide-and-Conquer Strategy for Communications Security," *Washington Post,* July 2, 1996, p. A6ff.

76. David Bank, "What Clicks?" *Wall Street Journal,* March 20, 1997, pp. R1, R4; http://www.infoplease.com/ipa/A0880773.html

77. www.walmart.com/catalog/catalog.gsp?cat=542413; Richard Tompkins, "Wal-Mart Plans Big On-line Expansion," *Financial Times,* March 27, 1997, p. 33. There have also been failures. Shopping 2000, a cyberclone of a traditional mall with 58 storefronts, failed because it was too cumbersome.

78. Diane Cyr, "Web Winners and Losers Strive to Make Sense of Selling on the Internet," *Catalog Age,* October 1, 1996, p. 1ff.

79. www.answers.com/topic/netflix-inc

80. David Pogue, "Awash in a Stream of Movies," *New York Times,* January 29, 2009.

81. Miguel Helft, "Amazon Claims 'Best Ever' Christmas (Whatever That Means). *New York Times,* December 26, 2008.

82. Elizabeth Corcoran, "What Intuit Didn't Bank On," *Washington Post,* June 22, 1997, p. H5.

83. David Streitfeld, "King of the Booksellers' Jungle: Amazon.com Proved That Readers and the Internet Can Click," *Washington Post,* July 10, 1998, pp. A1, A20.

84. Beth Berselli, "Gamblers Log On to Deal Themselves In," *Washington Post,* August 19, 1997, pp. A1, A8.

85. www.peakentertainment.com

86. Berselli, "Gamblers Log On," p. A1.

87. Michael Herman, "Huge Growth in Porn Websites," *The Press* (Christchurch, New Zealand), October 7, 2003, p. C7.

88. Wal-Mart has run into some resistance to expanding its economic base. See Jessica Hall and Jim Troy, "Wal-Mart, Go Home! Wal-Mart's Expansion Juggernaut Stumbles as Towns Turn Thumbs Down and Noses Up," *Warfield's Business Record,* July 22, 1994, vol. 9, section 1, p. 1ff.

89. All data are from http://walmartstores.com/sites/AnnualReport/2008/ (Walmart online investor relations site, linked off of walmart.com).

90. Ibid.

91. "Winning the Grocery Game," *Consumer Reports,* August 1997, pp. 10–17.

92. All data are from http://phx.corporate-ir.net/phoenix.zhtml?c=83830& p=irol-irhome&cm_re=1_en-_-Bottom_Nav-_-Bottom_investor&lang=en-US (Costco online investor relations site, linked off of costco.com).

93. "Winning the Grocery Game," pp. 10–17.

94. Some trace it much further back to the founding of FAO Schwartz in New York in the 1860s.

95. Richard Panek, "Superstore Inflation," *New York Times,* April 6, 1997, section 6, p. 66ff.

96. www.online.wsj.com/article/SB122350935030117311.html

97. Panek, "Superstore Inflation," p. 66ff.

98. Older cathedrals of consumption have suffered, as well. In early 2009, the venerable department store chain Macy's announced that it was closing 11 stores.

99. Stanley Cohen and Laurie Tayor, *Escape Attempts: The Theory and Practice of Resistance in Everyday Life,* 2nd ed., London: Routledge, 1992.

100. John Urry, "The 'Consumption' of Tourism," *Sociology* 24 (1990): 23–35.

101. Bob Dickinson and Andy Vladimir, *Selling the Sea: An Inside Look at the Cruise Industry,* New York: John Wiley, 1997.

102. Ibid., p. 111.

103. www.dot.gov/affairs/briefing.htm; MARAD 31-03; November 26, 2003.

104. Nancy Keates, "Cruise-Ship Delays Leave Guests High and Dry," *Wall Street Journal,* October 24, 1997, p. B8.

105. http://www.msnbc.msn.com/id/27196377

106. www.cruisemates.com/articles/feature/OasisPreview-061908.cfm

107. Robert J. Martin, "Historical Background," in International Gaming Institute, *The Gaming Industry: Introduction and Perspectives,* New York: John Wiley, 1996, pp. 3–48.

108. Kenneth Labich, "Gambling's Kings: On a Roll and Raising Their Bets," *Fortune,* July 22, 1996, p. 82.

109. Hank Burchard, "High-Rollin' on the River," *Washington Post,* December 14, 1997, p. E1.

110. http://www.daveandbusters.com/Locations/default.aspx?Loc=140

111. Linton Weeks and Roxanne Roberts, "Amusement Mall," *Washington Post,* December 7, 1996, p. C1.

112. Ibid., p. C5.

113. Mitchell Pacelle, "Skeletons, Subs and Other Restaurant Themes Do Battle," *Wall Street Journal,* May 21, 1997, p. B1.

114. http://www.hardrock.com/corporate/press/content.asp?id=253

115. David Wolitz, "Hard Rock Absurdity," *San Francisco Daily Online!* August 15, 1996.

116. Hard Rock Cafe Web site, http://www.hardrock.com/

117. Thorstein Veblen, *The Theory of the Leisure Class: An Economic Study of Institutions,* New York: Modern Library, 1899/1934, p. 36.

118. Planet Hollywood Web site, http://www.planethollywood.com/

119. VNU Business Media, Inc, "Got Game?" June 1, 2003.

120. http://www.rainforestcafe.com

121. David Sweet, "To Maximize On-Field Product, Try Hitting Ball Out of Park Often," *Wall Street Journal,* May 8, 1998, p. B1.

122. Thanks to Michael Friedman for bringing this to my attention.

123. Thanks to Bryan Bracey for insights into this.

124. David J. Kennedy, "Residential Associations as State Actors: Regulating the Impact of Gated Communities on Nonmembers," *Yale Law Journal 105* (1995): 761–793; Mike Davis, *City of Quartz: Excavating the Future in Los Angeles,* New York: Vintage, 1992, p. 246.

125. Arthur G. Powell, Eleanor Farrar, and David K. Cohen, *The Shopping Mall High School: Winners and Losers in the Educational Marketplace,* Boston: Houghton Mifflin, 1985.

126. Debbie Goldberg, "A Room for Every Lifestyle," *Washington Post–Education Review,* October 26, 1997, pp. 1, 8.

127. George Ritzer, "McUniversity in the Postmodern Consumer Culture," *Quality in Higher Education 2* (1996): 185–199.

128. Rene Sanchez, "Colleges Turning Virtual Classrooms Into a Reality," *Washington Post,* March 27, 1997, pp. A1, A18; https://www.wgu.edu/about_WGU/who_we_are.asp

129. http://welcome.phoenix.edu/online/default.asp

130. Christine Laine and Frank Davidoff, "Patient-Centered Medicine: A Professional Evolution," *Journal of the American Medical Association 275* (January 10, 1996): 152ff.

131. As well as theme parks; see Margaret J. King, "The Theme Park Experience: What Museums Can Learn from Mickey Mouse," *Futurist 25* (1991): 24–31.

132. http://www.metmuseum.org/store/index.asp?HomePageLink=store_l

133. Ada Louise Huxtable, *The Unreal America: Architecture and Illusion,* New York: New Press, 1997, p. 85.

134. http://shop.louvre.fr/

135. Margaret Crawford, "The World in a Shopping Mall," in Michael Sorkin (ed.), *Variations on a Theme Park,* New York: Hill and Wang, 1992, p. 30.

136. Claudia Dreifus, "Talking Shop," *New York Times*, April 6, 1997, section 6, p. 83ff.

137. Joshua Harris Prager, "Out of Ideas: Give a Goat or a Seaweed Body Wrap," *Wall Street Journal*, December 23, 1997, pp. B1, B11.

138. And it is beginning to use another new means of consumption—e-commerce—in order to raise funds. See Sharon Theimer, *Associated Press Online*, September 13, 2003.

139. Gustav Niebuhr, "Where Shopping-Mall Culture Gets a Big Dose of Religion," *New York Times*, April 16, 1995, pp. 1, 14; Linda Perlstein, "The Rock of Ages Tries the Rock of Youth," *Washington Post*, July 18, 1998, p. A3.

140. Niebuhr, "Where Shopping-Mall Culture," p. 1.

141. Ibid., p. 14.

142. James Barron, "A Church's Chief Executive Seeks the Target Audience," *New York Times*, April 18, 1995, p. A20.

Chapter 2

1. Stuart Ewen, *Captains of Consciousness*, New York: McGraw-Hill, 1976.

2. Paco Underhill, *Why We Buy: The Science of Shopping*, New York: Simon & Schuster, 2000; Paco Underhill, *Call of the Mall*, New York: Simon & Schuster, 2004.

3. As I will discuss in more detail later, credit cards are not a means of consumption, but they do facilitate their use by consumers.

4. There is a substantial literature on shopping, but it is only a part of our concern and does not well describe the relationship between consumers and many of the new means of consumption, especially cruise ships, casinos, theme parks, eatertainment centers, and so on. See Sharon Zukin, *Point of Purchase: How Shopping Changed American Culture*, New York: Routledge, 2004.

5. Because of the huge size of the American market, many products, especially imports like consumer electronics, are available at rock-bottom prices.

6. See a special issue of the *Journal of Consumer Culture 4*, 2 (2004), edited by Dan Cook on "children's consumer culture."

7. Ellen Goodman, "Zapping Christmas," *Washington Post*, December 20, 1997, p. A21.

8. Michael F. Jacobson and Laurie Ann Mazur, *Marketing Madness: A Survival Guide for a Consumer Society*, Boulder, CO: Westview, 1995.

9. In this, they are much like the tobacco companies and their efforts to hook teenagers on cigarettes.

10. Gary Cross, *Kids' Stuff: Toys and the Changing World of American Childhood*, Cambridge, MA: Harvard University Press, 1997.

11. Gary Cross, "The Plight Before Christmas: How the Toy Market Outgrew Grown-Ups," *Washington Post*, December 21, 1997, p. C1.

12. George Ritzer, *Expressing America: A Critique of the Global Credit Card Society*, Thousand Oaks, CA: Pine Forge Press, 1995; Robert Manning, *Credit Card Nation*, New York: Basic Books, 2000.

13. And the facilitating means themselves need facilitators. For example, wider scale credit card use on the Internet needed greater trust in the reliability of methods of encryption.

14. www.apple.com/itunes/store/

15. Abraham Genauer, "Airport Retailers Thrive Despite Post–9-11 Travel Dip," *The Hill,* May 14, 2003, p. 40.

16. Ann Smart Martin, "Makers, Buyers, and Users," *Wintherthur Portfolio 28* (1993): 141–157.

17. A number of other experts trace the origins of mass consumption in the United States to the 1920s, the shift from a mentality of scarcity to one of abundance and the rise of modern advertising.

18. William Leach, *Land of Desire: Merchants, Power, and the Rise of a New American Culture,* New York: Pantheon, 1993, p. 3.

19. Susan Strasser has analyzed the new means of consumption in turn-of-the-century America in the context of a larger discussion of the creation of a mass market for consumer goods. See Susan Strasser, *Satisfaction Guaranteed: The Making of the American Mass Market,* New York: Pantheon, 1989.

20. On the decline of the department store, especially in New York City, see Adam Gopnik, "Under One Roof: The Death and Life of the New York Department Store," *The New Yorker,* September 22, 2003, p. 92ff.

21. Leach, *Land of Desire,* p. 269.

22. Rosalind Williams, *Dream Worlds: Mass Consumption in Late Nineteenth-Century France,* Berkeley: University of California Press, 1982.

23. Americans are not the only ones obsessed with consumption. For a discussion of the Japanese case, see John Clammer, *Contemporary Urban Japan: A Sociology of Consumption,* Oxford, UK: Basil Blackwell, 1997.

24. April Witt, "Acquiring Minds: Inside America's All-Consuming Passion," *Washington Post Magazine,* December 14, 2003, p. W14.

25. Benjamin Barber, *Consumed: How Markets Corrupt Children, Infantilize Adults, and Swallow Citizens Whole,* New York: W. W. Norton, 2007.

26. For a diametrically opposite view on at least part of this, see Elizabeth Warren and Amelia Warren Tyagi, *The Two-Income Trap: Why Middle-Class Mothers and Fathers Are Going Broke,* New York: Basic Books, 2003.

27. Juliet B. Schor, *The Overworked American: The Unexpected Decline of Leisure,* New York: Basic Books, 1991, p. 109.

28. Clammer also uses the term *hyperconsumption* to describe contemporary Japanese consumption; see Clammer, *Contemporary Urban Japan,* p. 54.

29. Stephen E. Lankenau, *Native Sons: A Social Exploration of Panhandling,* doctoral dissertation, College Park, MD, 1997.

30. Given this focus on consumption, I have opted not to discuss the situation confronting the millions of people who work in or on behalf of the cathedrals of consumption. This is an important issue, worthy of a book of its own.

31. Robert Manning, *Credit Card Nation,* New York: Basic Books, 2000.

32. Robert J. Samuelson, "Shades of the 1920s?" *Washington Post,* April 22, 1998, p. A23.

33. "North Americans Swimming in Debt," *Ottawa Citizen,* January 6, 2004, p. D4.
34. Juliet B. Schor, *The Overspent American: Upscaling, Downshifting, and the New Consumer,* New York: Basic Books, 1998, p. 20.
35. Ritzer, *Expressing America.*
36. http://www.money-zine.com/Financial-Planning/Debt-Consolidation/Credit-Card-Debt-Statistics/
37. The Japanese have managed to engage in hyperconsumption while remaining largely opposed to debt and reliant on a cash economy. See Clammer, *Contemporary Urban Japan.*
38. http://www.synovate.com/news/article/2008/11/us-households-will-receive-one-billion-fewer-credit-card-offers-in 2008.html
39. Jacob N. Schlesinger, "Are Lenders Letting Optimism Go Too Far?" *Wall Street Journal,* April 20, 1998, p. A1. However, the number of such solicitations dropped a bit in 2003 due to, among other things, higher mailing costs and a declining response rate; see Reed Albergotti, "Something Missing from Your Mailbox?" *Chicago Sun-Times,* November 6, 2003, p. 3.
40. Schor, *The Overspent American,* pp. 20–21.
41. Marc Fisher, "Naming Your Price," *Washington Post,* June 30, 1997, p. C2.
42. See ibid., pp. C1, C2, for a discussion of at least one exception to this.
43. Another recent innovation designed to increase consumption is mechanisms built into products that demonstrate to consumers that it is time to replace them. Examples include razors with strips that fade indicating that the blade needs to be replaced, beer cans with brewing dates designed to encourage consumers to discard stale beer (even though beer can last for years), and toothbrushes with blue bristles that fade, indicating that it is time to replace the brushes. See Dana Canedy, "Where Nothing Lasts Forever," *New York Times,* April 24, 1998, pp. C1, C3.
44. Malcolm Gladwell, "The Science of Shopping," *New Yorker,* November 4, 1996, pp. 66–75.
45. Margaret Crawford, "The World in a Shopping Mall," in Michael Sorkin (ed.), *Variations on a Theme Park,* New York: Farrar, Strauss and Giroux, 1992, p. 13.
46. Marc Fisher, "Where Hunters Gather," *Washington Post Magazine,* September 3, 1995, p. 20.
47. Albert B. Crenshaw, "How Direct-Mail Marketers Are Pushing the Envelope," *Washington Post,* March 17, 1996, pp. H1, H5.
48. "Winning the Grocery Game," *Consumer Reports,* August 1997, pp. 10–17.
49. Of course, consumers do not always buy, or buy as much as they are "supposed" to. Furthermore, consumers may actively resist and rebel against the new means of consumption. They may also use the cathedrals in ways unanticipated by those who designed and manage them.
50. Émile Zola, *Au Bonheur des Dames,* Lausanne, Switzerland: Editions Rencontre, n.d.
51. See, for example, Alvin Toffler, *Future Shock,* New York: William Morrow, 1980; Philip Kotler, "Prosumers: A New Type of Consumer?" *Futurist 20* (1986):

24–29; Daniel Zwick, Samuel K. Bonsu, and Aron Darmody, "Putting Consumers to Work: 'Co-Creation' and New Marketing Govern-mentality." *Journal of Consumer Culture* 8 (2008): 163–196; Ashlee Humphreys and Kent Grayson, "The Intersecting Roles of Consumer and Producer: A Critical Perspective on Co-Production, Co-Creation and Prosumption," *Sociology Compass* 2 (2008): 963–980; Chunyan Xie, Richard P. Bagozzi, and Sigurd V. Troye, "Trying to Prosume: Toward a Theory of Consumers as Co-Creators of Value," *Journal of the Academy of Marketing Science* 36 (2008): 109–122; George Ritzer and Nathan Jurgenson, "Production, Consumption, Prosumption: The Nature of Capitalism in the Age of the Digital Prosumer." *Journal of Consumer Culture,* forthcoming; George Ritzer, "Focusing on the Prosumer: On Correcting an Error in the History of Social Theory." Keynote address presented at the Conference on Prosumption, Frankfurt, Germany, March 2009.

52. It could also be argued that prosumption has historically been the rule and that we have tended, in part because of the seeming predominance of production during and long after the Industrial Revolution, to not only distinguish production from consumption but also to privilege production. See George Ritzer, "Focusing on the Prosumer: On Correcting an Error in the History of Social Theory." Keynote address presented at the Conference on Prosumption, Frankfurt, Germany, March 2009.

53. Karin Knorr Cetina, "Postsocial Relations: Theorizing Sociality in a Postsocial Environment," in George Ritzer and Barry Smart (eds.), *Handbook of Social Theory,* London: Sage, 2001, pp. 520–537.

54. Although the Barbie's dominance was threatened by another American product, the hipper "Bratz" doll. See Charles Laurence, "Beat It Barbie," *Sunday Telegraph* (London), December 23, 2003, p. 01ff.; Ruth La Ferla, "Notice: Underdressed and Hot Dolls Moms Don't Love," *New York Times,* October 26, 2003, section 9, p. iff.

55. Kevin Sullivan, "Barbie Doll: Japan's New Look," *Washington Post,* December 16, 1996, p. A20.

56. However, there are limits to this, as Mars Inc. candy makers discovered in Russia, where its America-oriented ads, as well as a general return to "Russianness," led to a backlash and renewed interest in "real Russian chocolate." See Christian Caryl, "We Will Bury You . . . with a Snickers Bar," *U.S. News & World Report,* January 26, 1998, pp. 50, 52; see also Daniel Williams, "Advertisers Cash in on Things Russian," *Washington Post,* June 12, 1998, p. A16.

57. Edwin McDowell, "Bazaar; Megamalls; Dropping in to Shop," *Orange County Register,* August 4, 1996, p. D4.

58. Richard F. Kuisel, *Seducing the French: The Dilemma of Americanization,* Berkeley: University of California Press, 1993.

59. John Vidal, *Counter Culture vs. Burger Culture,* London: Macmillan, 1997.

60. McDonald's sued two members of Greenpeace for passing out leaflets critical of the company. The trial ran for more than 2 years, becoming the longest running trial in the history of Great Britain. The judge's decision in mid-1997 was

generally seen as a partial and Pyrrhic victory for McDonald's. The case became the rallying cry for a large number of individuals and groups critical of McDonald's on a wide variety of grounds.

61. Jane Perlez, "A McDonald's? Not in Their Medieval Square," *New York Times,* May 23, 1994, p. A4.
62. Of course, with capitalism now triumphant throughout virtually the entire world, the conditions (e.g., hyperexploitation) may be being put into place to allow for the reemergence of a radical alternative to capitalism.
63. http://asis.news.yahoo.com/031215/ap/d7vf2jn80.html; http://www.mcdonalds.com/corp/invest/pub/2007_annual_report.html
64. http://www.mcdonalds.com/corp/invest/pub/2007_annual_report.html
65. http://www.mcdonalds.com/corp/invest/pub/2007_annual_report.html
66. McDonald's Corporation, *The Annual: McDonald's Corporation Annual Report,* Chicago: Author, 1996.
67. http://www.mcdonalds.com/corp/invest/pub/2007_annual_report.html
68. Judith H. Dobrzynski, "The American Way," *New York Times,* April 6, 1997, section 6, p. 79ff.
69. Jim Fox, "Category Killers Mount Major Canadian Invasion; US Retailers in Canada," *Discount Store News,* vol. 34, July 17, 1995, p. 44ff.
70. Uri Ram, "McDonaldization," Chapter 6 in *The Globalization of Israel: McWorld in Tel Aviv, Jihad in Jerusalem,* New York: Routledge, 2008, pp. 179–205.
71. David Horovitz, "Big Macs Challenge the Cuisine of the Kibbutz," *Irish Times,* July 21, 1995, p. 8.
72. Michael Freeman, "Cubicov Zirconiumich: US-Produced Russian Home Shopping Show 'TV Style,'" *Mediaweek,* vol. 5, June 5, 1995, p. 12ff.
73. Avy Hoffman, "Dally by the Danube," *Jerusalem Post,* February 8, 2002, p. 26ff.
74. Robert Muraskin, "Hungary to Shop, American Style," *Washington Post,* November 29, 1996, p. B12.
75. Keith B. Richburg, "Attention, Shenzen Shoppers!" *Washington Post,* February 12, 1997, p. C14.
76. Mai Hoang, "The Americanization of Vietnam," *Washington Post,* May 11, 1997, p. A25.
77. Kevin Sullivan, "Saigon Goes to the Superbowl: American-Style Mall Draws Young, Newly Affluent Vietnamese," *Washington Post,* June 6, 1997, p. A29.
78. Jonathan Friedland, "Can Yanks Export Good Times to Latins?" *Wall Street Journal,* March 6, 1997, p. A11.
79. Ibid., p. A11.
80. Dana Thomas, "La Mall Epoque," *Washington Post,* January 3, 1997, p. D6.
81. Ibid., p. D6.
82. Ibid., p. D6.
83. Jeff Kaye, "Invasion of the Discounters: American-Style Bargain Shopping Comes to the United Kingdom," *Los Angeles Times,* May 8, 1994, p. D1ff.
84. Peter Jones, "Factory Outlet Shopping Centres and Planning Issues," *International Journal of Retail & Distribution Management,* vol. 23, January 1995, p. 12ff.

85. Kaye, "Invasion of the Discounters," p. D1ff.

86. Friedland, "Can Yanks Export Good Times to Latins?" p. A11.

87. Ibid., p. A11.

88. Clammer, *Contemporary Urban Japan,* p. 72.

89. Judith H. Dobrzynski, "The American Way," *New York Times,* April 6, 1997, section 6, p. 79ff.

90. http://www.wordspy.com/words/generica.asp

91. Gabriel Escobar and Anne Swardson, "From Language to Literature, a New Guiding Lite," *Washington Post,* September 5, 1995, p. A1ff.

92. Justin Arenstein, "Tourism Boom Expected for Mpumalanga," *Africa News,* May 27, 1997.

93. James L. Watson (ed.), *Golden Arches East: McDonald's in East Asia,* Stanford, CA: Stanford University Press, 1997.

94. Mary Yoko Brannen, "'Bwana Mickey': Constructing Cultural Consumption at Tokyo Disneyland," in Joseph Tobin (ed.), *Remade in Japan: Everyday Life and Consumer Taste in a Changing Society,* New Haven, CT: Yale University Press, 1992, pp. 216–234; John Van Maanen, "Displacing Disney: Some Notes on the Flow of Culture," *Qualitative Sociology 15* (1992): 5–35.

95. Thomas L. Friedman, "Big Mac II," *New York Times,* December 11, 1996, p. A21.

96. Kenneth J. Cooper, "It's Lamb Burger, Not Hamburger, at Beefless McDonald's in New Delhi," *Washington Post,* November 4, 1996, p. A14.

Chapter 3

1. It is increasingly difficult to separate them. In many of the new means of consumption, consumers produce their own consumption. For example, by pouring their own drinks or making their own salad, consumers are helping to produce their own meals.

2. Adam Smith, *The Wealth of Nations,* New York: Modern Library, 1789/1994.

3. Karl Marx, *Capital: Volume Two,* New York: Vintage, 1884/1981, p. 471.

4. Ibid., p. 471.

5. Ibid., p. 479.

6. Ibid., p. 479.

7. Smith (1789/1994, p. 938) does not make this error, labeling what Marx calls the means of consumption "consumable commodities." Marx, like Smith, is really dealing with consumer goods and not with the kinds of structures that are discussed in this book as the means of consumption.

8. However, as we have already seen and will have occasion to examine further, there is a sense in which we "consume" means of consumption such as the fast-food restaurant.

9. As the reader will see, I will waffle a bit on whether the consumer is, like the worker, exploited.

10. Georg Simmel, *The Philosophy of Money,* London: Routledge and Kegan Paul, 1907/1978, p. 477; Rosalind H. Williams, *Dream Worlds: Mass*

Consumption in Late Nineteenth-Century France, Berkeley: University of California Press, 1982, p. 95; Sharon Zukin, *Landscapes of Power: From Detroit to Disney World,* Berkeley: University of California Press, 1991.

11. Jean Baudrillard, *The Consumer Society,* London: Sage, 1970/1998.

12. Sheila Rothenberg and Robert S. Rothenberg, "The Pleasures of Paris," *USA Today* (Magazine), March 1993, p. 38ff.

13. Baudrillard also discusses the credit card, which is an important example of what has been termed *facilitating means.*

14. Mike Gane, *Baudrillard's Bestiary: Baudrillard and Culture,* London: Routledge, 1991, p. 65.

15. Paul Baran and Paul M. Sweezy, *Monopoly Capital: An Essay on the American Economic and Social Order,* New York: Monthly Review Press, 1966.

16. Juliet B. Schor, *The Overspent American: Upscaling, Downshifting, and the New Consumer,* New York: Basic Books, 1998, p. 20.

17. Ibid.

18. Ira Chinoy and Charles Babington, "Low-Income Players Feed Lottery Cash Cow," *Washington Post,* May 3, 1998, pp. A1, A22; Charles Babington and Ira Chinoy, "Lotteries Lure Players with Slick Marketing," *Washington Post,* May 4, 1998, pp. A1, A10.

19. Harry Braverman, *Labor and Monopoly Capital: The Degradation of Work in the Twentieth Century,* New York: Monthly Review Press, 1974; Richard Edwards, *Contested Terrain: The Transformation of the Workplace in the Twentieth Century,* New York: Basic Books, 1979.

20. Cited in Hans Gerth and C. Wright Mills (eds.), *From Max Weber,* New York: Oxford University Press, 1958, p. 128.

21. Or at least less. In fact, because the three types of authority are also "ideal types," each appears, at least to some degree, in all particular cases of the exercise of authority.

22. Max Weber, *Economy and Society,* 3 vols., Totowa, NJ: Bedminster, 1921/1968, p. 223.

23. Ibid., p. 1156.

24. Max Weber, *The Protestant Ethic and the Spirit of Capitalism,* New York: Scribner's, 1904–5/1958, p. 54.

25. However, as we will see, there is an important trend toward less objective, dematerialized means of consumption.

26. The idea of a "neon cage" has been employed by Lauren Langman to analyze one of the new means of consumption—the shopping mall. Langman takes a Marxian, rather than a Weberian, view of malls, but he nonetheless sees them as isolated structures in which everything—from temperature to merchant displays to people—is controlled. To his credit, Langman also sees malls as producers of fantasies and dreamlike states. See Lauren Langman, "Neon Cages: Shopping for Subjectivity," in Rob Shields (ed.), *Lifestyle Shopping: The Subject of Consumption,* London: Routledge, 1992, pp. 40–82.

27. Mark A. Schneider, *Culture and Enchantment,* Chicago: University of Chicago Press, 1993, p. ix.

28. Hans Gerth and C. Wright Mills, "Introduction," in Hans Gerth and C. Wright Mills (eds.), *From Max Weber*, New York: Oxford University Press, 1958, p. 51.

29. Schneider, *Culture and Enchantment*, p. ix.

30. Ibid., p. xiii.

31. It appears also in his writings on law. Weber argues, "Inevitably, the notion must expand that the law is a rational technical apparatus . . . and devoid of all sacredness of content." In other words, law grows increasingly disenchanted. Weber, *Economy and Society*, p. 895.

32. Max Weber, "Science as a Vocation," in Hans Gerth and C. Wright Mills (eds.), *From Max Weber*, New York: Oxford University Press, 1958, p. 139.

33. Colin Campbell, *The Romantic Ethic and the Spirit of Modern Consumerism*, Oxford, UK: Basil Blackwell, 1989.

34. Ibid.

35. This is so at least in the form of being emotional about not showing emotion.

36. Campbell, *The Romantic Ethic*, p. 153.

37. Of course, they are successful to varying degrees. Some consumers may find a cathedral of consumption quite enchanting, whereas others will fail to see its enchanting qualities. Most, of course, will stand somewhere in between.

38. Schneider, *Culture and Enchantment*, p. x.

39. Benjamin clearly relates arcades to religious structures. In one instance, he describes an arcade as a "nave with side chapel" (p. 37). Of course, the arcade is not the only cathedral of consumption to have this quality and character. Benjamin describes department stores as temples consecrated to religious intoxication (p. 61). It could be argued that all of the settings of consumption discussed by Benjamin, indeed many settings to this day, have such a religious quality, at least to some extent. See Walter Benjamin, *The Arcades Project*, Cambridge, MA: Belknap, 1999.

40. Benjamin discusses many other means of consumption such as "winter gardens, panoramas, factories, wax museums, casinos, railroad stations" (p. 405).

41. Walter Benjamin, "Paris, Capital of the Nineteenth Century," in *Reflections: Essays, Aphorisms, Autobiographical Writings*, New York: Schocken, 1986, pp. 146–147.

42. Cited in Susan Buck-Morss, *The Dialectics of Seeing: Walter Benjamin and the Arcades Project*, Cambridge, MA: MIT Press, 1989, p. 38.

43. Cited in ibid., p. 83; Benjamin, *The Arcades Project*, p. 37.

44. Cited in Buck-Morss, *The Dialectics of Seeing*, p. 83.

45. Cited in ibid., p. 92.

46. Cited in ibid., p. 23.

47. That is just what Michael Hardt and Antonio Negri (*Empire*, Cambridge, MA: Harvard University Press, 2000) do, although the proletariat is replaced by the "multitude" as the potentially revolutionary force.

48. Cited in Buck-Morss, *The Dialectics of Seeing*, p. 271.

49. Cited in ibid., p. 159.

50. Cited in ibid., p. 271.

51. Cited in ibid., p. 284.

52. William Leach, *Land of Desire: Merchants, Power and the Rise of a New American Culture,* New York: Pantheon, 1993, p. 15.

53. Cited in Buck-Morss, *The Dialectics of Seeing,* p. 33.

54. Wallace Fowlie, *Age of Surrealism,* Bloomington: Indiana University Press, 1950.

55. Williams, *Dream Worlds,* p. 67.

56. Although Williams's work is discussed in this section, her research does not fit comfortably under the heading of neo-Weberian theory. However, she is dealing with the issue of enchantment.

57. Williams, *Dream Worlds,* pp. 70–71.

58. Michael B. Miller, *The Bon Marché: Bourgeois Culture and the Department Store, 1869–1920,* Princeton, NJ: Princeton University Press, 1981.

59. Ibid., p. 68.

60. Ibid., p. 71.

61. Campbell, *The Romantic Ethic,* p. 227.

62. George Ritzer, *Postmodern Social Theory,* New York: McGraw-Hill, 1997.

63. Zygmunt Bauman, *Intimations of Postmodernity,* London: Routledge, 1992.

64. Eva Illouz, *Consuming the Romantic Utopia,* Berkeley: University of California Press, 1997, p. 13.

65. Baudrillard, *The Consumer Society.*

66. Pauline Marie Rosenau, *Post-Modernism and the Social Sciences: Insights, Inroads, and Intrusions,* Princeton, NJ: Princeton University Press, 1992, p. 6.

67. Jean Baudrillard, *The Mirror of Production,* St. Louis, MO: Telos Press, 1973/1975, p. 83.

68. Jean Baudrillard, *Symbolic Exchange and Death,* London: Sage, 1976/1993.

69. Clammer offers a powerful critique of Baudrillard by demonstrating the continued importance of the gift, and thereby symbolic exchange, in contemporary Japan. See John Clammer, *Contemporary Urban Japan: A Sociology of Consumption,* Oxford, UK: Basil Blackwell, 1997.

70. The reader might want to think of other aspects of the American society from this point of view. For example, this helps us understand the popularity, not too many years ago, of the television show and movie *The X-Files.*

71. Zygmunt Bauman, *Postmodern Ethics,* Oxford, UK: Basil Blackwell, 1993, p. 33.

72. Jean Baudrillard, *Fatal Strategies,* New York: Semiotext(e), 1983/1990, p. 51.

73. Illouz does much the same thing; see Illouz, *Consuming the Romantic Utopia,* p. 17.

Chapter 4

1. George Ritzer, *The McDonaldization of Society 5,* Thousand Oaks, CA: Pine Forge Press, 2008.

2. William Severini Kowinski, *The Malling of America: An Inside Look at the Great Consumer Paradise,* New York: William Morrow, 1985, p. 61.
3. Mark Marymount, "A Sound Idea: Music Catalogs Hit All the Right Notes for Some Shoppers," *Chicago Tribune—Your Money,* April 5, 1995, p. 1ff.
4. Sandra S. Vance and Roy V. Scott, *A History of Sam Walton's Retail Phenomenon,* New York: Twayne, 1994, p. 135.
5. Robert Bryce, "Merchant of Death," *Texas Monthly,* June 1996, p. 58ff.
6. Dean Takahashi, "Little Caesar's Plans 'Big! Big!!' Pizzas, While Keeping the Price Structure the Same," *Wall Street Journal,* September 2, 1997, p. B10.
7. George Ritzer, "McDonald's Cooks Up a Fresh Serving of PR," *Newsday,* March 17, 2004, p. A41.
8. Philip Elmer-DeWitt, "Fat Times," *Time,* January 16, 1995, pp. 60–65.
9. "Loose slots" are those that pay out the most frequently.
10. The desire to offer low prices puts great pressure on manufacturers, especially in Third World countries, to keep costs and wages low.
11. Although, as we will see, Disney World is also in a sense a shopping mall oriented to getting people to spend far more than they do on their daily pass.
12. G. Bruce Knecht, "Book Superstores Bring Hollywood-Like Risks to Publishing Business," *Wall Street Journal,* May 29, 1997, pp. A1, A6.
13. Chris Anderson, *The Long Tail: Why the Future of Business Is Selling Less of More,* New York: Hyperion, 2006.
14. Marc Fisher, "Where Hunters Gather," *Washington Post Magazine,* September 3, 1995, pp. 31–32. Used with permission.
15. Christina Binkley, "A Day with a High Roller," *Wall Street Journal,* May 1, 1998, p. W1.
16. Margaret Webb Pressler, "2 With Reservations at the Gourmet Table," *Washington Post,* April 24, 1998, pp. F1, F4.
17. http://ir.papajohns.com/phoenix.zhtml?c=115556&p=irol-irhome
18. Richard Gibson, "Popular Pizza Chain's Gimmick Is Taste," *Wall Street Journal,* April 28, 1997, pp. B1, B10.
19. Ibid., pp. B1, B10.
20. George Ritzer, *The McDonaldization Thesis: Explorations and Extensions,* London: Sage, 1998.
21. Robin Leidner, *Fast Food, Fast Talk: Service Work and the Routinization of Everyday Life,* Berkeley: University of California Press, 1993, pp. 45–47.
22. David Wolitz, "Hard Rock Absurdity," *San Francisco Daily Online!* August 15, 1996.
23. Paul Goldberger, "The Sameness of Things," *New York Times,* April 6, 1997, section 6, p. 56ff.
24. Ibid., p. 56ff.
25. Wal-Mart exercises the usual kinds of control McDonaldized systems have over customers, as well as one that is fairly unique. It censors the words and images on CDs sold in its stores. Some disks are marked:

"Sanitized for your protection." Customers are not allowed to decide for themselves whether they want to listen to the forbidden lyrics or view the proscribed images. See "American Survey," *The Economist,* November 23, 1996, pp. 27–28.

26. Vance and Scott, *A History of Sam Walton's Retail Phenomenon,* p. 93.

27. Kowinski, *The Malling of America.*

28. Margaret Crawford, "The World in a Shopping Mall," in Michael Sorkin (ed.), *Variations on a Theme Park,* New York: Farrar, Straus and Giroux, 1992, p. 14.

29. Kowinski, *The Malling of America,* p. 359.

30. Ibid., p. 349.

31. Ibid., p. 354.

32. Ibid., p. 343.

33. William G. Staples, *The Culture of Surveillance: Discipline and Social Control in the United States,* New York: St. Martin's, 1997.

34. David Dillon, "Fortress America: More and More of Us Are Living Behind Locked Gates," *Planning* 60 (1994): 8ff.

35. Karen E. Klein, "Code Blues: Rules That Govern Life in Homeowners Associations Are Being Challenged in Court by Angry Owners," *Los Angeles Times,* March 5, 1995, p. K1ff.

36. Cited in Staples, *The Culture of Surveillance,* p. 64.

37. Judith A. Adams, *The American Amusement Park Industry: A History of Technology and Thrills,* Boston: Twayne, 1991, p. 111.

38. Michel Foucault, *Discipline and Punish: The Birth of the Prison,* New York: Vintage, p. 216.

39. Mike Davis, *City of Quartz,* London: Verso, 1990.

40. Foucault, *Discipline and Punish,* p. 298.

41. John O'Neill, "The Disciplinary Society: From Weber to Foucault," *British Journal of Sociology* 37 (1986): 42–60.

42. George Ritzer, "Islands of the Living Dead: The Social Geography of McDonaldization," *American Behavioral Scientist* (special issue) 47(2, 2003): 119–136.

43. Erving Goffman, *Asylums,* Garden City, NY: Anchor, 1961, p. xiii.

44. Louis A. Zurcher Jr., "The Sailor Aboard Ship: A Study of Role Behavior in a Total Institution," *Social Forces* 53 (1965): 389–400.

45. Gary Gumpert and Susan J. Drucker, "From the Agora to the Electronic Shopping Mall," *Critical Studies in Mass Communication* 9 (1992): 186–200.

46. Laura Billings, "Click on Triple Rinsed Mesclun," *New York Times,* April 6, 1997, section 6, p. 34ff.

47. Although in other contexts, *rationality* and *reason* are often used interchangeably, they are here employed to mean antithetical phenomena.

48. Cited in Vance and Scott, *A History of Sam Walton's Retail Phenomenon,* p. 126.

49. Rene Sanchez, "Colleges Turning Virtual Classrooms into a Reality," *Washington Post,* March 27, 1997, pp. A1, A8.

50. Laura Esquivel, *Like Water for Chocolate*, New York: Doubleday, 1992, pp. 10–11.

51. Ibid., p. 39.

52. Ibid., pp. 241–242.

53. As we will see, great spaces, large sizes, and the like can have, or be made to appear to have, a magical character.

54. Ada Louise Huxtable, *The Unreal America: Architecture and Illusion*, New York: New Press, 1997, p. 61.

55. Christina Binkley, "Starless Nights in the 'New' Las Vegas," *Wall Street Journal*, May 9, 1997, p. B1.

56. This can be traced to the first Ferris wheel at the 1893 Chicago Exposition, and perhaps even before that. But whatever its origins, we are amazed by the new technologies.

Chapter 5

1. Teena Hammond, "Inland Empire Focus: Entertaining the Shopper," *The Business Press/California*, September 23, 1996, p. 1.

2. James Bernstein, "Retailers: Let Us Entertain You, Too," *Newsday*, October 20, 1996, p. F8ff.

3. Mike Featherstone, *Consumer Culture and Postmodernism*, London: Sage, 1991, p. 103.

4. Kevin Fox Gotham, "Marketing Mardi Gras: Commodification, Spectacle, and the Political Economy of Tourism in New Orleans," *Urban Studies 39* (September 2002): 1735–1756.

5. Michael B. Miller, *The Bon Marché: Bourgeois Culture and the Department Store, 1869–1920*, Princeton, NJ: Princeton University Press, 1981, p. 173.

6. William Leach, *Land of Desire: Merchants, Power, and the Rise of a New American Culture*, New York: Pantheon, 1993.

7. Guy Debord, *The Society of the Spectacle*, New York: Zone, 1967/1994.

8. Ibid., p. 16.

9. Ibid., p. 16.

10. Ibid., p. 26.

11. Ibid., p. 26.

12. David Chaney, *Fictions of Collective Life*, London: Routledge, 1993.

13. M. M. Bakhtin, *Rabelais and His World*, Cambridge: MIT Press, 1968; P. Stallybrass and A. White, *The Politics and Poetics of Transgression*, London: Methuen, 1986.

14. Another of Chaney's distinctions is between spectacular society and the society of the spectacle.

15. Although we often talk in this book as if the cathedrals of consumption act, it is clearly the case that it is those people who design, control, and work in them who take the actions. We must be wary of reifying the new means of consumption.

16. On the importance of crowds to consumption, see John Clammer, *Contemporary Urban Japan: A Sociology of Consumption,* Oxford, UK: Basil Blackwell, 1997.

17. William N. Thompson, J. Kent Pinney, and John A. Schibrowsky, "The Family That Gambles Together: Business and Social Concerns," *Journal of Travel Research 34* (1996): 70–74.

18. Ann Conway, "Siegfried Without His Roy," *Los Angeles Times,* December 2, 2003, p. E1.

19. Kenneth Labich, "Gambling's Kings: On a Roll and Raising Their Bets," *Fortune,* July 22, 1996, p. 82.

20. Rick Bragg, "Las Vegas Is Booming After City Reinvention," *New York Times,* May 4, 1997, p. 22.

21. Neil Postman, "The Las Vegasizing of America," *National Forum,* Summer 1982, p. 6.

22. Hugh Hart, "Dave & Buster's Offers Fun by Day for the Whole Family," *Chicago Tribune,* April 4, 1997, p. 73.

23. Rainforest Cafe Web site, www.rainforestcafe.com/

24. Glenn Collins, "Egg McMuffins, Priced to Move," *New York Times,* April 4, 1997, p. C1.

25. Doris Hajewski, "Gurnee Mills Aiming to Give Shoppers Fun Time," *Milwaukee Journal Sentinel, Business,* March 12, 1997, p. 1.

26. Paul Goldberger, "The Store Strikes Back," *New York Times,* April 6, 1997, section 6, p. 45ff.

27. www1.toysrus.com/TimesSquare/dsp_home.cfm; thanks to Jon Lemich for bringing this and much else to my attention.

28. Goldberger, "The Store Strikes Back," p. 45ff.

29. Roxanne Roberts, "High-Browse Fun," *Washington Post,* April 3, 1997, p. C1.

30. Ibid., p. C8.

31. Ibid., p. C8.

32. Goldberger, "The Store Strikes Back," p. 45ff.

33. Ann Carrns, "Skyscrapers Try to Top Same Old Thrill," *Wall Street Journal,* April 11, 1997, p. B1.

34. Jean Baudrillard, *Simulations,* New York: Semiotext(e), 1983, p. 4.

35. Ibid., p. 15.

36. Ibid., p. 23.

37. Unfortunately, for lovers of simulations, it has recently been closed, but there are many others to choose from at a Disney theme park.

38. Christina Binkley, "Gambling on Culture: Casinos Invest in Fine Art," *Wall Street Journal,* April 15, 1998, p. B10.

39. Ada Louise Huxtable, *The Unreal America: Architecture and Illusion,* New York: New Press, 1997, pp. 64, 65.

40. Ibid., p. 3. Unlike Baudrillard, Huxtable does have a sense of the real as, for example, "an architecture integrated into life and use" (p. 3).

41. Ada Louise Huxtable, "Living With the Fake and Liking It," *New York Times,* March 30, 1997, section 2, p. 1. Used with permission.

42. Ibid., p. 40. Used with permission.
43. Huxtable, *The Unreal America,* p. 50.
44. Ibid., p. 101.
45. Robin Leidner, *Fast Food, Fast Talk: Service Work and the Routinization of Everyday Life,* Berkeley: University of California Press, 1993.
46. Alfred Schutz, *The Phenomenology of the Social World,* Evanston, IL: Northwestern University Press, 1932/1967.
47. Amy Waldman, "Lonely Hearts, Classy Dreams, Empty Wallets: Home Shopping Networks," *Washington Monthly* 27 (June 1995): 10ff.
48. Now, lamentably, all but defunct.
49. Of course, the real Old West has been filtered for so long through the simulations of movies and television shows that it is difficult to even have a glimmer of what it "really" was.
50. Norman K. Denzin, *The Cinematic Society: The Voyeur's Gaze,* London: Sage, 1995.
51. Don Kaplan, "Retail Hot Spots: New Retail Centers Differentiate Themselves From Megamalls," *Daily News Record,* February 10, 1997, p. 22.
52. This is the site, by the way, of the haunted hotel in the classic horror novel-cum-movie *The Shining.*
53. Kaplan, "Retail Hot Spots," p. 22.
54. Mark Gottdiener, *The Theming of America,* Boulder, CO: Westview, 1997, p. 147.
55. David Littlejohn, "They Took Manhattan—To the Desert," *Wall Street Journal,* January 21, 1997, p. A16.
56. William Booth, "Planet Mouse: At Disney's Tomorrowland, the Future Is a Timid Creature," *Washington Post,* June 24, 1998, pp. D1, D8.
57. Peter Carlson, "At Animal Kingdom, a Disney Critic Smells a Rat," *Washington Post,* June 24, 1998, p. D7.
58. Alexander Stille, "Virtual Antiquities Could Help Real Icons Stand Test of Time," *Washington Post,* December 25, 1995.
59. Sam Walker, "Hair Salons, Hot Tubs and . . . Oh, Yeah, Basketball," *Wall Street Journal,* March 27, 1998, p. W6.
60. Gottdiener, *The Theming of America.*
61. *Ossi* was the easterners' slang term for East German citizens.
62. Cited in Benjamin R. Barber, *Jihad vs. McWorld,* New York: Times Books, 1995, p. 133; italics added.
63. www.frys.com
64. Kathy M. Newbern and J. S. Fletcher, "Leisurely Cruise the Caribbean," *Washington Times,* August 27, 1995. All is not lost; the McDonald's built on the island was forced (by lack of business) to close after 6 months.
65. Susan Carey, "Ersatz Isles Lack Local Color, but the Bathrooms Shine," *Wall Street Journal,* February 16, 1996, pp. B1, B5.
66. Ibid., p. B1.
67. Ibid., p. B1.
68. Ibid., p. B1; italics added.

69. Ibid., p. B5. They probably would if they were simulated.
70. Huxtable, *The Unreal America*, p. 82.
71. Shelby Grad, "Irvine With a Down Home Side? It's All in the Master Plan," *Los Angeles Times, Orange County Edition*, July 8, 1996, p. B3.
72. Russ Rhymer, "Back to the Future: Disney Reinvents the Company Town of Celebration, FL," *Harper's Magazine*, October 1996, p. 65ff.
73. Mike Williams, "Living With the Magic Kingdom," *Atlanta Journal and Constitution*, September 29, 1996, p. 14ff.
74. Rhymer, "Back to the Future," p. 66. Used with permission.
75. Ibid., p. 67. Used with permission.
76. Ibid., p. 68. Used with permission.
77. Ibid., p. 75. Used with permission.

Chapter 6

1. Like much else to do with the cathedrals of consumption, implosions are not new, although they have accelerated in recent years. For example, a century and a half ago, the department store was created as a result of the implosion of boundaries separating a wide range of specialty shops.
2. Jean Baudrillard, *Simulations*, New York: Semiotext(e), 1983, p. 57.
3. Malcolm Waters, *Globalization*, London: Routledge, 1996.
4. Umberto Eco, *Travels in Hyperreality*, San Diego: Harcourt Brace Jovanovich, 1986.
5. Daniela Deane, "Theaters Explore Mergers, Fancy Megaplexes," *Washington Post–Business*, December 31, 2003, pp. E1, E5.
6. Peter McKay and Maryann Haggerty, "Entertaining New Mall Ideas," *Washington Post*, June 19, 1998, pp. F1, F10.
7. Anne Friedberg, *Window Shopping: Cinema and the Postmodern*, Berkeley: University of California Press, 1993, p. xi.
8. Laura Bird, "Huge Mall Bets on Formula of Family Fun and Games," *Wall Street Journal*, June 11, 1997, pp. B1, B12.
9. Ibid., p. B12.
10. Michael Pretes, "Postmodern Tourism: The Santa Claus Industry," *Annals of Tourism Research* 22 (1994): 1–15.
11. Reuters, "American Express, America Online Hook Up," *Washington Post*, January 31, 1995, p. D3.
12. "Fast Food Speeds Up the Pace," *Time*, August 26, 1985, p. 60.
13. Christina Binkley, "Huge Casino Project Does the Unthinkable: It Rattles Las Vegas," *Wall Street Journal*, December 4, 1997, pp. A1, A10.
14. This may even be more true of the Japanese.
15. Andy Dworkin, "Jurassic Jostling: Two Giant Malls Threaten to Steal Others' Thunder," *Dallas Morning News*, July 24, 1996, p. 1D.
16. David Segal, "Our Love Affair With the Mall Is on the Rocks," *New York Times*, January 31, 2009.

17. Edwin McDowell, "Bazaar: Megamalls; Dropping in to Shop," *Orange County Register*, August 4, 1996, p. D4.
18. Segal, "Our Love Affair With the Mall"; Terry Pristin, "Commercial Real Estate: Giant Mall of America Plans to Be Even Bigger," *New York Times*, August 27, 2003, p. C5.
19. McDowell, "Bazaar: Megamalls," p. D4.
20. Rachel Spcvack, "Nike in N.Y.: In the Starting Blocks," *WWD*, October 29, 1996, p. 4ff.
21. Naedine Joy Hazell, "The Sailings Grow in Popularity, Cruises and More, Seagoing Vacations Enhanced With Country Music, Irish Culture, Cigar Smoking," *Hartford Courant*, September 15, 1996, p. F1.
22. Judith Evans, "Catering to the Quick Food Fix," *Washington Post–Business*, May 19, 1997, pp. 12–13.
23. Margaret Webb Pressler, "Retailing's Quick Fix," *Washington Post*, June 13, 1998, pp. D1, D3.
24. Richard Panek, "Superstore Inflation," *New York Times*, April 6, 1997, section 6, p. 66ff.
25. Ibid., p. 66ff.
26. Lori Lincoln, "Scenes From a Mall," *Business Traveler*, June 1998, p. 51.
27. Margaret Webb Pressler, "Retailers, Restaurants Aim to Grab Some of Travelers' Time," *Washington Post*, July 16, 1997, p. F12.
28. www.mspupdate.com/northstarcrossing.htm
29. Lincoln, "Scenes From a Mall," pp. 48–51.
30. Ibid., pp. 48–51.
31. Sam Walker, "Hair Salons, Hot Tubs and . . . Oh, Yeah, Baseball," *Wall Street Journal*, March 27, 1998, pp. W1, W6.
32. Ibid., p. W6.
33. Ibid., p. W6.
34. Dave Kindred, "Luxurious New Ballparks Monuments to Greed," *Atlanta Journal and Constitution*, March 23, 1997, p. 03G.
35. Paul Newberry, "Stadium Pace Has Questions," *Chattanooga Free Press*, February 12, 1997, p. H8.
36. Michelle Hiskey, "The Ballpark: It's Entertaiment," *Atlanta Journal and Constitution*, March 23, 1997, p. 02G.
37. Ibid., p. 02G.
38. I. J. Rosenbergh, "No Mickey Mouse Operation: Braves Are Going to Disney World," *Atlanta Journal and Constitution*, February 24, 1997, p. 01C. Disney owned the Anaheim Angels, and its Edison Stadium was refurbished to include a Disneyesque simulated rock formation beyond the centerfield fence.
39. Derived from www.magictrips.com/beyond/wwos.shtml
40. Peter Applebome, "Franchise Fever in the Ivory Tower," *New York Times Educational Life Supplement*, April 2, 1995, section 4A, p. 16; cited in Mark Gottdiener, *The Theming of America*, Boulder, CO: Westview, 1997, p. 91.

41. Anne Friedberg, *Window Shopping: Cinema and the Postmodern,* Berkeley: University of California Press, 1993, p. xii.

42. Arthur G. Powell, Eleanor Farrar, and David K. Cohen, *The Shopping Mall High School: Winners and Losers in the Educational Marketplace,* Boston: Houghton Mifflin, 1985.

43. Ibid., p. 8.

44. Ibid., p. 8.

45. Ibid., pp. 8–9.

46. Ibid., p. 10.

47. Jim Carlton, "A Vancouver Condo Irks the Neighbors, but Nobody Cares," *Wall Street Journal,* March 8, 1998, p. A1.

48. John M. Goshko, "New York Wrestles With King Kong–Size Retail Dilemma: Superstores," *Washington Post,* April 13, 1997, p. A3.

49. James T. Yenckel, "New York by Night: The New Times Square; The City Hasn't Dropped the Ball," *Washington Post–Travel,* April 13, 1997, p. E6.

50. Gary A. Warner, "Times Square Now 'Great Whitewashed Way': Heart of New York Gets G-Rated Refurbishment," *Arizona Republic,* July 27, 1997, p. T14ff.

51. See, for example, Scott Lash and John Urry, *Economies of Signs and Space,* London: Sage, 1994; Roger Friedland and Deirdre Boden (eds.), *NowHere: Space, Time and Modernity,* Berkeley: University of California Press, 1994.

52. Anthony Giddens, "A Reply to My Critics," in D. Held and J. B. Thompson (eds.), *Social Theory of Modern Societies: Anthony Giddens and His Critics,* Cambridge, UK: Cambridge University Press, 1989, pp. 249–301.

53. For more on this idea, see Chapter 3.

54. David Harvey, *The Condition of Postmodernity: An Inquiry Into the Origins of Cultural Change,* Oxford, UK: Basil Blackwell, 1989, p. 284.

55. As such, they are an early example of making consumption "fun."

56. These experienced something of a revival, at least for a time. See Jacqueline L. Salmon, "Break Out the Tupperware: Home Is Where the Sell Is," *Washington Post,* March 24, 1997, pp. A1, A12.

57. Bloomberg News, "'Do-Not-Call' Gets Hearing," *Los Angeles Times,* November 11, 2003, p. C9.

58. Caroline E. Mayer, "Telemarketers Just Beginning to Answer Their Calling," *Washington Post,* August 31, 1997, p. H1.

59. Bloomberg News, "'Do-Not-Call' Gets Hearing," p. C9.

60. Being online has brought with it yet another type of intrusion into the home— "spam," or unwanted junk e-mail often designed to lure recipients into buying goods or services.

61. Johnny Johansson, *In Your Face: How American Marketing Success Fuels Anti-Americanism,* Upper Saddle River, NJ: Prentice Hall, 2004.

62. Amy Waldman, "Lonely Hearts, Classy Dreams, Empty Wallets: Home Shopping Networks," *Washington Monthly* 27 (June 1995): 10ff. Used with permission.

63. See, for example, Alvin Toffler, *Future Shock,* New York: William Morrow, 1980; Philip Kotler, "Prosumers: A New Type of Consumer?" *Futurist 20* (1986): 24–29; Daniel Zwick, Samuel K. Bonsu, and Aron Darmody, "Putting Consumers to Work: 'Co-Creation' and New Marketing Govern-mentality." *Journal of Consumer Culture 8* (2008): 163–196; Ashlee Humphreys and Kent Grayson, "The Intersecting Roles of Consumer and Producer: A Critical Perspective on Co-Production, Co-Creation and Prosumption," *Sociology Compass 2* (2008): 963–980; Chunyan Xie, Richard P. Bagozzi, and Sigurd V. Troye, "Trying to Prosume: Toward a Theory of Consumers as Co-Creators of Value," *Journal of the Academy of Marketing Science 36* (2008): 109–122; George Ritzer and Nathan Jurgenson, "Production, Consumption, Prosumption: The Nature of Capitalism in the Age of Digital Prosumer." *Journal of Consumer Culture,* forthcoming; George Ritzer, "Focusing on the Prosumer: On Correcting an Error in the History of Social Theory." Keynote address presented at the Conference on Prosumption, Frankfurt, Germany, March 2009.

64. Murray Melbin, "Night as Frontier," *American Sociological Review 43* (1978): 3–22.

65. As Juliet Schor has pointed out, the validity of this assertion depends on one's point of comparison.

66. Linton Weeks, "In U.S., Nighttime Is the Right Time," *Washington Post,* July 20, 1997, p. A1.

67. Ibid., p. A16.

68. This also goes for credit cards as facilitating means.

69. Colin Campbell, *The Romantic Ethic and the Spirit of Modern Consumerism,* Oxford, UK: Basil Blackwell, 1987.

70. College students without jobs are often offered credit cards, however. Modern "bankers" eager to get as many credit cards issued as possible ask, Why should the lack of a job be an impediment to obtaining credit?

71. It is true that the merchant must pay the credit card companies a small fee (2% to 4%, in general) on each transaction—a fee that would not be incurred in a cash transaction. However, it is also the case that many transactions take place that would not have were it not for credit cards.

72. Larry Fox and Barbara Radin Fox, "Floating a Loan," *Washington Post,* March 16, 1997, p. E4.

73. Although its presence seemingly everywhere one turns and throughout much of the world is spectacular; see below.

74. Michelle Wong, "Virtual Inventory," *Star Tribune* (Minneapolis, MN), August 6, 1996, p. 1D.

75. www.hotel-online.com/Trends/ChiangMaiJun00/CustomizationHospitality.html

76. logosoftware.com

77. Some of the other new means of consumption also serve to render time zones less relevant, or even irrelevant. If one is watching HSN or QVC, or shopping by catalog, it does not matter whether it is 9 A.M. on the East Coast or 6 A.M.

on the West Coast. If one is shopping on the Internet, it is of no consequence whether one is doing it in the United States or at the same time in Australia, which is more or less a day later.

78. Weeks, "In U.S., Nighttime Is the Right Time," pp. A1, A16; see also www.24hour-mall.com

79. It is interesting to note that these first three very different worlds are literally next door to one another on the Las Vegas Strip.

80. http://investor.starbucks.com/phoenix.zhtml?c=99518&p=irol-IRHome

81. Dina ElBoghdady, "Pouring It On: The Starbucks Strategy? Locations, Locations, Locations," *Washington Post,* August 25, 2002, p. H1ff.

82. Dave McNary, "New High-Tech Arcades Aim to Redefine Theme Parks," *Pittsburgh Post-Gazette,* May 3, 1997, p. D8.

83. William Severini Kowinski, *The Malling of America: An Inside Look at the Great Consumer Paradise,* New York: William Morrow, 1985, pp. 216–217.

84. Ibid., p. 218.

85. Although the opportunity to see and explore huge spaces may draw us to the mall, once there, it is also necessary to break this huge expanse up into manageable spaces so that the consumer is impressed, but not overwhelmed, by the physical confines of the mall. The malls usually have wings, often anchored by a department store. Customers are simultaneously led to believe that they are in physically manageable settings and that they are in a much larger, nearly infinite shopping space to explore later or at some future date. The sense conveyed is that outside of a manageable wing is a seemingly infinite space yet to be explored.

86. Pristin, "Commercial Real Estate," p. C5.

87. Edwin McDowell, "Sailings Worldwide: Not Just Cruise Ships Anymore," *New York Times,* February 2, 1997, section 5, p. 13ff.

88. www.cruisereviews.com/rci/

89. www.webprowire.com/summaries/585722.html

90. Larry Fox and Barbara Radin Fox, "Your Destiny Awaits," *Washington Post,* December 8, 1996, p. E4.

91. http://www.cruiseweb.com/CUNARD-QUEEN-MARY-2.HTM

92. Rory Nugent. "Hope Floats," *The Atlantic,* June 2009.

93. It is worth remembering that it characterized the early arcades.

94. Edward William Henry Jr., *Portman: Architect and Entrepreneur,* doctoral dissertation, University of Pennsylvania, 1985, p. 162.

95. John Portman and Jonathan Barnett, *The Architect as Developer,* New York: McGraw-Hill, 1976, pp. 74–76.

96. Ibid., p. 10.

97. Henry, *Portman: Architect and Entrepreneur,* p. 202.

98. http://www.bloomingtonmn.org/mallofamerica.html

99. Richard Panek, "Superstore Inflation," *New York Times,* April 6, 1997, section 6, p. 66ff.

100. "American Survey," *The Economist,* November 23, 1996, pp. 27–28.

Chapter 7

1. This term has been used by others, most notably Sharon Zukin, *Landscapes of Power: From Detroit to Disney World*, Berkeley: University of California Press, 1991; see also John Brinckerhoff Jackson, *A Sense of Place, A Sense of Time*, New Haven, CT: Yale University Press, 1994. However, as we will soon see, what Zukin means by this concept is not crystal clear and in any case is not precisely the same as the specific way it will be employed here. We could also think in terms of "landscapes of production"—for example, industrial parks or industrial zones—but that is not our concern here.

2. Although, as we will see immediately, this distinction is *not* neat and clean.

3. Walter Benjamin, *The Arcades Project*, Cambridge, MA: Belknap, 1999, p. 827.

4. The older, downtown area around Fremont Street and encompassing a number of older casinos was, as we have seen, redeveloped some years ago. The goal was to create a landscape of consumption that was more competitive with the Strip.

5. George Ritzer and Todd Stillman, "The Postmodern Ballpark as a Leisure Setting: Enchantment and Simulated DeMcDonaldization," *Leisure Sciences* 23 (2001): 99–113.

6. Suzette Barta, Jason Martin, Jack Frye, and Mike D. Woods, "Trends in Retail Trade," *OSU Extension Facts*, WF-565, n.d., p. 2.

7. In terms of intellectual resources for this work, mention must also be made of the now almost forgotten Chicago school of urban ecology. It clearly anticipated the current interest in spatiality, and its effort to map the city in terms of a center, concentric zones, radial sectors, specialized enclaves, and so on is clearly useful.

8. Edward W. Soja, *Postmodern Geographies: The Reassertion of Space in Critical Social Theory*, London: Verso, 1989.

9. Ibid., p. 1.

10. Ibid., p. 6.

11. Ibid., p. 1.

12. Michel Foucault, "Questions on Geography," in C. Gordon (ed.), *Power/Knowledge: Selected Interviews and Other Writings, 1972–1977*, New York: Pantheon, 1980, p. 70.

13. Michel Foucault, "Of Other Spaces," *Diacritics*, Spring 1986, p. 22.

14. Henri Lefebvre, *The Production of Space*, Oxford, UK: Basil Blackwell, 1991.

15. Ibid., p. 410.

16. Ibid., p. 405.

17. Zukin, *Landscapes of Power*.

18. Mike Crang, *Cultural Geography*, London: Routledge, 1998, p. 15.

19. Ibid., p. 15.

20. Zukin, *Landscapes of Power*, p. 16.

21. Ibid., p. 19.

22. Ibid., p. 269.

23. The poor consumer is worth separate discussion.

24. Zukin, *Landscapes of Power,* p. 6.

25. Ibid., p. 254.

26. Joseph Schumpeter, *Capitalism Socialism and Democracy,* New York: Harper and Bros., 1950.

27. We are focusing here on shopping streets, but there are many other types of landscapes of consumption. For example, the Broadway theater district in New York City, as well as its counterpart in London-Soho, could be considered more specific landscapes devoted to the consumption of theatrical performances.

28. Of course, the church or cathedral, very early means of consumption, can be seen as offering experiences to the "consumer."

29. This magnificent opera and concert venue, constructed between 1776 and 1778, could also be seen as a cathedral, this time for the consumption of music and opera.

30. This is a term for those who wander about various locales, including centers for shopping. It is found in the work of classic sociologists such as Georg Simmel and Walter Benjamin.

31. The religious significance of this, as well as much else about arcades and settings for consumption such as malls, should not be missed by the reader.

32. John Pomfret, "Tempest Brews Over Coffee Shops: U.S. Chain Stirs Ire in Beijing's Forbidden City," *Washington Post,* November 23, 2000, p. A40.

33. Ray Oldenburg, *The Great Good Place,* New York: Paragon House, 1989.

34. Barta et al., "Trends in Retail Trade," p. 2.

35. Underhill does not see this as so new; see Paco Underhill, *Call of the Mall,* New York: Simon & Schuster, 2004, p. 210.

36. Jim Welker, "Visionary's Quest," *The Columbus Dispatch,* June 9, 2002, Business, p. 01E.

37. Ibid., p. 01E.

38. Edmund Mander, "Columbus Discovers Streetscape Concept," *Shopping Centers Today,* www.icsc.org/srch/sct/current/sct1001/page1c.html

39. Ibid.

40. John Urry, "Tourism, Europe and Identity," in *Consuming Places,* London: Routledge, 1995, p. 123.

41. Underhill, *Call of the Mall,* p. 209.

42. Michael Barbaro, "Retailers Embrace the Great Outdoors," *Washington Post–Business,* December 1, 2003, pp. E1, E12.

43. Eric M. Weiss, "'Big-Box' Stores Leave More Than a Void," *Washington Post,* January 20, 2004, pp. B1, B3.

44. Other lifestyle centers such as Bowie Town Center in Maryland do much the same thing. For example, its food court also resembles an old local train station, and above a woman's clothing shop is a sign reading "Bowie School, est. 1881." See Barbaro, "Retailers Embrace the Great Outdoors," p. E12.

45. Ibid., p. E12.

46. Mander, "Columbus Discovers Streetscape Concept."

47. Robert F. Worth, "Laid-Off Foreigners Flee as Dubai Spirals Down," *New York Times,* February 12, 2009.

48. www.ameinfo.com/133896.html

49. Delays in many projected completion dates would not be surprising.

50. www.madinatjumeirah.com/shopping; retrieved December 24, 2008.

51. www.dubailandparks.com/

52. Actually, they are simulations of simulations; second- (or third-) order simulations. The Venetian, Macau is a simulation of the "original" Venetian, Las Vegas, which, of course, is a simulation of the "real" Venice (itself now largely a simulation created for tourists).

53. USATODAY.com, June 19, 2007; retrieved December 23, 2008.

54. www.venetianmacau.com/en; retrieved December 23, 2008.

55. Christopher Dickey, "Financial Paradise Becomes a MIRAGE," *Newsweek,* December 15, 2008, p. 46.

56. Which is part of a developing landscape of consumption called "Downtown Burj Dubai."

57. www.burjdubaiskyscraper.com

58. Andrew Ross Sorkin, "Cash Crunch Halts Work on Dubai Skyscraper," *New York Times Deal Book,* January 14, 2009; http://dealbook.blogs.nytimes.com/2009/01/14/cash-crunch-halts-work-on-dubai-skyscraper

59. Dickey, "Financial Paradise Becomes a MIRAGE," p. 46.

60. Mark McDonald, "Chinese Officials Gamble, and Their Luck Runs Out," *New York Times,* January 15, 2009, p. A10.

61. www.time.com/time/printout/0,8816,1857376,00.html

62. A similar development has occurred in Branson, Missouri, among other places; see below.

63. Another major entrance into the national park lies in North Carolina via, among other routes, the Blue Ridge Parkway.

64. There are some beautiful spots within view of Las Vegas or only a short drive from it (e.g., Red Rock Canyon), but relatively few visitors can be drawn away from the Strip and its casinos.

65. Michael Flannagan, "Merchants Mull Future of Gatlinburg," *Knoxville News Sentinel,* June 8, 2003, p. C1ff.

Chapter 8

1. What the then-head of the Federal Reserve, Alan Greenspan, called the economy's "irrational exuberance."

2. Terry Pristin, "Miami Monuments to Excess: Condo Colossus Becomes Symbol of a Building Boom Gone Bust," *New York Times,* March 11, 2009, p. B7.

3. Sheryl Gay Stolberg and Helene Cooper, "Obama Says Failure to Act Could Lead to a 'Catastrophe,'" *New York Times,* February 10, 2009, p. A1ff.

4. Joel Garreau, "Big Box and Beyond," *Washington Post*, November 16, 2008, pp. M1, M6.

5. Stephanie Rosenbloom, "Malls Test Experimental Waters to Fill Vacancies," *New York Times*, April 5, 2009, p. A22.

6. Hiroko Tabuchi, "In Japan's Stagnant Decade, Cautionary Tales for America," *New York Times*, February 13, 2009.

7. *Need* is in quotes here because as Baurdrillard has argued, much of consumption has little to do with what people need. See Jean Baudrillard, *The Consumer Society*, London: Sage, 1970/1998.

8. Kristina Shevory, "Mini Versions of Big-Box Stores," *New York Times*, May 20, 2009, p. B5.

9. Cited in Shevory, "Mini Versions of Big-Box Stores," p. B5.

10. www.shopping.yahoo.com/articles/vshoppingarticles/244/summer-top-pop-up-shops

11. Stephanie Rosenbloom, "Don't Ask. You Can Afford It," *New York Times*, May 2, 2009, pp. B1, B5.

12. Alessandra Stanley, "A Dose of Deference and Earnest Showbiz," *New York Times*, February 23, 2009.

13. Dubai is not a significant producer of oil, but its neighbors, including others of the United Arab Emirates, are.

14. Federal Reserve, "Credit Market Debt Outstanding," March 6, 2008. Retrieved April 10, 2008, from http://www.federalreserve.gov/Releases/z1/Current/z1r-4.pdf. Bureau of Economic Analysis at the U.S. Department of Commerce, "GROSS DOMESTIC PRODUCT: FOURTH QUARTER 2007 (FINAL)." Released March 27, 2008. Accessed April 10, 2008, from http://www.bea.gov/newsreleases/national/gdp/2008/pdf/gdp407f.pdf

15. Thomas L. Friedman. "China to the Rescue? Not!" *New York Times*, December 21, 2008, p. 10.

16. "A Few Good Machines," *The Economist*, March 13, 2008.

17. Richard Florida, *The Rise of the Creative Class: And How It's Transforming Work, Leisure, Community and Everyday Life*, New York: Basic Books, 2003.

18. Daniel Bell, *The Coming of Post-Industrial Society*, New York: Basic Books, 1973; Jerald Hage and Charles H. Powers, *Post-Industrial Lives: Roles and Relationships in the 21st Century*, Newbury Park, CA: Sage, 1992.

19. George Ritzer and Craig Lair, "Outsourcing: Globalization and Beyond," in George Ritzer (ed.), *The Blackwell Companion to Globalization*, Malden, MA: Blackwell, 2007, pp. 307–329.

20. Benjamin R. Barber, "The Economic Crisis Isn't All Bad; It's a Chance for Us and Obama to Reimagine How We Live Our Lives," *The Nation*, January 28, 2009.

21. Both Dollar General and Dollar Tree are among the 500 largest companies in the United States; see Rosenbloom, "Don't Ask. You Can Afford It."

22. T. R. Witcher, "The Good Times Stop Rolling: Vegas Meets the Recession," *Time*, December 29, 2008; www.time.com/time/business/article/0,8599,1868932,00.html

23. Ashley Powers, "Recession Tests Las Vegas Bet on Luxury's Lure," *Seattle Times,* December 28, 2008; http://seattletimes.nwsource.com/html/travel/2008560966_vegas26.html

24. www.vegastodayandtomorrow.com/citycenter.htm

25. Paul Baran and Paul M. Sweezy, *Monopoly Capital: An Essay on the American Economic and Social Order,* New York: Monthly Review Press, 1966.

26. Monica Zurowski, "V Stands for Value in Las Vegas: Deals, Discounts Abound in Sin City," *Calgary Herald,* March 2, 2009.

27. Adding to its difficulties is the fact that in recent years, after flirting with being more family oriented, Las Vegas is returning (if it had ever changed) to its more sinful image and ways. The recent slogan, "What happens in Vegas stays in Vegas" is a reflection of this regression.

28. One of the attractions of cruises is their highly McDonaldized character, and predictability (e.g., of the cost) is a key aspect of McDonaldization. See George Ritzer, *The McDonaldization of Society 5,* Thousand Oaks, CA: Pine Forge Press, 2008.

29. http://cannmoney.printthis.clickability.com/pt/cpt?action=cpt&title=dead+stores+and+mall

30. David Segal, "Our Love Affair With Malls Is on the Rocks," *New York Times,* January 31, 2008, Business, p. 1ff.

31. http://cnnmoney.printthis.clickability.com/pt/cpt?action=cpt&title=Credit+crisis%2C+spec

32. Stephanie Rosenbloom, "Malls Test Experimental Waters to Fill Vacancies," *New York Times,* April 5, 2009, p. A22.

33. Rory Nugent, "Hope Floats," *The Atlantic,* June 2009.

34. Sean B. Gregory, "The Last Shopping Mall?" http://news.yahoo.com/s/time/20090309/us_time/08599188354600

35. Ibid.

36. Ibid.

37. Andrew Martin, "Empty Tables Threaten Some Restaurant Chains," *New York Times,* April 4, 2009.

38. Rosalind Williams, *Dream Worlds: Mass Consumption in Late Nineteenth Century France,* Berkeley, University of California Press, 1982/1991.

39. Nelson D. Schwartz, "In Spain's Falling Prices, Early Fears of Deflation," *New York Times,* April 21, 2009, pp. A1, A3.

40. Rosenbloom, "Malls Test Experimental Waters to Fill Vacancies."

41. Terry Pristin, "Miami Monuments to Excess: Condo Colossus Becomes Symbol of a Building Boom Gone Bust," *New York Times,* March 11, 2009, p. B7.

42. Ibid.

43. It is difficult to imagine huge spaces that can be built and run economically.

44. www.nytimes.com/2009/04/05mall.html

45. See, for example, Alvin Toffler, *Future Shock,* New York: William Morrow, 1980; Philip Kotler, "Prosumers: A New Type of Consumer?" *Futurist 20* (1986): 24–29; Daniel Zwick, Samuel K. Bonsu, and Aron Darmody, "Putting Consumers to Work: 'Co-Creation' and New Marketing Govern-mentality." *Journal of*

Consumer Culture 8 (2008): 163–196; Ashlee Humphreys and Kent Grayson, "The Intersecting Roles of Consumer and Producer: A Critical Perspective on Co-Production, Co-Creation and Prosumption," *Sociology Compass* 2 (2008): 963–980; Chunyan Xie, Richard P. Bagozzi, and Sigurd V. Troye, "Trying to Prosume: Toward a Theory of Consumers as Co-Creators of Value," *Journal of the Academy of Marketing Science 36* (2008): 109–122; George Ritzer and Nathan Jurgenson, "Production, Consumption, Prosumption: The Nature of Capitalism in the Age of the Digital Prosumer." *Journal of Consumer Culture,* forthcoming; George Ritzer, "Focusing on the Prosumer: On Correcting an Error in the History of Social Theory." Keynote address presented at the Conference on Prosumption, Frankfurt, Germany, March 2009.

Index

About the Author

George Ritzer is Distinguished University Professor at the University of Maryland, where he has also been a Distinguished Scholar-Teacher and won a Teaching Excellence Award. He was also awarded the 2000 Distinguished Contributions to Teaching Award by the American Sociological Association, and in 2004, he was awarded an honorary doctorate by LaTrobe University, Melbourne, Australia. He is perhaps best known for *The McDonaldization of Society* (translated into over a dozen languages and now in its 5th edition) and several related books, including *Expressing America: A Critique of the Global Credit Card Society* and *The Globalization of Nothing2* (2007). He edited *The Encyclopedia of Social Theory* (2005) and the 11-volume *Encyclopedia of Sociology* (2007), and he is the founding editor of the *Journal of Consumer Culture*.